# Essays on Shelley

# Essays
# on Shelley

*Edited by*

MIRIAM ALLOTT

BARNES & NOBLE BOOKS
TOTOWA, NEW JERSEY

*First published in the USA 1982 by*
*BARNES & NOBLE BOOKS*
*81 ADAMS DRIVE*
*TOTOWA, NEW JERSEY, 07512*

Copyright © 1982 by
Liverpool University Press

ISBN 0-389-20127-8


First published 1982

**Library of Congress Cataloging in Publication Data**
Essays on Shelley.

   (Liverpool English text and studies)
   Bibliography: p.
   Includes index.
   Contents: Attitudes to Shelley: the vagaries of a critical reputa-
tion/Miriam Allott—Shelley's "Gothick" in St. Irvnye and after/
David Seed—The Shelleyan psycho-drama: "Julian and
Maddalo"/Vincent Newey—Speech and silence in The Cenci/
Michael Worton—[etc.].
   1. Shelley, Percy Bysshe, 1792–1822—Criticism and interpreta-
tion—Addresses, essays, lectures. I. Allott, Miriam. II. Series:
Liverpool English texts and studies.

(Totowa, N.J.)
PR5438.E8   1982       821'.7       81-12885
ISBN 0-389-20127-8              AACR2

Text set in 11/12 pt Monophoto Baskerville by
Willmer Brothers Limited, Birkenhead
Printed and Bound in Great Britain by
Camelot Press, Southampton

# Contents

# Preface

This collection of essays, written for the most part by members of the Department of English Literature at Liverpool University, has grown out of a renewed interest in Shelley, stimulated initially by the contributors' engagement with his work in their role as teachers and quickened further by recent critical reappraisals and the dedicated scholarship which since the 1950s has marked a new stage in the history of Shelley's reputation. The names of those who have helped to set moving our own inquiries appear often in the following pages and are recorded in the Select Bibliography. At the same time, it is right to say that much of the impetus in this book springs from the interplay of independent thinking and corporate enthusiasm which sometimes develops among people who for some time have worked fairly closely together in a particular field. Moreover many of the present contributors have already shared the experience of working together in this kind of enterprise, which allows a subject of common interest to be explored from different, individually chosen, points of view. For myself as editor of this volume, it was the nature of the topics chosen and the emphasis given to particular aspects of Shelley's achievement which held attention as the various essays first came in. Apart from their intrinsic qualities and concerns, they seemed to promise that the collection as a whole would have considerable historical value as an index to some representative modern attitudes to this often misunderstood Romantic poet.

The essays, which are arranged more or less according to the chronological order of the principal works chosen for discussion, run from an account of Shelley's 'Gothick' in his early prose romances to a reading of his unfinished last poem, 'The Triumph of Life', and are prefaced by a survey of his critical reputation from his own day to the present. What emerges from these differently conceived pieces is general agreement about, and admiration for, Shelley's conscious craftsmanship, his disciplined originality in handling and reworking traditional forms and the

striking 'modernity' distinguishing his major work. In his
'Shelley's "Gothick" in *St. Irvyne* and after', David Seed discovers
this gifted Eton schoolboy already making individual use of
existing Gothic tales and employing his own fictions to express,
while obliquely commenting upon, that liking for the marvellous,
the wonderful and the macabre, which remained with him to the
end (as allusions in several other of the essays help to remind us).
For Vincent Newey in 'The Shelleyan Psycho-drama: "Julian
and Maddalo" ', the interest of the poem (written in 1818 after
Shelley's first meeting with Byron) centres in the relation
between 'objective' and 'subjective' or confessional elements: the
theme of confinement; and the modernity of its psychological
empiricism and its celebration of experience. Again, it is the
nature of the 'modern' in *The Cenci* (1819) which is fastened on by
Michael Worton, a colleague formerly working in the School of
French at Liverpool (he now teaches modern French literature at
University College, London), who is attracted by the play's
strong influence in the revolutionary theatres of the twentieth
century. His 'Speech and Silence in *The Cenci*' aims to show by a
close reading of the text that the play's modernity could be said to
lie essentially in its alertness to the limitations of language, an
argument supported by his summary of facts about major foreign
productions mounted since the 1890s, including those by Karel
and Josef Çapek in Prague in 1922 and Antonin Artaud in Paris
in 1935.

In 'Shelley's Magnanimity', Kenneth Muir celebrates the
reformist idealism dramatised in *Prometheus Unbound*, written
during Shelley's *annus mirabilis*, which occupied the period from
October 1818 to December 1819 (thus more or less coinciding
with the flowering of Keat's '1819 temper' in his own 'living
year'); Professor Muir is also concerned with the relationship
between his work and the theme and style of other writings
produced during the prolific time with, additionally, a glance
forward to Shelley's last poems composed in the period from 1820
to 1822. Shelley's 'modern' vision, he reminds us, led Maynard
Keynes in 1920 to quote from *Prometheus Unbound* when
illustrating the parallel between the aftermath of the Napoleonic
Wars and the years following the war of 1914–1918. Shelley's
'magnanimity' is looked at in another way by Ann Thompson in
her 'Shelley's "Letter to Maria Gisborne": tact and clutter', an

essay reinforcing latterday recognition of, and sympathetic response to, Shelley's qualities of grace, lightness and 'urbanity', once much neglected but now seen as rendering particularly attractive this expression of 'easy and relaxed intimacy with his correspondent'. Lightness of manner and gaiety of intention in another poem of the same year, 'The Witch of Atlas' (1820), are again saluted by Brian Nellist in 'Shelley's Narratives and "The Witch of Atlas" ', but they are also seen here as playing a part in what is, notwithstanding, a highly complex narrative structure. This discussion searches out Shelley's various efforts, from the time of *The Revolt of Islam* (1817) onwards, to overcome the limitations of 'story' in the interests of accommodating the shifts and turns of personal feeling, the conflict between the inner and outer, and the contrarieties in experience to which this temperament, with its ardent yearning for wholeness and harmony, was keenly and unremittingly sensitive. Its urgent movement towards anti-dualism stands out forcefully for Geoffrey Ward in his discussion of aspects of Shelley's Romanticism in 'Transforming Presence: Poetic Idealism in *Prometheus Unbound* and *Epipsychidion* [1821]', which is essentially an inquiry into the shifting relationship between 'language' and 'reality' characterising these two poems. The peculiar difficulties confronting this complicated creative intelligence in its search for appropriate expression, and its resourcefulness in employing the craftsman's disciplines placed at its service, are further explored by Bernard Beatty in 'The transformation of discourse: *Epipsychidion, Adonais* [1822] and some lyrics', which argues that Shelley manipulates his reader's experience of his poems by changes of tempo inducing an excitement that may suggest a mood or confirm a belief.

As it turns out, my own essay, 'The Reworking of a Literary Genre: Shelley's "The Triumph of Life" [1822]' has a good deal in common with issues raised by fellow contributors, including a central theme in Vincent Newey's 'Julian and Maddalo', that is the movement in Shelley towards self-dialogue of the kind which characterizes much of the literature of the Victorian years, from *Sartor Resartus* to Arnold, Browning, Tennyson and beyond. It has affinities, too, with Ann Thompson's view of Shelley's flexible personal use of a specific literary genre; Brian Nellist's interest in Shelley's movement between the narrative and lyrical modes, and between public issues and private dubieties; and Bernard Beatty's recognition of Shelley's effort to sustain the disciplines of a considered discourse which yet constantly modifies, at the same time that it is modified by, pressures of lyrical feeling of the kind to which Geoffrey Ward also attends in his own 'discourse'.

To what extent, if at all, these essays fit into the outline of Shelley's reputation mapped out in the opening survey, 'Attitudes to Shelley: the vagaries of a critical reputation', must be left to the reader to decide. My emphasis lies chiefly in Shelley and the Victorians, a subject hitherto not much attended to, even though his presence among them is almost as pervasive and ambiguous as Wordsworth's. But it could perhaps be said that the general temper of the present collection accords with my closing summary of contemporary response to Shelley, which seem to me to take their rise principally from close attentiveness to what he actually wrote and respect for the hardworking craftsmanship which recent, equally hardworking, scholarly examination of Shelley's manuscript materials has done so much to confirm. Our thanks to those who have helped us in putting the book together are set out formally below but it needs to be emphasised again here that our major debt, after all, is to those who have worked closely on Shelley's texts and have based seminal critical studies on their findings. The names of many such scholars—Geoffrey Matthews, Donald Reiman, Timothy Webb and Judith Chernait among them—appear, as I have said, from time to time in these pages, but this is only a small indication of the stimulus provided by their work and the debt of gratitude owed to them by their fellow Shelleyans.

# Acknowledgements

As the editor of this volume, I am deeply grateful to my fellow contributors, including Keith Durham who compiled our chronological outline, for their interest in the project from the start and for the patience, care and skill which they have brought to the work throughout. But above all, as colleagues working in or near the Liverpool Department of English Literature, we are, as always, warmly thankful for the support of our secretarial staff, expecially Joan Welford and Cathy Rees, who do far more than type out our essays (often from very foul papers indeed). In fact they take on much of the hard editorial work of tidying up the typescript, keeping the pages in order and dealing forbearingly with our second, third, and fourth thoughts. It is difficult to see how we should have got on without them.

Finally I would like to thank Mrs. Rosalind Campbell of Liverpool University Press, who, since she joined the Press in 1977, has worked hard to maintain the high standards of presentation to which readers of Liverpool English Texts and Studies have long been accustomed, and who was sympathetic and helpful when we ran into difficulties which postponed the arrival of the typescript on her desk for longer than we had thought likely at the beginning of this session.

M. A.

*Department of English,*
*Liverpool.*
*December* 1980

# Note

The text used throughout for the poetry (unless otherwise stated) is *Shelley: Poetical Works*, Oxford Standard Authors, ed. Thomas Hutchinson (1904), revised G. M. Matthews (1970). This is referred to in the notes as *Poetical Works*. The text used for the prose is *Shelley's Prose, or the Trumpet of a Prophecy*, ed. David Lee Clark (Albuquerque, 1954), and for the letters, *The Letters of Percy Bysshe Shelley*, ed. F. L. Jones (2 vols., Oxford, 1964), referred to in the notes respectively as *Clark* and *Letters*.

# Chronology

| *Shelley's Life* | *Other Publications and Historical Events* |
|---|---|

1811 (*January*) *St. Irvyne; Or, the Rosicrucian* published (probably written 1810).

(*February*) Publishes *The Necessity of Atheism* which leads to his and Hogg's expulsion in March, and to the stopping of his father's allowance.        Jane Austen, *Sense and Sensibility*

(*29 August*) Marries 16-years-old Harriet Westbrook after eloping with her to Edinburgh. This autumn tours England and Wales with Harriet and Hogg.

(*December*) Visits the Lake District, meets Southey and stays with him at Keswick.

1812 (*February*) To Ireland. Becomes involved with radicals. Publishes *An Address to the Irish People* and pamphlets supporting Catholic Emancipation and Repeal of the Union.        Byron, *Childe Harold's Pilgrimage* Dickens and Browning born.

Returns to live successively in Wales, Devon and again in Wales (Tremadoc), where he is involved in schemes for building an embankment and a model village.

(*September*) Meets Godwin and Peacock. Writing *Queen Mab*.

1813 (*April*) To London (after briefly revisiting Ireland).        Jane Austen, *Pride and Prejudice*. Southey, *The Life of Nelson*.

(*May*) *Queen Mab* privately published.

(*June*) Daughter Ianthe born.

1814 (*27 July*) Elopes with Mary Godwin. Journeys to Switzerland with Mary and her stepsister Claire Clairmont. From this time on becomes increasing liable to Godwin's demands for money.        Congress of Vienna

(*13 September*) Returns to London.        Scott, *Waverley*

(*30 November*) Birth of son Charles to Harriet.        Invention of steam printing machine facilitates wider distribution of newspapers and journals.

*Shelley's Life*

**1815** (*22 February*) Mary's first child born; dies two weeks later.
(*June*) Death of grandfather. Granted allowance by father. Is told he is dying of consumption.
(*August*) Moves to Bishopsgate and writes 'Alastor'.

Battle of Waterloo.
Wordsworth, *Collected Poems*.

**1816** (*24 January*) Birth of son, William to Mary.
(*February*) *Alastor and other Poems* published.
(*June–July*) Journeys to Geneva. Meets Byron (through Byron's relationship with Claire Clairmont).
(*late June*) Writes 'Hymn to Intellectual Beauty'.
(*late July*) Writes 'Mont Blanc'
(*8 September*) Returns to England and settles at Marlow. Friendly with Leigh Hunt.
(*9 October*) Mary's half-sister Fanny Imlay commits suicide.
(*10 December*) Harriet found drowned in the Serpentine, London (committed suicide 9 November).
(*30 December*) Marries Mary.

Spa Fields Riot.
Jane Austen, *Emma*.
Peacock, *Headlong Hall*.
Scott, *Old Mortality*.
Byron leaves England; publishes *The Prisoner of Chillon*.
Charlotte Bronte born.

**1817** (*12 January*) Birth of Allegra, Byron's daughter by Claire Clairmont.
(*February*) Meets Keats. At this time begins association with Leigh Hunt, Keats and other members of the 'Hampstead set'.
(*March*) Loses fight for custody of Ianthe and Charles, his children by Harriet. Settles at Marlow. Publishes *A Proposal for Putting Reform to the Vote*.
(*2 September*) Daughter Clara born. This month 'Laon & Cythna' finished, 'Rosalind and Helen' begun. Publishes *History of a Six Weeks Tour*.
(*December*) 'Laon and Cythna' published and withdrawn.

Coleridge, 'Christabel', 'Kubla Khan'.
Start of series of articles in *Blackwood's Magazine* on 'The Cockney School of Poetry'.
Jane Austen dies.

1818 (*January*) *The Revolt of Islam* published (revised version of 'Laon and Cythna').
(*11 March*) To Italy with Mary, William, Clara, Claire and Allegra.
(*28 April*) Allegra sent to Byron.
(*9 May*) At Leghorn; meets the Gisbornes.
(*11 June*) To Bagni di Lucca; completes 'Rosalind and Helen: A Modern Eclogue'.
(*July*) Translates Plato's *Symposium*.
(*August*) Begins essay on the manners and customs of the ancient Greeks. Visits Byron at Venice which inspires 'Julian and Maddalo'.
(*24 September*) Clara dies. This autumn works on *Prometheus Unbound*, 'Julian and Maddalo', 'Lines written among the Euganean Hills'.
(*11 December*) Settles in Naples after visiting Ferrara, Bologna, Rome. This month writes 'Stanzas written in Dejection'.

Mary Shelley. *Frankenstein* (Preface by Shelley).
Peacock, *Nightmare Abbey* (in which Shelley appears as Scythrop Glowry)
Keats, *Endymion*.
Hazlitt, *Lectures on the English Poets*.

1819 (*5 March*) Settles at Rome (after visiting Paestum and Pompeii in February and March).
(*March–April*) Finishes Acts II and III of *Prometheus Unbound*.
(*May*) Finishes 'Julian and Maddalo'. 'Rosalind and Helen' published.
(*7 June*) Son William dies.
(*10–17 June*) Leaves Rome, settles at Leghorn. Working on *The Cenci* (period of composition May–8 August).
(*September*) Writes *The Mask of Anarchy* (published 1832), inspired by the Peterloo Massacre.

Peterloo massacre in St. Peter's Fields, Manchester, 19 August.

|  | *Shelley's Life* | *Other Publications and Historical Events* |
|---|---|---|
|  | (*20 October*) Moves to Florence. Writes *Peter Bell the Third*. 'Ode to the West Wind. (*November*) Finishes *Prometheus Unbound*. Begins *A Philosophical View of Reform* (published 1920). (*12 November*) Son Percy Florence born. (*December*) 'England in 1819' written. |  |
| 1820 | (*26 January*) Moves to Pisa. *The Cenci* published this spring. (*15 June–4 August*) Moves to Leghorn. During this period writes 'The Sensitive Plant', 'Ode to Liberty', 'The Cloud', 'To a Sky-lark' and 'Letter to Maria Gisborne'; translates Homeric *Hymn to Mercury*. (*August*) Moves to Baths of San Guiliano near Pisa. Writes 'The Witch of Atlas', 'Ode to Naples', *Swellfoot the Tyrant*. *Prometheus Unbound* published (*31 October*) Returns to Pisa. (*December*) Friendship with Emilia Viviani; probably begins *Epipsychidion*. | Keats, *Poems* (includes the major Odes). Clare, *Poems Descriptive of Rural Life and Scenery*. |
| 1821 | (*13 January*) Jane and Edward Williams arrive in Pisa. (*February–March*) Working on *A Defence of Poetry* (published 1840). (*11 April*) Hears of Keats's death. (*April–July*) Writes and publishes *Adonais*, elegy on Keats. (*May*) *Epipsychidion* published. (*August*) Visits Byron at Ravenna. (*October*) Writes *Hellas*. (*November*) Arrival of Byron at Pisa. | Napoleon dies. Keats dies at Rome 23 February. |

|  | *Shelley's Life* | *Other Publications and Historical Events* |
|---|---|---|
| 1822 | (*January*) Meets Trelawny. (*February*) *Hellas* published. Writes the poems to Jane Williams. (*20 April*) Allegra Byron dies. This spring translates scenes from Goethe's *Faust* and Calderon. (*30 April*) Moves with Jane and Edward Williams to the Casa Magni at Lerici. (*May–June*) Sailing on his recently purchased boat, the *Don Juan*. Writing *The Triumph of Life* (possibly begun in February and left unfinished at his death). (*8 July*) Drowned with Williams when sailing back from Leghorn after visiting Leigh Hunt. | Matthew Arnold born. |
| 1824 | Publication of *Posthumous Poems*, edited by Mary Shelley. | |

# Attitudes to Shelley: the vagaries of a critical reputation

## MIRIAM ALLOTT

### I

Surveys of Shelley's critical reputation have been growing in number since the 1960s—Frederick Pottle's influential 'The Case of Shelley', first published in 1952, was revised in 1960[1]— and their appearance signals the arrival of a fresh stage in the movement of opinion about this poet, a movement itself affected by the 'revaluations' of the 1930s when Shelley began to receive special attention as a poet whose achievement had in any case always aroused a certain degree of critical strife. Perhaps the nearest modern equivalent so far as his early reputation is concerned is found in D. H. Lawrence, who used to be looked on by impassioned early readers as either a Satan or a Messiah. As a recent critic put it, when writing in 1968 about Shelley's early reviewers, 'the declarations have in common the same fervour, the fervour that drapes Shelley in the borrowed robes of either angel or atheist'.[2] That initial violence died away but the reasons for the dissension remained. It can be said, I hope without too much damaging simplification, that the history of Shelley's reputation falls into five principal stages: the first covering the contemporary and immediately posthumous years; the second and third covering successive, complexly interrelated, phases in the earlier and later Victorian years; and the fourth and fifth belonging to the past forty years of this century.

My chief concern in this essay is with the second and third phases, that is to say with Shelley and the Victorians, a subject which has not hitherto received as much attention as Shelley and the Moderns, though Roland Duerksen in his *Shelleyan Ideas in Victorian Literature* of 1966 gave us a valuable pioneering study of

Victorian attitudes to Shelley's major political and moral ideas. But among the general points which need to be made about the course of Shelley's reputation from his own day to ours is that common to all the 'phases' just referred to, though looked at in a new light in recent years, is a preoccupation with 'the two Shelleys', one of them a poet passionately committed to reformist principles (largely the Shelley of Durksen's survey), the other a lyrical poet capable of great melodic purity and poignancy of feeling. The 'lyrical' Shelley has never wanted admirers, even among the most hostile early critics for whom the 'extra-aesthetic' Shelley's revolutionary ideas were a 'hideous blasphemy' signifying 'a wretched infirmity of mind' and arousing in many readers the 'mixture of sorrow, indignation and loathing' experienced by the reviewer in the *Literary Gazette* who found himself exposed for the first time to *Queen Mab* when it was reprinted in 1821 (it had first appeared in 1813). But this critic was not alone in also finding in the same writer passages of 'genuine poetry' which were 'sublime', 'visionary', 'brilliant', 'noble'.[3] The other Shelleys, if one may put it so, among them the humorous stylist of the 'Letter to Maria Gisborne', the penetrating psychologist of 'Julian and Maddalo' and the sombre poet of 'The Triumph of Life', have all had to wait until our own day for critical recognition. This recognition has encouraged our habit of looking askance at clear-cut distinctions of the kind once made between the 'aesthetic' and the 'extra-aesthetic' Shelley.

But this is by no means to say that modern criticism has a monopoly of literary insight. Allowing for shifts of taste and emphasis brought about by historical and social change, the sectarianism of periodicals housing much of our 'critical heritage' and the late arrival of professional criticism with its carefully cultivated analytical coolness, it still seems true to say that the qualities of Shelley's poetry we fasten on and debate about now are largely the qualities fastened on and debated about from the beginning. The differences today are less a matter of breaking radically with earlier opinion than of establishing new procedures of critical inquiry along with fresh terms of reference to accommodate them.

Our folklore about the neglect or incomprehension of gifted writers in their lifetime owes a good deal to those cries of pain at 'the shock of the new' which often greets the first appearance of original talent. An anthology of nineteenth-century utterances of this sort, easy enough to compile, would certainly suggest to an uninitiated reader that the entire period suffered a total dearth of literary sensibility, most dramatically apparent perhaps in its critical response to new writers—Keats, Shelley, the Brontës, let us say—who did not live long enough to survive the squalls. The collection would be sure to include Lady Eastlake's notorious, though far from typical, attack in 1848 on *Jane Eyre* and *Wuthering Heights*,[4] together with the piece by the reviewer who aimed to kill two birds with one stone by abusing Shelley's *Adonais* as an elegy on 'a radically presumptuous profligate', and its author as one of a band of 'notorious libellers, exiled adulterers and avowed atheists'.[5] Keats, the 'radically presumptuous profligate', himself believed that England produced 'the finest writers in the world' because 'the English world ill-treated them during their lives and foster'd them after their deaths', so they were obliged to fend for themselves and 'see the festerings of Society'.[6] Shelley certainly saw 'the festerings of society', but did so at first because of his quick imaginative feeling for the victims of social wrong and later through the choice of life pressed on him by the laws of his own temperament.

In fact it is hard to assess the degree of 'ill-treatment', if such there be. Frederick Pottle thought 'the commonly held view that as a poet Shelley was ignored in his lifetime does not correspond with the facts',[7] but his fellow critic, James Barcus, editor of the *Critical Heritage* volume published in 1975, speaks of Shelley's 'lack of reputation, even among his literary contemporaries'.[8] The difference of opinion is understandable if only because of the many variables to reckon with, including matters such as the print runs of various editions, the readership of periodicals carrying reviews, and the incidence and influence of the literary coteries where new writers might become fashionable topics of conversation. With Shelley, the size of the editions was small, ranging, it seems, from 100 copies of *Epipsychidion* and 250 copies each of *Queen Mab, Adonais* (for which he paid himself), and *The Cenci*, to 750 copies of *The Revolt of Islam* in its first version as *Laon and Cythna*. *The Cenci* went into a second edition, but many copies of his other works were left unsold at his death.[9] Moreover the later poems, notably *Epipsychidion, Hellas*, and *Adonais*, were written after Shelley had settled in Italy and received few reviews in England. 'The Triumph of Life' was of course not known in his lifetime and in any case was more or less ignored until relatively recently in this century.

Clearly, though, Shelley's gifts were never wholly unappreciated. It is the rule rather than the exception to find lively tributes struck off even by readers who were seriously disturbed by his urgent polemics. Few of these compare perhaps with William Howitt's dazzling description of Keats's poetry as 'a vivid orgasm of the intellect'[10] (this appeared in 1848, the year of Lady Eastlake's piece about the Brontës 'coarseness' and want of propriety), but as early as the 1820s there are many attempts in the reviews to define the nature of Shelley's 'genius' (the word most often used about him); and in 1831 appeared Hallam's remarkable commentary—written when he was himself only twenty-one—on the poetry of Shelley, Keats, and Tennyson, his friend and contemporary.[11] In 1821 the *London Magazine and Theatrical Inquisitor* carried a review of *Queen Mab* which left Shelley's 'palpably absurd and false' opinions for others to judge, seeing the 'prominent features' of his poetical character to be 'energy and depth' and—in the spirit, if not the style, of William Howitt—finding that 'All Mr Shelley's thoughts are feelings. He certainly communicates to a reader the impression made on his own mind, and gives it . . . all the vividness and strength with which it struck his own fancy'.[12] Again, the *London Magazine and Monthly Critical and Dramatic Review* in its 1820 review of *Prometheus Unbound* despaired of conveying 'any idea of its gigantic outlines', but found the poem 'one of the most stupendous of those works which the daring and vigorous spirit of modern poetry and thought has created . . . It is a vast wilderness of beauty . . . yet the boundaries . . . are all cast by the poet . . . the wildest paths have a certain and noble direction; and the strangest shapes which haunt its recesses, voices of gentleness and wisdom'.[13] These statements are only a few years away from the commentary by that intelligent and somewhat mysterious, contributor to *Knight's Quarterly Magazine* who praised Shelley not only for his poetic genius but also for the ethical integrity of his ideas, which everywhere express

> love for others, belief in the immutability of value . . . and in the final happiness and exaltation of human nature, to be

brought about by the exertions and self-sacrifices of the good
and wise . . . If this is not religion, it is something not wholly
unallied to it . . .[14]

This is the voice, in effect, of one 'agnostic angel' saluting
another. The author is known from records as 'E. Haselfoot' but
may be the W. S. Walker who wrote an unfavourable review in
the *Quarterly* of 1821 and who resigned his Trinity College
Fellowship for religious reasons in 1829.[15] If this is right, the
reviewer must be seen as a forerunner of the distinguished and
sizeable company of Victorian devout sceptics, of whom George
Eliot and Matthew Arnold were among the most eminent. As
such he seems to have been a good deal readier than many to
recognize Shelley's affinity with his own brand of non-dogmatic
Christianism.

Shelley was fortunate too in the serious, and influential,
attention accorded him by his fellow writers. Among his early
reviewers were Leigh Hunt, Lockhart, Hazlitt, and Hallam, who
with Tennyson introduced his work to new readers at Cambridge
in the early 1830s. Again, various *obiter dicta* disseminated
themselves in literary talk. 'Shelley was one of the best *artists* of us
all: I mean in workmanship of style', Wordsworth is known to
have said, adding that he put him above Byron, though he
disliked his principles and thought that, like Keats, he would
please only the young.[16]

## II

The latter judgment has turned out to be a familiar feature in
Shelley criticism. Most poet-critics who have discussed Shelley
with individual qualities of insight and imagination—the list
reaches from Matthew Arnold and Browning to Yeats, T. S. Eliot
and some of our best known contemporary poets—have
acknowledged the attraction which his poetry held for them in
their youth and the cooler feelings it prompted in their later
years. This shifting enthusiasm is associated with the similarly
persistent inquiry into the relationship between the reader's
judgment of Shelley's poetry and his attitude to the social and
political ideas it expresses. T. S. Eliot in 1933 is discovered still
trying to resolve this matter for himself (a trifle disingenuously

perhaps) in the chapter on Shelley and Keats in his *The Use of Poetry and the Use of Criticism:*

> . . . the reason that I was intoxicated by Shelley's poetry at the age of fifteen, and now find it almost unreadable, is not so much that at that age I accepted his ideas, and have since come to reject them, as that at that age 'the question of belief or disbelief', as Mr Richards puts it, did not arise . . . I can only regret that Shelley did not live to put his poetic gifts, which were certainly of the first order, at the service of more tenable beliefs—which need not have been, for my purposes, beliefs more acceptable to me . . .[17]

To these perennial concerns must be added the frustration commonly experienced by Shelley's readers, early and late, when attempting to make out the meaning of particular passages in his work, which is not necessarily the same thing as attempting to make sense of his ideas. 'The mind, fatigued and perplexed, is mortified by the consciousness that its labour has not been rewarded by the acquisition of a single distinct conception'. says W. S. Walker in the *Quarterly Review* of October 1821,[18] and the frustration is still felt in sympathetically defensive interpretations a century later. For I. J. Kapstein 'Mont Blanc' is a poem with 'tensions that disrupt its logic and obscure its meaning', and the tensions are attributed to 'hidden conflict':

> Shelley struggles to assert the freedom of his mind against his conviction that nothing in the universe is free. It is this conflict which is responsible for the ambiguities and equivocations in phrasing that make 'Mont Blanc' such difficult reading . . .[19]

For all this, 'ambiguities and equivocations' have been traced often enough to less esoteric sources, notably Shelley's grammatical peculiarities and his elliptical, often careless syntactical constructions. 'Shelly is more careless than Wordsworth or Milton', declares Frederick Pottle 'but he is less careless than Keats or Shakespeare'. On the other hand he 'appears to have been innocent of any construction in English grammar: he writes just as he talked and his conversational idiom

(Eton), though good, was not at all points identical with the formal written statement'.[20]

Still more common as an explanation of the difficulty experienced in understanding Shelley is his alleged making of darkness visible by a highly idiosyncratic use of figurative language, where tenor and vehicle may any moment change places, begetting with bewildering speed and intensity a fresh chain of similarly hermaphroditic ideas and images. Recent criticism has been deeply interested in this matter of Shelley's imagery. Moreover it has more or less finally decided against the charges of muddle-mindedness and arbitrary association levelled by F. R. Leavis in the 1930s[21] and by prominent formalist critics during the next two decades. There is an uncanny resemblance between the latter and certain critics of that first phase in the 1820s and early 1830s, a period which has two landmarks making for minor 'revaluations' of its own: the first being the reprinting of *Queen Mab* in 1821, which encouraged a certain amount of retrospective reviewing; and the second Mary Shelley's publication of the *Posthumous Poems* in 1824, which produced a similar effect. Hazlitt opens his review of the 1824 volume with a substantial general analysis of Shelley's personal qualities, saluting him as a man of genius, 'sincere in all his professions', but damaged by his 'desertion of nature and truth' to deal in 'dark sayings' and in 'allegories and riddles'. He exempts 'Julian and Maddalo' because it is written in his 'best and *least* mannered manner' (thus foreshadowing a modern enthusiasm), but 'The Witch of Atlas', 'The Triumph of Life' and 'Marianne's Dream', examples of stanza-poetry where his Muse 'chiefly runs riot', are 'rhapsodies . . . full of fancy and fire . . . but difficult to read from the disjointedness of the materials, the incongruous metaphors and violent transitions, and of which . . . it is impossible in most instances to guess the drift or the moral'.[22] *Prometheus Unbound*, published in 1820, was recognized as a portentous new departure though in what direction remained a puzzle, not least because of its complex system of imagery. But W. S. Walker in his *Quarterly* article of 1821, looking at the poem in the earlier of the two 'retrospective' periods, decided to illustrate 'the incoherence which prevails in his metaphors' not from 'that great storehouse of the obscure and unintelligible' but from the opening of 'A Vision of the Sea', with its description of the storm:

> . . . when lightning is loosed like a deluge from Heaven,
> She sends the black trunks of the water-spouts spin
> And bend, as if heaven were ruining in
> Which they seem'd to sustain with their terrible mass
> As if ocean had sunk from beneath them: they pass
> To their graves in the deep with an earthquake of sound,
> And the waves and the thunders made silent around,
> Leave the wind to its echo . . . (ll.4–11)

Walker thought the style 'cumbersome and uncouth', wondered who 'She' could be and found 'the funeral of water-spouts' to be 'curious enough', and 'an earthquake of sound' 'as difficult to comprehend as a cannon of sound, or a fiddle of sound'. As for,

> . . . the screams
> And hissings crawl fast o'er the smooth ocean-streams,
> Each sound like a centipede . . .., (ll.146–48)

this is still harder to take ('the comparison of sound to a centipede would be no small addition to a cabinet of poetical monstrosities').[23] This is fairly typical as a response to the novelties of synaesthesia, to which readers had yet to become acclimatized as a critical and imaginative concept of peculiar importance in the evolution of Romantic poetry and Romantic poetic. In this century, long familiar with 'organicism' as a literary concept, the process can be carried to the opposite extreme, with 'synaesthesia' supplying ontological interpretation for the entire Shelley canon (for example in Glenn O'Malley's *Shelley and Synaesthesia* of 1964). Allowing for this 'novelty' it still seems strange that certain aspects of Shelley's metaphorical language should have caused so much difficulty for so long. James Barcus's *Critical Heritage* volume incorporates a curious comment on what appears to be a passage from *The Cenci* to the effect that the 'fault' of Shelley's imagery lies in the substitution of the poet's '*own impression* of the thing for the thing itself', the root cause being in 'that subjective tendency whose excess is lamented by Goethe and Schiller, and which is one of the main distinctions between ancient and modern poetry'. The remark has its interest as the reflection of one kind of anxiety experienced by Victorian writers about their romantic legacy.[24] Anxiety about 'the subjective tendency' surfaces in a new form in certain twentieth century readings, or more properly misreadings, of Shelley, notably T. S. Eliot's in 1928 of the fifth stanza of 'To a Skylark'; Leavis's in 1935 of the description of clouds in the second section of the 'Ode to the West Wind'; and Alan Tate's in 1941 of the lyrical poem 'When the lamp is shattered'.[25] All these see only incoherence and self-indulgent arbitrariness in the ordering of the imagery. But in what I have called the fifth and latest period of Shelleyan criticism there is some determined settling to the task of repudiating these charges by equally close but less inflexible—if still not always finally convincing—readings of the texts, the aim being to make a case for Shelley's coherent thinking and accurate observation of external reality, a critical position strengthened by the enthusiasm for current scientific theory which recent Shelleyan scholarship has been at pains to confirm. Desmond King-Hele's *Shelley, His Mind and Thought* (1962) was looked on as a landmark, if only because its arresting meterological analysis of the cloud imagery in the 'Ode to the West Wind' seriously damaged the authority of Leavis's reading.

### III

This twentieth-century concern with Shelley's imagery could be said to revive rather than sustain uninterrupted debate about a particular theme. It certainly looks so when set beside the preoccupation which strikingly links the 'first' to the 'second' period of Shelley's critical reputation, that is to the earlier Victorian years. It is probably too much to claim that the intellectual and aesthetic history of the Victorians could be written in terms of their response to Shelley, a claim often made with a good deal of justice about their response to Wordsworth, which was complex, ambivalent, and enormously influential. All the same, it comes as something of a surprise to discover how strongly Shelley's presence makes itself felt in Victorian political literature and critical discussion. Broadly, and in roughly chronological sequence, it shows itself in four principal areas: (1) through the political writings of his early imitators, the brand of predominantly Chartist poets belonging to the period from the 1830s to the 1840s; this response is the least ambiguous and—apart from occasional 'Spasmodic' elements—critically perhaps the least interesting of any, but nevertheless carries considerable historical and social weight; (2) through his re-creation as a fictional character in various novels of more or less the same early Victorian period (Ladislaw in *Middlemarch* (1872) is uncharacteristically. late as an example, though of course 'correct' for the Reform Bill England in which George Eliot sets her novel); (3) through the echoes and influences from his poetry found in the early work of major Victorian poets (these are clearly traceable in the early poems of Tennyson, Arnold and Browning); (4) through critical discussions about the nature of his poetic gifts sporadically carried on during the entire period by his fellow poets, from the days of the youthful Hallam and Tennyson, through Arnold's and Clough's friendship and correspondence in the 1840s, to the beginning of Yeats's career, where Shelley was a potent creative influence, and also indeed to that of Joyce, whose Stephen Dedalus invokes recollections of Shelley when explaining his theory of the 'epiphany' to his Dublin fellow students.[26]

One feature of the 'extra-aesthetic' Shelley's posthumous nineteenth-century life, briefly glanced at above, is the apparent reluctance of eminent Victorian 'devout sceptics', Arnold and Clough among them, to recognize Shelley as a forerunner, though in many ways he is their John the Baptist. Few followed 'Haselfoot-Walker' in responding to Shelley's exhortation 'to fear ourselves and love all humankind' with the declaration that 'if this is not religion it is something not wholly unrelated to it'. Nor did many emulate Henry Crabb Robinson's thoughtful progress from believing in 1821 that Shelley's 'polemical hatred of Christianity [in *Prometheus Unbound*] is as unpoetical as it is unnatural', to finding in 1828, when re-reading the poem, that 'no man had ever had more natural piety' and concluding in 1836, when re-reading *Queen Mab* and other poems, 'that the God he denies seems to be after all but the God of the superstitious'.[27] Nor indeed were there many to pronounce with Coleridge, 'His discussions would not have scared *me* . . . I have ever thought that sort of atheism the next best religion to Christianity'.[28] It was left to George Macdonald (not notable as one of the age's agnostic angels) to quote Coleridge with strong approval in the 1860s when compiling his article on Shelley for the *Encyclopaedia Britannica*, a piece reprinted with minor stylistic alterations in his collection of essays on the imagination, *A Dish of Orts* (1893). For him, 'All [Shelley's] attacks on Christianity are . . . directed against evils to which the true doctrines of Christianity are more opposed than those of Shelley could possibly be . . . Shelley's own feelings towards others, as judged from his poetry, seem to be tinctured with the very essence of Christianity'. He celebrates the brilliancy of Shelley's youthful achievement, concluding that he 'had in him that element of wide sympathy and lofty hope for his kind which is essential both to the *birth* and the subsequent *making* of the greatest of poets'.[29] His own work diffusely suggests Shelley's influence: for instance the consciously shared delight in reflected images (though he uses mirrors more often than water) and the similarities in *Phantastes*, which has an epigraph from 'Alastor' ('The oak/Expanding its immense and knotty arms,/ Embraces the light beech' (ll.431–33)), and sees to it that there shall be certain resemblances between Amados's odyssey and that of Shelley's lonely poet.

Neither George Lewes in his 1841 review of Shelley's posthumous poems, nor George Eliot, who sympathetically projects Shelleyan virtues in Will Ladislaw, goes as far as this in celebrating the 'extra-aesthetic' Shelley. Lewes emphasizes his benevolence with something of 'Haselfoot-Walker's' spirit in the important forty-one page review which he wrote for the *Westminster Review*, but in vindicating the ideas he also stresses Shelley's 'want of objectivity'—he finds his mind 'sensitive and reflective, rather than plastic and creative'—and the suggestion, as a recent critic rightly points out, is that for Lewes this 'intensely subjective' quality was likely to exclude the reader by making the ideas too 'elusive'.[31] George Eliot's Will Ladislaw is 'elusive' too, judging by the many readers over the years who have found him less solidly realized than the other principal characters. He is refracted for the most part through the sensibilities of other Middlemarchers, none of whom are made to see him as an unadulterated Shelleyan. Mr Brooke finds him 'a sort of Burke with a leaven of Shelley' and tells Mr Casaubon,

> He seems to me a kind of Shelley you know . . . I don't mean as to anything objectionable—laxities or otherism, or anything of that kind, you know . . . But he has the same sort of enthusiasm for liberty, freedom, emancipation—a fine thing under guidance—under guidance, you know . . .[32]

He remains 'under guidance' from his creator too, since her carefully considered public concerns direct her away from contrasting too explicitly an ardently Shelleyan spokesman for spiritual truth and leadership with mild clerics like Cadwallader and Farebrother, whose moments of worldliness or weakness leave intact the human decencies which are to be reassuring agents of social cohesiveness in the rapidly changing world of the 1830s. This order of anxiety is at the heart of the matter for most of the age's devout sceptics, who had their work cut out to maintain the equilibrium achieved by whatever honourable system of moral and spiritual belief they could forge for themselves without trying also to accommodate Shelley's restless and disturbing categorical imperatives.

It was left, then, to Shelley's Chartist followers to respond most directly to his ideas, though their attention is necessarily directed to his strong reformist principles rather than the Christianism intended as the principles' combined rationale and outcome. The ideas which had troubled the first readers came powerfully into their own in that region of early-Victorian culture where the condition-of-England question was more urgently felt than by even the most serious minded 'social' novelists customarily associated with the late 1840s and early 1850s. Perhaps a dozen or so of these activist Shelleyans survive in literary history but their significance is stronger than the number and quality of their writing might suggest. Marx saw Shelley as the inspirer, if not the only begetter, of the Chartist movement and, Kenneth Muir reminds us in his early essay on 'Shelley's Heirs', *Queen Mab* certainly came to be known as 'the Chartists' Bible'.[33] The better known of these revolutionary poets include the Sheffield Corn Law rhymer, Ebenezer Elliot, whose 'too sadly beautiful' factory hands on their day out in his 'Preston Mills' ('Thousands and thousands, all so white!/With eyes so glazed and dull!') present a much sadder spectacle than Mrs. Gaskell's Manchester cotton operatives on their rare holiday walk in Green Hays Fields at the opening of *Mary Barton*; and Thomas Wade (also an admirer of Keats) who in his 1835 collection of poems concluded his sonnet to Shelley with the lines,

> I have heard thee Dreamer styled—
> I've mused upon their wakefulness—and smiled.

Again, there is Richard Hengist Horne, best known for his long epic *Orion* (1843), an allegory of 'the contest between the intellect and the senses' whose hero is 'a type of the struggle of man with himself . . . a Worker and Builder for his fellow-men', and in which the perfervid style, in spite of avowed intentions towards reason and restraint, betrays the writer's predilection for the surges of feeling associated with the Spasmodics (especially his admired fellow poet Philip Bailey, the author of *Festus*, published in 1839). Of those most closely involved with the movement many came from strikingly different backgrounds. Thomas Cooper, variously teacher, Methodist minister, and political journalist, was imprisoned in 1843 after addressing Staffordshire coal miners out on strike and later versified his speech (which 'might be called "Variations on a theme of Shelley" ')[34] as 'The Purgatory of Suicides'. This was a lengthy poem in Spenserians which Disraeli, himself a curious example of early-Victorian Shelleyanism, helped to get into print. 'Slaves, toil no more', exhorts Cooper in fine 'Mask of Anarchy' style,

> Shout as one man: 'Toil no more renew,
> Until the Many cease their slavery to the Few.'

There were also the self-taught Gerald Massey, author of *Cries of '48*, a collection reflecting the last flare-up of Chartism, who with Cooper was part-inspirer of the eponymous self-educated tailor-poet of Charles Kingsley's *Alton Locke* (1850); Ebenezer Jones, the sadly over-worked and emotionally over-taxed 'Spasmodic' poet, whose *Studies of Sensation and Event* (1843) was acclaimed by Rossetti; and the lawyer Ernest Jones, the upper-class Shelleyan *jusqu'au-boutiste*, who was imprisoned as an agitator and, forbidden paper and books, used feathers found in the prison yard for pens, leaves torn from prayer-books for writing paper, and seemingly at times his own blood for ink. His Shelleyan *The Revolt of Hindustan* was one outcome of this dedication; another was his refusal to be bought off by his uncle's promise of a handsome legacy. Shelleyan idealism could hardly go further. He was rewarded by the Chartists' enthusiastic recitation of his songs at meetings and by Landor's salute to his 'noble' *Battle Cry*.

This Shelleyan sub-culture has its links with the mainstream through the fellow-travelling interest of various major Victorian figures who offered practical aid to the Chartist poets and then went on to explore their own ideas about the 'aesthetic' as well as the 'extra-aesthetic' Shelley'. The influence of the latter works its way throughout the period, emerging clearly here and there, for instance in John Stuart Mill's admiration for Shelley's libertarianism, (which was encouraged by his Harriet's enthusiasm, though he thought 'Shelley, so far as his powers were developed in his short life, was but a child compared with what she eventually became');[35] in William Rossetti, whose *Democratic Sonnets* (1907) reflect Shelley's influence and to whose work on Shelley throughout the period from 1868 to the early 1900s Shelleyan scholarship was deeply indebted; and in Swinburne's general agreement—rare among late-Victorian poets—with Shelley's social ideas. So there is a traceable continuity between the Shelleyan ideologies of the 1830s and 1840s and the late-Victorian arrival of the Fabians, who 'used to carry in their pockets copies of Shelley's poems';[36] the advent of Shaw, the last and most articulate of literary enthusiasts for the 'political' Shelley; and certain features of twentieth-century socialism. Shelley was deeply despondent in his last months of life about his power for general good—'I write little now,' he said, 'Imagine Demosthenes reading a Phillipic to the waves of the Atlantic',[37]—and would have been astonished and delighted by the enthusiasm of his 'heirs' in the 1830s and 1840s, the founding of the Shelley Society in 1886, and the description of him in the 1940s as 'a greater influence of nineteenth-century opinion—if not on poetic style—than either Keats or Wordsworth'.[38]

## IV

The Shelley who figures in the mainstream is altogether a more ambiguous figure. One writer to bridge the two cultures is the young Disraeli (he finally allied himself with Toryism after failing to secure a Radical seat in 1832). Besides supporting the Chartist poet Thomas Cooper, he turned to the composition of his own Shelleyan poem, *The Revolutionary Epic*, which was published in 1843 and remains one of the curiosities of literature (to echo the title of his father's book).[39] It is cast in quasi-Miltonic style but owes a great deal to Shelley's symbolic apparatus in *Queen Mab*, *The Revolt of Islam*, and *Prometheus Unbound*. The grandiose intention was to produce a modern Homeric epic about the climactic struggle between Federalism and Feudalism under Napoleon, but the poem opens in Shelleyan style with allegorical figures representing these and other related conceptions appearing before Demogorgon to plead their cause. Asia too is prominent, though in somewhat unShelleyan guise, since for Disraeli Asia's relationship with Europe was an absorbing and urgently topical political theme. The poem, unsurprisingly, was ill-received and left unfinished, though the author reprinted its three Cantos with stylistic revisions in 1864, thus adding something to Shelleyan lore in later Victorian years.

More influential and also more complexly interesting is Disraeli's fictional portrait of Shelley as Marmion Herbert, the character in his novel *Venetia* (1837) which can be reckoned the first substantial representation of this kind to appear (earlier attempts are Peacock's Scythrop in his satirical *roman à clé Nightmare Abbey* (1817) and Mary Shelley's portrayal of her husband in *The Last Man* (1826) and *Lodore* (1834)). Disraeli's aim, as stated in his Preface, was 'to shadow forth . . . two of the most renowned and refined spirits that have adorned these our later days', that is Byron and Shelley, and the depicting of Herbert as the older and wiser of the two is something of a double-edged tribute. Marmion's daughter Venetia falls in love with the Byron figure, young Lord Plantagenet Cadurcis, who looks up to Marmion as an intellectual and moral mentor and as a greater poet himself. But the Shelley thus admired is a man tamed by time and suffering to accept private happiness instead of struggling for unattainable public good. 'I will not give up a jot of my conviction of a great and glorious future for human destinies', he tells Cadurcis, 'but its consummation will not be so rapid as I once thought, and in the meantime I die . . . Once I sacrificed my happiness to my philosophy, and now I have sacrificed my philosophy to my happiness'.[40] Herbert as a youth is courageous, impetuous, and honourable but alienates his wife through his unconventionalism. He goes off to fight with the revolutionaries in the American War of Independence, covering himself with glory and winning the respect even of the English, though as a 'traitor' he must live in exile and chooses Italy. He has a mistress, a relationship treated as normal in the circumstances ('It is a habit to which very young men, who are separated from or deserted by their wives, occasionally have recourse. Wrong, no doubt as most things are, but it is to be hoped venial . . .').[41] At the end he is reunited with his wife and daughter, who effects the reconciliation, and also with his daughter's lover Cadurcis, so that a charmed, devoted *modus vivendi* in Italy is looked forward to. But, true to the historically tragic ending, Disraeli finally drowns Marmion in the Bay of Spezzia, and Cadurcis along with him. After a period of anguish, largely inspired by Mary Shelley's graphic record of the terror-stricken hunt for Shelley and Williams after their failure to return from Leghorn, Venetia and her mother return sorrowingly home to England.

Disraeli's reworking of recent biographical and literary material for this modestly readable story presented for the first time to a wide novel-reading audience a gifted, sympathetic figure; and also a cultural world which though unconventional was nevertheless guided by honourable principle. The main sources were Trelawny's admiring reminiscences, Mary Shelley's records, the recollections of Byron's servant Falcieri and Thomas Medwin's Shelley papers, which incorporated various passages from Shelley's prose writings not yet published in full, including the *Discourse on the Manners of the Ancients* (written in 1818 and first published in full in 1931) and *A Defence of Poetry* (1840). From these Disraeli pieced together his portrait of Shelley both as a man (who first appears as late as the second chapter of Book IV, remaining offstage till then as a mysterious figure thought to be the perpetrator of unnameable crimes), and as a creative intelligence (first seen at close quarters in Book VI in company with Lord Cadurcis when, like their originals, the friends discuss art and literature while sailing in the Bay of Spezzia). Marmion's sayings are taken from Medwin's selected prose passages and the sequence in the eighth chapter of Book VI closes with Herbert answering Cadurcis's 'what is poetry but a lie, and what are poets but liars', with 'Poets are the unacknowledged legislators of the world',[42] a statement not to be known in its proper context in *A Defence of Poetry* for another three years. On the other hand Herbert's demurring views about his own work, though plausibly Shelleyan in relation to his known views about Byron, are largely his creator's and have a familiar ring if we remember Arnold on the limitations of Romantic poetry. 'I am not altogether void of the creative faculty', Herbert tells Cadurcis, 'but mine is a fragmentary mind. I produce no whole. Unless you do this you cannot last; at least you cannot materially affect your species'. His praise for Cadurcis, on the other hand, is taken directly from the Sonnet to Byron: 'What I admire in you is that . . . your creative power is vigorous, prolific and complete; your creations rise "fast and fair like perfect worlds" ' (the sonnet has, '. . . his creations rise as fast and fair/As perfect worlds at the Creator's will.').[43] What is clear from allusions such as these, including the account in Book VI of Herbert's youthful verse—it evokes a 'society of immaculate purity and unbounded enjoyment which he believed was the natural inheritance of the unshackled man', its stanzas glitter 'with refined images and [are] resonant with subtle sympathy'—is Disraeli's intimate familiarity with Shelley's work, as Richard Garnett later on recognized in the seminal paper on Shelley and Disraeli which he read for the Shelley Society in 1887.[44]

Disraeli's mingled admiration and misgiving, at its sharpest benevolently paternalistic, is a different matter from Charles Kingsley's emotionalism, whose movements run *pari passu* with the notorious disequilibrium in his spiritual history. His Shelleyan graph seems at first sight perhaps to follow the customary curve from youthful enthusiasm, as in *Yeast* (1848) and the 'Chartist' *Alton Locke* (1850), to a certain dismissiveness, as in 'Thoughts on Shelley and Byron' (1853),[45] where Byron is the stronger and more admired figure, and *Two Years Ago* (1857), where the poet Elsley Vavasour ('Elsley' being a near-anagram of 'Shelley') is an effete figure who hides under the pseudonym John Briggs, abandons his wife and children, tries and fails to escape to Italy, and dies by drowning. But the 1853 essay is infected by the anti-Romanism gripping this muscular Christian now restored to the arms of the Established Church. Shelley, it is claimed, would probably have become an 'Oratorian' or a 'Passionist', once his 'intense self-opinion had deserted him, and the emotional charge signals the aftermath of Kingsley's drift to disbelief at Cambridge, its arrest by his strong attraction to Rome, and his counter-balancing detestation of both saintliness and celibacy: 'not God's idea of a man but an effeminate starveling's ideal'.[46] Inextricably mixed up as he is with these confused feelings, Shelley remains an obsessive presence in Kingsley's work. In the opening chapter of *Yeast* Lancelot Smith transcribes in his diary lines by 'the divine Shelley' from 'The Sensitive

Plant' (ll.84-5), in chapter II Argemone aspires to be 'a female Alastor', while Claude Mellot's aesthetic theories, announced in chapter III, retain a strong Shelleyan flavour: 'Truth of form, colour, chiaroscuro . . . that which they express is eternal . . . . If I am to get at the symbolic unseen, it must be through the beauty of the symbolizing phenomenon . . .' The flavour persists even in the 1853 essay, which salutes the 'rightness' of the moral fervour, however 'wrong' the means to the ends. What is more, in *Two Years Ago* Kingsley continues to familiarize readers with Shelley's verse by relying on him as often before to heighten his narrative effects. In *Yeast* he had vivified Claude Mellot's habits of thought by quoting lines from the 'Hymn to Intellectual Beauty' (ll.13-14), with the comment 'as poor Shelley has it, and much peace of mind it gave him', and Launcelot's love for Argemone by lines from 'Alastor' about the girl in the vision (ll.488-92); in *Alton Locke* he had seen to it that *The Revolt of Islam* should come as readily to the lips of Sandy Mackay, Alton's guide and mentor, as 'Alastor' to Alton's. Now, in *Two Years Ago*, where Claude Mellot reappears, his West Country Sybil, Grace Harvey, gazes out to sea, at the coming storm 'with such a countenance as that "fair-terror" of which Shelley sang', the picture being filled out with the help of lines from the first stanza of 'On the Medusa of Leonardo da Vinci'. Another girl, Valentia, with 'magnificent beauty' and 'magnificent voice', occasions a quotation from 'To Constantia Singing' (stanza IV, 'I have no life, Constantia, now, but thee . . .'); and Shelley's opium-drugged fictional *alter ego*, Elsley Vavasour, is provided towards the end of his life with an epigraph—grudgingly acknowledged by an unsympathetic bystander—which incorporates a stanza from *Adonais* (including the line 'our Adonais hath drunk poison . . .').

## V

If Disraeli and Kingsley link the 'two cultures', Browning and Arnold, both of whom among the major poets have much more to say about Shelley than Tennyson, can be said to link two areas out of the four I have sketched out, that is the portrayal of Shelley and Shelleyan ideas in imaginative literature and the analysis of Shelley's poetic qualities in critical debate. Browning's feelings once again are complex, partly at first because of his battle with his own youthful religious questionings. As early as *Pauline* (1833), though, the first rawness was over and his early enthusiasm could be freely recollected in the long impassioned address to Shelley (ll.151–229), beginning 'Sun-treader, life and light be thine for ever', and ending,

> I awoke
> As from a dream . . . 'twas beautiful,
> Yet but a dream; and so adieu to it . . .

The distance widens in *Paracelsus* (1835) and *Sordello* (1840), but Browning still creates Shelleyan characters, Alastor-like pursuers of ultimate truth who come to grief because of their retreat from the finite realities of the everyday world: the scientist Paracelsus seeks the universal principle behind all things and Aprile, the idealistic Shelleyan poet who 'would love infinitely and be loved', seeks absolute beauty with a peculiarly Shelleyan form of Platonic earnestness though he has to admit,

> Knowing ourselves, our world, our task so great,
> Our time so brief, 'tis clear if we refuse
> The means so limited, the tools so rude
> To execute our purpose, life will fleet,
> And we shall fade, and leave our task undone
>
> (ll.497–501).

The opening passages of *Sordello* similarly convey regret for the falling away of a high ideal:

> Stay—thou spirit, come not near
> Now—not this time desert thy cloudy place
> To scare me, thus employed, with that pure face!
> I need not fear this audience, I make free
> With them, but then this is no place for thee!
>
> (ll.57–62)

Browning's reading of Shelley's socio-religious position in his critical essay written eleven years later lights up the 'simultaneous perception of Power and Love in the absolute, and of Beauty and Good in the concrete', and there is praise for his power of throwing between both 'swifter, and more numerous films for the connection of each with each, than have been thrown by any modern artificer of whom I have knowledge . . .'

These sympathies are now guaranteed by Browning's renewed allegiance to orthodoxy: 'I shall say what I think—had Shelley lived he would have finally ranged himself with the Christians'. His reading of the 'aesthetic' Shelley has a similarly personal impetus and is used to justify his own progress from the early 'confessional' poems to the 'objectivity' of his dramatic monologues and lyrics. He sees Shelley as the subjective poet who

> is impelled to embody the thing he perceives, not so much with reference to the many below as to the one above him, the supreme Intelligence which apprehends all things in the absolute truth . . . ,

and contrasts Shakespeare as

> the type of the objective poet—seeking to reproduce things eternal . . . with an immediate reverence . . . to the common eye and apprehension of his fellow men.

Neither kind is superior, but in certain periods the subjective poet may be needed to rouse consciousness above the phenomenal and to approach its 'exacter significance', while in other periods, notably Browning's own, there is an

> imperative call for the appearance of another sort of poet, who shall at once replace this intellectual rumination of food swallowed long ago by a supply of a fresh and living swathe . . .[48]

It seems clear that Browning hoped and believed that this was what he was doing in the poetry of the period we now think of as his best, that is when he published *Dramatic Lyrics* (1842), *Dramatic Romances and Lyrics* (1845), and *Men and Women* (1855). His Fra Lippo Lippi exalts the richness of particulars,

> —The beauty, and the wonder and the power,
> The shapes of things, their colours lights and shades,
> Changes, surprises . . . (ll.283–85)

Browning's 1852 essay, then, reaches into that fourth area where Shelley's fellow writers debate his poetic practice as often as not with an eye to their own creative stance. The most destructive critics were writers of prose who had less of the fellow practitioner's insight into what was being tried for. Carlyle and Ruskin are both vehement anti-Shelleyans, Ruskin's feelings representing an extreme case of disgust at the festered lily. An unpublished passage of his autobiography relates that as a child he was carried away by Shelley's descriptions of sea and mountain and 'imagined Pisa and Lucca and La Spezzia from him, as . . . Venice from Byron'.

> In my nascent and vulgarly sensuous taste, liking richness and sweetness . . . I fed upon him like a fly, till I was sick and sticky. He clogged all my faculties and infested all my imagination—he is to me now comparable in memory only to a dream I had . . . of putrid apple-blossoms with a smell which was to that of real apple blossom as that of rotten cabbage to fresh lettuce . . . I began in my own verses to imitate his affected diction, and to make myself miserable over the plots of the *Cenci* and *Prometheus*; mixed up with deadly arsenic out of the juvenil[e] blasphemies of *Queen Mab*.[49]

Ruskin cast aside this 'Voltaire powdered and mixed with redcurrant jelly and julap'. As for Carlyle, 'Poor Shelley always was, and is, a kind of ghastly object', who sounded 'shrieky' and 'frosty, as if a ghost were trying to sing to us', and in temperament was 'spasmodic, hysterical, instead of strong and robust . . . fine affectations and aspirations, gone all such a road . . . infinitely too weak for that solitary scaling of the Alps which he undertook . . .'.[50] In *Characteristics* he mourned, 'The Godhead has vanished from the world', leaving instead a Shelley 'filling the earth with inarticulate wail . . . like the inarticulate grief and weeping of forsaken children' (an image which Tennyson may have remembered in the lines from *In Memoriam*, 'An infant crying for the light/And with no language but a cry . . .')[51] Yet, as Roland Duerksen has reminded us in his *Shelleyan Ideas in Victorian Literature*, Carlyle's idea of the artist still remains Shelleyan: he is the 'spiritual light of the world' and as 'Prometheus Vinctus' the 'bitterest aggravation of his wretchedness is that he is conscious of Virtue, but finds himself the victim not of suffering but of injustice'.[52] Moreover his own 'dialogue of the mind with itself', inaugurated with *éclat* in *Sartor Resartus* (1836), reinforces the habit of self-debate which increasingly exerts stylistic and formal influences on Shelley's later poems.

In those of Shelley's nineteenth-century fellow poets who are at once drawn to and uneasy about his poetic practice the personal engagement is capable of prompting shrewd insights, as it does indeed, after all, in Browning and again in the young Matthew Arnold. Arnold's 'beautiful *and ineffectual* angel, beating in the void his luminous wings in vain' is of the 1880s,[53] when the elegiac poet had long ago yielded to the master of prose and reason who was distressed to find from Dowden's recent and lushly sentimental biography that 'data' for our 'ideal Shelley, 'the angelic Shelley' which 'we had and knew long ago' was being overshadowed by new 'data for the unattractive Shelley'. 'What a set!' he said, reflecting on Dowden's account of the domestic behaviour of Shelley's circle. But the young Arnold's criticisms spring in particular from worries about his own poetry and in general from Victorian anxieties about 'the function of poetry at the present time'. 'I am glad you like the Gipsy Scholar', he tells Clough in a famous letter, 'but what does it *do* for you? Homer *animates*—Shakespeare *animates*—the Gipsy Scholar at best awakens a pleasing melancholy. But this is not what we want.'[55] So in 'Stanzas from the Grande Chartreuse'—Shelley is mournfully rebuked:

> What boots it, Shelley! that the breeze
> Carried thy lovely wail away
> Musical through the Italian trees
> Which fringe thy soft blue Spezzian bay?
> Inheritors of thy distress
> Have restless hearts one throb the less? (ll. 139–44)

This Victorian worry—'the art which leaves the soul in despair is laming to the soul', George Eliot declared,[56] though certainly in her case with no immediate thought of Shelley in mind—is associated in Arnold with the requirement that art should aim for a Sophoclean seeing of life steadily and seeing it whole. Shelley's poetry by such standards suffers from a want of *architectonicè* and fails to move towards wholeness and harmony:

> Keats and Shelley were on a false track when they set themselves to reproduce the exuberance of expression, the charm, the richness of imagery, the felicity, of the Elizabethan poets. Yet critics cannot get to learn this, because the Elizabethan poets are our greatest, and our

canons of poetry are founded on their works. They still think that the object of poetry is to produce exquisite bits and images—such as Shelley's *clouds shepherded by the slow unwilling wind* and Keats passim.

It is the '*contents*' of poetry that matter. Tennyson, Keats, Shelley, '*et id genus omne*' are bad models for young poets, because poetry must be 'a complete magister vitae' like the poetry of the ancients, with the style accordingly 'plain, direct and severe'; it must not lose itself 'in parts and episodes and ornamental work, but must press forwards to the whole'.[57] Shelley fails in this high seriousness, his major poetic gift is his musicality, the quality singled out admiringly in Arnold's 1865 Oxford lecture on Maurice de Guérin.

> It always seemed to me that the right medium for Shelley's genius would be the sphere of music, not of poetry; the medium of sounds he can master, but to master the more difficult medium of words he has neither intellectual force enough nor sanity enough . . .[58]

'The man Shelley, in very truth, is not entirely sane', he was to say again in 1888, 'and Shelley's poetry is not entirely sane either'.[59]

Arnold's attitude is consistent with his sense that the Romantic poets 'didn't know enough', a view which he first put forward publicly in 'The Function of Criticism at the Present Time' (1864). It is wholly opposed to Hallam's enthusiastic 1831 essay, though the nature of the disagreement makes it hard to believe that Arnold was unaffected by his young predecessor's essay. Hallam on Wordsworth—'much has been said of him which is good as philosophy, powerful as rhetoric but false as poetry'[60]— foreshadows Arnold on the need to save Wordsworth from the Wordsworthians, which culminated in his 1880 *Poems of Wordsworth* with its widely influential introductory essay. Again Hallam's diagnosis of the prevailingly 'melancholy' temper of the age is close to Arnold's in the 1853 Preface: ('the cheerfulness, the disinterested objectivity [of 'the great monuments of early Greek genius'] have disappeared; the dialogue of the mind with itself has commenced . . . we hear . . . the doubts, we witness the discouragement, of Hamlet and of Faust'). Hallam sees ushered in at the end of the eighteenth century an era of powerful struggle to bring our over-civilised condition of thought into union with the fresh productive spirit that brightened the morning of our literature. But repentance is unlike innocence . . . . Those different powers of poetic disposition, the energies of Sensitive, of Reflective, of passionate Emotion, which in former times were intermingled, and derived from mutual support an extensive empire over the feelings of men, were now restrained within separate spheres of agency. The whole system no longer worked harmoniously . . .[61]

Hallam, in effect, is occupied with the notion of 'dissociated sensibility' nearly a century before T. S. Eliot's use of the phrase in his essay on the metaphysical poets set the fashion for discussing it (not always fruitfully) in the 1920s and 1930s. 'In one or two passages of Shelley's *Triumph of Life*, in the second *Hyperion*' he declared then, 'there are traces of a struggle toward unification of sensibility. But Keats and Shelley died, and Tennyson and Browning ruminated'.[62] For Hallam, though, Shelley, Keats, Tennyson, *'et id genus omne'* so far from suffering the disability, if such it be, are the great unifiers of 'sensation and thought'. Shelley and Keats are 'of opposite genius', Shelley being 'vast, impetuous, sublime', while Keats 'cannot sustain a lofty flight: he does not generalize, or allegorize nature'. Yet within the 'formal opposition there is a groundwork of similarity . . . constituting a remarkable point in the progress of literature. They are both poets of sensation rather than reflection'.[63] If this gives us pause, Keats for many readers being reflective in a way that Shelley is not, Hallam justifies the 'groundwork of similarity' in a manner recalling Howitt's 'orgasm of the intellect' and Aubrey de Vere's 'His [Keat's] body seemed to think'. In both poets (the italics are mine),

> So vivid was the delight attending the simple exertions of eye and ear that it became mingled more and more with their trains of active thought, and tended to absorb their whole being into the *energy of sense.*[64]

As Geoffrey Matthews reminds us, Hallam sees the best poetry as ' "a sort of magic", working through images and symbols which demand strenuous activity from the participating reader', a line of argument which 'appealed strongly to the pre-Raphaelites, and to the young Yeats'.[65] It is perhaps what could be termed his 'modernism' that makes Hallam, surprisingly perhaps, among the most arresting (if also long-winded) nineteenth-century commentators on the second generation of the Romantic poets. Certainly he travels a fair way towards grasping the paradoxical nature of Shelley's poetry, which is inspired at once by a vivid sense of particulars (the quality denied him by Browning), a feeling for colour, texture, light and dark, for 'contrasts and surprises', and by an equally vigorous intellectual and imaginative yearning for totality and harmony. Hallam's Shelley is in keeping with one's own image of his creative intelligence as it struggles to wrestle all-into-one while retaining activity, energy, process. The subversions of an expected order in his poems—good may well up from below instead of descending from the sky, a serpent may become an emblem of purity instead of evil, a vision of light may be a portent of disaster—are signs and symbols of unremitting effort to reconcile contrarieties. That the later Shelley found it increasingly difficult to effect this resolution seems clear from the last poems: the shifting moods in *Hellas* and the poems for Jane, for example, and the unresolved ambiguities in the tone and tenor of the last, unfinished, poem 'The Triumph of Life'.

It is tempting to believe that if Hallam had not died so young, the presence of this maturing critical intelligence might have encouraged Tennyson to find in himself livelier and more substantial things to say about poetry and poets in general and about Shelley in particular. As it is his comments (recorded for the most part *passim* in his son's memoir) are sparse and disappointingly predictable. Shelley, for all his 'splendid imagery and colour' and his achievement in *Epipsychidion* (which Tennyson liked 'as much as anything by him'), was 'often too much up in the clouds' and his 'Life of Life' was characteristic in that it 'seemed to go up, and burst'.[66] Furthermore Tennyson was adamant in disclaiming any influence from Shelley on his own poetry, though even in the early 1830s there were those who saw resemblances.[67] Present-day critics have certainly noted many echoes, most of these, significantly, clustering in poems written during the 1830s and early 1850s, that is during the period of Hallam's essay, his death shortly afterwards and the long years of mourning and writing the *In Memoriam* lyrics which followed. In the most fully annotated edition of Tennyson's poetry yet to appear (Christopher Ricks's *The Poems of Tennyson*, published in

1969), there are some fifty references in the editorial commentary
to scattered Shelleyan verbal echoes and parallels in poems
worked on by Tennyson from the 1820s (for example in 'The
Coach of Death' and 'Timbuctoo') to the 1850s (for example in
*Maud* and a handful of the *In Memoriam* lyrics). The references
diminish after this. A critic in the 1890s saw 'indisputable signs of
an early study of Shelley' in Tennyson's 'voluptuous affection for
nature, the warm overloaded phraseology, and long-drawn
eloquence of melancholy passion', and this still stands up as an
account of the prevailing temper in much of Tennyson's earlier
poetry.

The age's growing 'sense of the weight of things' which Hallam
diagnosed in 1831 had become more acute by the time Tennyson
flung his rallying cry against it at the close of *In Memoriam*.
Among later critics, Walter Bagehot's alertness to its presence in
Shelley was sharpened by his own feeling for what Henry James
saw as the constantly encroaching 'imagination of disaster'. It is
not the nature of Shelley's ideas as such which does the weighing
down but the hopelessness of bringing them to fruition. And so, as
with so many ordinary Victorian readers of poetry, and for
similar reasons, Bagehot finds himself celebrating the 'extra-
aesthetic' Shelley of the lyrical poems. Most of Shelley's works, he
wrote in 1856, are '*disjecta membra* . . . It is absurd to expect from a
man who dies at thirty a long work of perfected excellence . . . His
success is in fragments; but the best of these fragments are lyrical.
Yet even the lyrical rapture is short lived':

> The rigid frame of society, the heavy heap of traditional
> institutions, the solid slowness of ordinary humanity,
> depress the aspiring fancy . . . . It is characteristic of Shelley,
> that the end of his most rapturous and sanguine lyrics there
> intrudes the cold consciousness of this world.

He cites the chorus from *Hellas*, including the lines which inspired
Yeats,

> A loftier Argo cleaves the main,
>     Fraught with a later prize;
> Another Orpheus sings again,
>     And loves and weeps and dies:
> A new Ulysses leaves once more
> Calypso for his native shore . . . (ll. 1072–77)

and the dying fall with which it ends,

> The world is weary of the past,
>     Oh, might it die or rest at last! (ll.1100–1)

'In many of his poems', Bagehot comments, 'the failing of the feeling is as beautiful as its short moment of hope and buoyancy'.[68]


## VI

One might say that the 'two Shelleys' of nineteenth-century critical tradition reached their apotheosis with the arrival of a playwright and a poet who became famously active in the later nineteenth and earlier twentieth centuries. If Shaw represents the last and most unambiguous commitment to the 'extra-aesthetic' Shelley since the days of the political poets of the 1830s and 1840s, Yeats celebrates above all, it would seem,- the 'aesthetic' Shelley. But things rarely fall out so neatly. For one thing Yeats's 'aesthetic' Shelley displays qualities of imagery and symbolism which answer to his own individual poetic temper as also to some prevailing modernist preoccupations which Yeats himself at once reflects and fosters. Then again there is at the turn of the century an odd departure from a customary pattern in the late-arriving Shelleyanism of Yeats's older contemporary Hardy (whose familiarity with Shelley's poetry was in fact not properly documented until the 1950s).[69] His gesture of Shelleyan optimism towards the Immanent Will in his late work *The Dynasts* (1904–8) is posed against the prevailing scepticism of his novels, and so reverses the familiar reductive process. Echoes of *Prometheus Unbound*, for example, stir in the chorus of the Pities with which the drama ends.

> But—a stirring thrills the air
> Like sounds of joyance there
>     That the rages
>     Of the ages
> Shall be cancelled, and deliverance offered from the
>     doubts that were,
> Consciousness the Will informing; till It fashions all
>     things fair!

By contrast, the course of Yeats's Shelleyan history at first appears to be in many respects fairly traditional. His initial enthusiasm is one symptom of reaction against the Victorian scepticism informing his childhood and youth. Mill escaped from the effects of his father's tutelage through the 'salvation' he discovered in Wordsworth. Yeats in turn recognized that Shelley had 'reawakened in himself the age of faith'.[70] The difference is that the habit of reading Shelley reached back through two generations of Yeats's family and that he was first made familiar with *Prometheus Unbound* in very early years through Jack Yeats's habit of reading passages from it aloud. It became 'my sacred book' as the poet of 'Alastor' became 'my chief of men'.[71] Later, when puzzled by its 'deep meanings, which I felt more than understood', he tells us that 'a learned scholar' informed him that it was 'Godwin's *Political Justice* put into rhyme and that Shelley was a crude revolutionist'. His reply points to the direction of his own early Shelleyanism:

> I quoted the lines which tell how the halcyon ceased to prey on fish, and how poisonous leaves became good for food to show that he foresaw more than any political regeneration.[72]

In *Ideas of Good and Evil* it is clear that his is a mystical Shelley who perhaps had doubts, 'as the saints have doubts', but had heard the commandment, 'If ye know these things, happy are ye if ye do them'. *Prometheus Unbound*, then, is a 'mysterious song' expressing in 'a form suitable to a new age' the Blake-like belief that 'the holy spirit is "an intellectual fountain", and that the kinds and degrees of beauty are images of its authority'.[73] But by 1933 (the year, as it happens, of T. S. Eliot's *The Use of Poetry and the Use of Criticism*), his perspective, as he looks back over his Shelleyan past, has dramatically altered and what he says has its own value for the historian of Shelley's reputation:

> When I was in my early twenties Shelley was much talked about. London had its important Shelley Society. The Cenci had been performed and forbidden, provincial sketching clubs displayed pictures by young women of the burning of Shelley's body . . . . He had shared our curiosities, our political problems, our conviction that despite all experience to the contrary, love is enough; and

unlike Blake, isolated by an arbitrary symbolism, he seemed to sum up all that was metaphysical in English poetry . . .

Reflecting about him again in 'middle life', Yeats finds him a destructive force:

> . . . when I thought of the tumultuous and other tragic lives of friends or acquaintance I attributed to his direct or indirect influence their Jacobin frenzies, their brown demons.

Moreover Shelley was, after all, 'not a mystic, his system of thought was constructed by his logical faculty to satisfy desire, not a symbolical relevation received after the suspension of all desire . . .'[74] In the years separating these divergent images of Shelley, Yeats's running debate with him is reflected in his sombre poetic reworking of Shelleyan images and ideas. The stanza from *Hellas* quoted just now is recast with a different register in 'Two Songs from a Play'.

> Another Troy shall rise and set,
> Another lineage feed the crow,
> Another Argos painted prow
> Drive to a flashier bauble yet . . . (ll.9–12)

The parallel with the passage from *Prometheus Unbound*—

> The good want power, but to weep barren tears.
> The powerful goodness want: worse need for them.
> The wise want love; and those who love want wisdom;
> . . . (I.ll.625–27)

—found in 'The Second Coming'—

> The blood-dimmed tide is loosed, and everywhere
> The ceremony of innocence is drowned;
> The best lack all conviction, while the worst
> Are full of passionate intensity . . .—(ll.5–8)

occurs in a bleak vision of the future totally at variance with the emotional direction of Shelley's poem, that 'mysterious song' and 'sacred book' of Yeats's youthful admiration.

By the time we reach this 'Second Coming', so to say, we are well advanced into those modern stages of Shelley's critical history which have engaged attention in recent Shelleyan 'overviews'. My own concern is less substantive since, as I have said, interest in this essay lies chiefly with Shelley as he figured in the century before our own. In my introductory outline, however, the story of Shelley's recent reputation was described as falling into two stages (the 'fourth and fifth phases' of my sketch), and it is at the interrelationship between these that I want to glance at before concluding, since the second and most recent phase—the period that is, of sympathetic reappraisal—owes a good deal to reaction against the first. The New Critics of the 1930s and 1940s, who can be said to have revived Shelley in order to demolish him, ironically brought about the counter-movement which has helped to establish Shelley's unprecedented poetic 'respectability', the term which perhaps best suggests the balanced perspective in which his gifts are now generally viewed. Respectful admiration is common enough now but on the evidence so far in this respect is rarely quickened by the warmth which still characterizes general attitudes to Keats, the fellow poet and contemporary with whom Shelley's name has so often been linked since the first days of their brief creative life. The New Critics, observing the stringent Cambridge School procedures which finally put paid to the *belle lettrism* of the early 1900s ('the rise of this and the fall of that' as E. M. Forster once put it), produced critiques which have become notorious for those uncompromising and sometimes surprisingly unalert readings which were glanced at earlier in this essay. The roll-call of the famous in this context includes in America Allen Tate, Kenneth Burke, and John Crowe Ransome, and in England T. S. Eliot and F. R. Leavis. 'We can have a multiple meaning through ambiguity', declares Allen Tate in his analysis of the last stanza of 'When the lamp is shattered . . .', 'but we cannot have an incoherent structure of images'. As he sees it, 'The ravens in the second line are eagles in the sixth . . . . Are we to suppose that other birds come by and mock the raven (eagle), or are we to shift the field of imagery and see "thee" as a woman? . . . . Shelley, in confusion, or carelessness, or haste, could not sustain the nest-bird metaphor . . . he changed the figure and ruined the poem'.[75]

In England T. S. Eliot parallels Tate in his reply to Leonard Martin on the resemblance between Crashaw and Shelley: 'Crashaw's images even when entirely preposterous . . . give a kind of intellectual pleasure . . . . But in 'The Skylark' there is no brainwork . . . sound exists without sense'. On re-reading the stanza,

> Keen as are the arrows
> Of that silver sphere,
> Whose intense lamp narrows
> In the white dawn clear
> Until we hardly see—we feel that it is there . . .,

he can only say, 'I am ignorant to what sphere Shelley refers, or why it should have silver arrows, or what the devil he means by an intense lamp narrowing in the bright dawn.'[76] In the soon-to-follow 'corrective' period another poet-critic, Donald Davie, writing in the early 1950s about Shelley's 'urbanity', finds it 'typical of Shelley's obscurity that . . . I find no difficulty here, but only the accurate register of a sense-perception—the fading of the morning star'.[77] But Shelley is not after all referring to a 'star'. It is an amusing and instructive gloss on these readings to discover that T. S. Eliot's and Donald Davie's Victorian predecessor Matthew Arnold, certainly encountering 'no difficulty' with Shelley's 'sphere', takes it to be not a star but the moon, an image which had sufficiently impressed itself on his memory to have inspired the passage in his early poem 'Mycerinus':

> . . . the deep-burnish'd foliage overhead
> Splinter'd the silver arrows of the moon (ll.98–99)

Eliot's more substantial account of Shelley appears in the chapter in *The Use of Poetry and the Use of Criticism* which follows Hallam in acknowledging Shelley's 'passionate apprehension of abstract ideas' and salutes the approach to a 'unified sensibility' in the last poem 'The Triumph of Life'. But he judges finally that Shelley's 'mind was in some ways a very confused one', to the degree that he could be 'at once and with the same enthusiasm an eighteenth-century rationalist and a cloudy Platonist'.

If Donald Davie in 1952 negotiates the challenge about Shelley's 'obscurity' by coming at it from another angle of vision, John Holloway a decade or so later on in this stage of Shelley's story does the same for the challenge about Shelley's allegedly 'dissociated sensibility'. So far from *not* possessing a 'unified sensibility', this poet has in fact rather too much of this supposedly good thing. Shelley is 'hard to read' partly because 'there is, with trying regularity, a tension and eagerness about [his language] that leads the reader hardly to expect the control which he often finds'. The remark is indeed perceptive:

> One might almost put this point by saying that Shelley's sensibility was too emphatically unified to be altogether tolerable. No one ought to feel so passionately, so intensely as this, and yet move in thought with such virtuosity.[79]

A high price is paid for these powers in the 'excessive demand which Shelley makes on his readers', but the greatness itself is not in question. The essay was written as an introduction to a selection of the poems aimed at the rapidly growing academic audience of students and scholars and reflects the measured modern temper which aims to cool uncritical zestfulness while encouraging in the less enthusiastic the spirit of soberly responsible scholarly enquiry (Shelley is 'clearly great'; equally clearly he is 'not supremely great'; his work has 'a major and highly distinctive place in our literature').[80] The piece contrasts arrestingly with this critic's recent book *Narrative and Structure: Exploratory Essays*, which illustrates the most up-to-date phase of all, since its structuralist explorations include a commentary on 'The Triumph of Life', a poem which has suddenly become a research station for constructionists and deconstructionists alike.

Criticism of Shelley in these these essays by Donald Davie and John Holloway takes its direction to a considerable extent from their interest in his use of language. On another front the challenge is met by searching out the coherency of Shelley's symbolism and the firmness of his poetry's underlying structure. At first attending to the text with a closeness perfectly in keeping with the severest demands of the New Criticism, these appraisals scrutinised recurrent images, variations, and transformations in the use of metaphorical language, and the imaginative and mythical topography which the language defines. But this kind of interpretative analysis, it turns out, can become vulnerable to the very charge it undertakes to refute in Shelley through its own indulgent yielding to the side-winds of inspiration. The capturing ingenuity of many of its readings are hardly in doubt, portraying as they often do an arresting, archetypal, *paysage moralisé* vivified by mountains and caves, oceans and rivers, winds and volcanoes, the bright and the dark, spirits of harmony, and spirits of discord. But the excitement generated in sculpturing from the poems these models of reality can take over from the sometimes extremely arduous business of attending to what the poet is really trying to say. (It is hardly novel to claim that this has happened more than once in the seminal readings of Romantic literature undertaken by such distinguished critics in this field as Harold Bloom or Earl Wasserman. Not is it of course by any means unfamiliar in various poststructuralist readings.

## VII

An ideal methodology, we might now hazard in the light of this long story of Shelley's reputation, would need to take principally into account four types of approach. If we accept, as I think we should, the 'Bloom-Wasserman' procedure as one of the most quickening influences for our sense of an ordered complexity in Shelley, then to reduce its inherent risks it should perhaps be practised in association with three other, mutually corrective, disciplines found usefully at work in the most recent stages of Shelley criticism: (1) attentiveness to the poet's language, diction, and syntax, of the sort found in John Holloway's introductory essay or Donald Davie's *Purity of Diction in English Verse*, which broke new ground by demonstrating Shelley's ability to work successfully on the different stylistic levels of the urbane, the sublime, the witty, the low, the middle, and the elevated; (2) the equally valuable, and closely related, critical investigation of the traditional literary 'kinds' on which Shelley consciously drew and which he reworked (often subversively) for his own purposes. This habit of critical investigation, lately adapted for special purposes in some structuralist criticism, was impressively inaugurated by A. C. Bradley in his *Oxford Lectures in Poetry* (1909), particularly in 'The Long Poem in the Age of Wordsworth' and in the distinctions drawn between Shelley and Keats in his 'Shelley's View of Poetry' and 'The Letters of Keats'. A creative writer's deliberate taking over of a literary 'kind' usually involves some degree of self-dialogue, a fact which has an important bearing on the still debated question of Shelley's allegedly unbalancing subjectivity; (3) the careful study of manuscript material, which is again of prime importance since so much of the work left uncollected at Shelley's death is either fragmentary or exists in much worked-over holograph drafts. It is our good fortune that Shelley has at last attracted the attention of dedicated scholars (the example set by Geoffrey Matthews and Donald Reiman has been followed by such Shelleyans as Timothy Webb and Judith Chernaik) who have helped to supply reliable texts for us. It seems right to say that without this kind of scholarship no line of inquiry can properly be pursued. A conveniently economical and now well known instance is the *nature* of Shelley's 'subjectivity' in the line 'I die, I faint, I fail' (once commonly assumed to be the personal utterance of a sensibility too refined to sustain the harsh realities of existence), a matter on which useful light is shed by manuscript evidence establishing that this is part of a song from a play, the singer being an Indian woman grieving for her lover.[81]

The image of Shelley in the popular mind has derived much of its strength from his gift for composing yearning songs of this nature and was certainly fostered in the last century by poetasters, owners of keepsake albums, young ladies of refined sensibility, and singers at the pianoforte in Victorian *soirées*. (The blameless Indian Army officer's wife, who wrote her palpitant but by no means unappealing Indian Love Lyrics under the pseudonym 'Laurence Hope', seems to situate herself modestly in this tradition: her lovers 'swoon', the air about them 'quivers', the ladies have pale hands waving farewell or regard themselves as less than the dust beneath the loved one's chariot wheel). This idea of Shelley is of course associated with the brand image of the Romantic Poet, unwittingly fostered by the 'lyrical Shelley' in his own person, but more influentially still during the last century by the poet of his 'Alastor', with strong reinforcement from the folklore gathering round the work and life of his young, equally fated, contemporaries, Byron and Keats. The image dies hard and is much in evidence still in some kinds of fiction and in plays for the stage and television where 'sensitive' characters are recognized by their ability to quote passages from Shelley and Keats (often delivered in reverential tones or with a studied off-handedness designed to indicate deep feeling under control). By an irony of history Coleridge's picture of the poet in 'Kubla Khan'—'he on honey dew hath fed/And drunk the milk of Paradise'—has done more to foster this image than the intellectual and formal disciplines, the tough-mindedness and the complexities of the creative act, which emerge from his own critical inquiries into the nature of the poetic process (inquiries which professional criticism in this century has finally caught up with and interrogated along its own lines). Whether the 'professional' and the 'popular' idea of the poet are likely to draw more closely together is another story and may be left for future 'overviewers' to decide about.

## NOTES

1. Frederick A. Pottle, 'The Case of Shelley', *PMLA,* lxvii (1952), repr. (i) original version, *Shelley: Modern Judgements,* ed. R. B. Woodings (London, 1968; referred to below as *Woodings*), 35–50; (ii) revised version, M. H. Abrams, *English Romantic Poets* (New York, 1960), 289–306 and (extracts) *Shelley: Shorter Poems and Lyrics,* ed. Patrick Swinden (London, 1976; referred to below as *Swinden*), 19–33.

2. *Woodings,* Introduction, 11.

3. Unsigned review, *The Literary Gazette and Journal of Belles Lettres,* (19 May 1821) no. 226, 305–8, repr. James E. Barcus, *Shelley: The Critical Heritage* (London and Boston, 1975), 74–80.

4. In the *Quarterly Review* (Dec. 1848), lxxxiv, 153–85, repr. *The Brontës: The Critical Heritage,* ed. Miriam Allott (London, 1974), 105–112.

5. Unsigned review of Shelley's *Adonais, The Literary Gazette and Journal of Belles Lettres* (8 Dec. 1821), cclv, 772, repr. *Keats: The Critical Heritage,* ed. G. M. Matthews (London, 1971), 245–6.

6. Letter to Sarah Jeffrey, 9 June 1819, *The Letters of John Keats, 1814–1821,* ed. Hyder Rollins (Harvard University Press and Cambridge University Press, 1958), ii. 115.

7. See Frederick A. Pottle, 'The Case of Shelley' (1950), *Woodings,* 35, and for his 1968 rewording *Swinden* 19.

8. James E. Barcus, Introduction, *Shelley: The Critical Heritage,* ed. cit., 2.

9. Cp. Barcus loc. cit., 2–3.

10. William Howitt, *Homes and Haunts of the Most Eminent British Poets* (1846) i. 425–31, repr. *Keats: The Critical Heritage,* ed. cit., 311.

11. Arthur Henry Hallam, 'On Some of the Characteristics of Modern Poetry, and on the Lyrical Poems of Alfred Tennyson', *Englishman's Magazine* (Aug. 1831) i. 616–21, repr. (extracts) *Keats: The Critical Heritage,* 264–72.

12. Unsigned review, *The London Magazine and Theatrical Inquisitor,* (March, 1821) iii. 278–81, repr. *Shelley: The Critical Heritage,* 71–2.

13. Unsigned review of *Prometheus Unbound . . . with other poems, The London Magazine and Monthly Critical and Dramatic Review,* Sept.–Oct. 1820, ii. 306–8, 382–91, repr. *Shelley: The Critical Heritage,* 243–4.

14. Review by 'E. Haselfoot' of Shelley's *Posthumous Poems, Knight's Quarterly Magazine,* Aug. 1824, repr. (extracts) (ed.) Theodore Redpath, *The Young Romantics and Critical Opinion 1807–24* (London, 1973), 399–400.

15. On the pros and cons of the argument for W. S. Walker's authorship of the review see Theodore Redpath, op. cit., 323–4 *n.* The conjecture is that Walker adopted 'a tortuous white-sheet procedure' because of his changed views.

16. 'Conversations and Reminiscences recorded by the Bishop of Lincoln', *The Prose Works of William Wordsworth*, ed. A. B. Grossart (1876) iii. 458–67.

17. *The Use of Poetry and the Use of Criticism*, 89–90.

18. *The Quarterly Review* (October, 1821), xxvi. 168–80, repr. *Shelley: The Critical Heritage*, 254–67. Walker is referring to one of Shelley's 'three different styles: one which can be generally understood; another which can only be understood by the author; and a third which is absolutely and intrinsically unintelligible' (*Critical Heritage*, 254).

19. I. J. Kapstein, 'The Meaning of Shelley's *Mont Blanc*', *PMLA*, lxii (1947), repr. (extracts) *Swinden*, 165–77 (for the passage quoted see 165).

20. Frederick A. Pottle, loc. cit., repr. *Woodings*, 47, *Swinden*, 27.

21. See F. R. Leavis, *Revaluation* (London, 1936), 203–32.

22. William Hazlitt, review of *Posthumous Poems*, *Edinburgh Review* (July, 1824) xi. 496–516, repr. *Shelley: The Critical Heritage* (ed. cit.), 335–45; for the passages quoted see 335, 340, 341.

23. See Walker, loc. cit. (above *n.* 18), and for the passages quoted *Shelley: The Critical Heritage*, 258–9.

24. The comment is attributed (via a secondary source) to James Russell Lowell and the passage cited from *The Cenci*—which runs 'Do you not see that rock there which appeareth/To hold itself up with a throe appalling,/And, through the very pang of what it feareth,/So many ages hath been falling, falling?—roughly approximates to *The Cenci* III.i, 227–35, which like the rest of the play is in blank verse. See *Shelley: The Critical Heritage*, ed. cit., 224. Details concerning this mysterious attribution have been assembled too late for the press and will be discussed elsewhere.

25. T. S. Eliot in 'A Note on Richard Crashaw', *For Lancelot Andrews* (London, 1928), repr. *Swinden*, 70–71; F. R. Leavis, *Revaluation*, ed. cit., 204–8; Allan Tate, 'Understanding Modern Poetry', *Reason in Madness* (1941), repr. *Swinden*, 76–7. See further Bernard Beatty, 'The transformation of discourse: *Epipsychidion*, *Adonais* and certain lyrics', pp. 213–38 below.

26. 'The mind in that mysterious instant Shelley likened beautifully to a fading coal . . . the cardiac condition which the Italian physiologist Luigi Galvani, using a phrase almost as beautiful as Shelley's called 'the enchantment of the heart', *A Portrait of the Artist as a Young Man*, chap. V, the Viking Critical Library (New York, 1968), ed. Chester G. Anderson. (For Anderson's gloss on Joyce and Shelley see 536).

27. 'E. Haselfoot' (W. S. Walker?), review of *Posthumous Poems*, *Knight's Quarterly Magazine* (Aug. 1824), repr. ed. Theodore Redpath, *The Young Romantics and Critical Opinion 1807–24* (1973), 403; Henry Crabb Robinson, diary entries 28 Dec. 1821, 2 March 1828, 10 Jan. 1836; repr. *Shelley: The Critical Heritage*, 267, 268, 94.

28. S. T. Coleridge, Letter to John E. Reade, Dec. 1830, *The Collected Letters of Samuel Taylor Coleridge*, ed. G. L. Griggs (1971), vi. 849–50, repr. *Shelley: The Critical Heritage*, 354.

29. George Macdonald, 'Shelley', *A Dish of Orts* (1893), 271, 281 (*Encyclopaedia Britannica*, eleventh edition, 1042–3).

30. Parallels with 'Alastor' are referred to by Robert Lee Woolf, *The Golden Key: A Study of the Fiction of George Macdonald* (New Haven, 1961), 46, 55, 86, 92, 94.

31. For G. H. Lewes's review see *The Westminster Review* xxxv (April 1841), 303–44 and for the comment on Lewes's attitude to Shelley, *Woodings*, Introduction, 16–17.

32. *Middlemarch* Book IV, chap. 37 Riverside edn, ed. Gordon Haught (1956).

33. Kenneth Muir, 'Shelley's Heirs', *Penguin New Writing* No. 26 (1946), 117. I am much indebted to this essay for many of the following points about the Chartist poets.

34. Kenneth Muir, loc. cit., 127.

35. J. S. Mill, *Autobiography* (London, 1878), 186.

36. Kenneth Muir, loc. cit., 132.

37. Letter to John Gisborne, 18 June 1822, *Letters* ii. 434.

38. Kenneth Muir, loc. cit., 132. On the membership of the Shelley Society see Newman Ivy White '. . . about four hundred members, among them Robert Browning, George Bernard Shaw, W. M. Rossetti, H. B. Forman, F. J. Furnivall and T. J. Wise. For two years this society flourished and published volumes by or about Shelley, besides managing public productions of both *Hellas* and *The Cenci* . . . By 1887 forty or fifty of lyrics had been set to music, as well as all the choral parts of *Hellas*', *Shelley* (New York, 1940) ii. 412.

39. Isaac D'Israeli's *Curiosities of Literature* first appeared 1791–3.

40. *Venetia*, Book VI, chapter iv (Collected edition of the Novels and Tales [1871]), 415, 418.

41. Book IV, chapter ii (ed. cit., 220).

42. Book VI, chapter viii (ed. cit., 438).

43. Book VI, chapter viii (ed. cit., 438).

44. Richard Garnett, 'Shelley and Lord Beaconsfield' (1887), repr. in his *Essays of an Ex-Librarian* (London, 1901).

45. Charles Kingsley, 'Thoughts on Byron and Shelley', *Fraser's Magazine* (Nov. 1853), repr. *Miscellanies* (1860), I 304–24.

46. *Miscellanies* (1860), i. 311, 212.

47. For these Shelley references in *Yeast* see Kingsley's Novels (Macmillan ed. 1889–90), vol. I, 1, 9, 15, 26; and in *Two Years Ago*, ed. cit., vol. II, chap. ii, 24; chap. xv, 124; chap. xv, 124; chap. xxiv, 188.

48. Robert Browning's *An Essay on Percy Bysshe Shelley*, first pub. in the (spurious) *Letters of Percy Bysshe Shelley* (1852), repr. H. F. B. Brett-Smith with Shelley's *Defence of Poetry* and Peacock's *The Four Ages of Poetry* (Oxford, 1921). The passages referred to here are incorporated in *Browning*, ed. Kenneth Allott (Oxford, 1967), Appendix 191–6.

49. See Samuel E. Brown, 'The Unpublished Passages in the Manuscript of Ruskin's Autobiography', *Victorian Newsletter*, No. 16 (Autumn, 1959), 12.

50. *Reminiscences*, ed. J. A. Froude (1881), ii. 325.

51. *Critical and Miscellaneous Essays*, Centenary Edition (1899), iii. 31.

52. Duerksen, op. cit., 125; Carlyle, *On Heroes, Hero-Worship and the Heroic in History*, ed. cit., v. 159.

53. Arnold first described Shelley as 'a beautiful *and ineffectual* angel, beating in the void his luminous wings in vain' in his essay on Byron (1881), repr. *The*

*Complete Prose Works of Matthew Arnold*, ed. R. W. Super, (Ann Arbor, 1960–77), i. 237 and repeated it in his essay on Shelley (1888), repr. *Complete Prose Works*, xi. 327.

54. *Complete Prose Works*, xi. 308, 320, 323.

55. *The Letters of Matthew Arnold to Arthur Hugh Clough*, ed. H. F. Lowry (Oxford, 1932), 146.

56. 'Notes on Tragedy' (1885), *George Eliot's Life*, ed. J. W. Cross, vol. II, chapter xv, p. 48.

57. *Letters to Clough*, 97, 124.

58. *Complete Prose Works*, iii. 34 *n.*

59. 'Shelley', op. cit., xi. 327.

60. Arthur Hallam, 'On Some of the Characteristics of Modern Poetry and on the Lyrical Poems of Alfred Tennyson', *Englishman's Magazine* (Aug. 1831), 266.

61. *Keats: The Critical Heritage*, 271. For the passage from Arnold's 1853 Preface see *Complete Prose Works*, i. 1.

62. 'The Metaphysical Poets' (1921), repr. in his *Selected Essays* (London, 1932), 288.

63. *Keats: The Critical Heritage*, 267.

64. Ibid.

65. Ibid., 264.

66. Hallam Tennyson, *Alfred Lord Tennyson: A Memoir by His Son* (New York and London, 1897), ii. 70; ed. Hallam Tennyson, *Tennyson and His Friends* (London, 1911), 269.

67. *Memoir*, i. 256–7.

68. 'Percy Bysshe Shelley', *The National Review* (1856), repr. *Literary Studies*, 2 vols. ed. G. Sampson (London, 1911); for the passages quoted see i. 97–8, 100–1.

69. See Phyllis Bartlett, ' "Seraph of Heaven": A Shelleyan Dream in Hardy's Fiction', *PMLA*, lxx (Sept. 1955), 624–35, and her 'Hardy's Shelley', K-SJ iv (Winter, 1955), 15–29.

70. Yeats, 'The Philosophy of Shelley's Poetry' (1900), repr. *Essays and Introductions* (London, 1961), 77.

71. See Yeats, *Autobiographies* (London, 1955), 11.

72. Yeats, 'The Philosophy of Shelley's Poetry', loc. cit., 65–6.

73. Ibid., 77–8.

74. Yeats, 'Prometheus Unbound', *The Spectator* Cl (17 March 1935), 367.

75. Allen Tate, from 'Understanding Modern Poetry', *Reason in Madness* (New York, 1941), repr. *Swinden*, 76–7.

76. T. S. Eliot, 'A Note on Richard Crashaw', *For Lancelot Andrewes* (London, 1928), repr. *Swinden*, 1979.

77. Donald Davie, from *Purity of Diction in English Verse* (London, 1952), repr. *Swinden,* 1979.

78. *The Use of Poetry and the Use of Criticism*, 89–90.

79. John Holloway in 'The Poetry of Shelley', Introduction to his *Selected Poems of Percy Bysshe Shelley* (London, 1960), repr. *Swinden*, 142.

80. Ibid.

81. For a notable illustration of the interplay of scholarship and criticism in this field see Geoffrey Matthews, 'Shelley's Lyrics', *The Morality of Art: Essays Presented to G. Wilson Knight*, ed. D. W. Jefferson (London, 1969), 195–209.

# Shelley's 'Gothick' in
# *St. Irvyne* and after

## DAVID SEED

Apart from a private edition of some poems which he and his sisters had written, it is often forgotten that Shelley's first published work was a prose romance. *Zastrozzi* (1810) was part of an outburst of creative activity in 1809 and 1810 which produced a companion prose piece—*St. Irvyne*—miscellaneous shorter poems and 'The Wandering Jew'. All of these works bear clear marks of influence from the Gothic literature Shelley was reading at the time and partly for this reason they have been either ignored or written off as juvenile sensationalism. F. R. Leavis is typical in linking them to 'the trashy fantasies and cheap excitements of the Terror school'.[1] He is certainly right about the Gothic influence but far too hasty in his dismissal. These early writings have at least the importance of showing Shelley's first attempts at literary expression. An important factor in his struggle to find a subject and an individual style was how to come to terms with the Gothic. Even when he seems to be revamping sensational themes, as he does in *Zastrozzi*, Shelley was in fact selecting from the Gothic materials at his disposal, since this first prose work excluded the supernatural. *St. Irvyne* is, even by the standards of these first writings, a disjointed and uneven romance, but then it would be a mistake to expect a fully achieved work so early in Shelley's literary career. However, the very unevenness of *St. Irvyne* has a value since it indicates that it was a transitional piece of writing which demonstrates Shelley's growing restlessness with conventional Gothic themes and his attempts to modify and reduce Gothic modes of expression.

Throughout his childhood Shelley had shown a constant interest in the Gothic. A copy of Lewis's *Tales of Terror* (1799) was found in the library at Field Place, the Shelley family home.[2] Not content with reading, however, Shelley would spend whole nights trying to lay ghosts and to cast spells, as Richard Holmes reminds us in his lively recent biography,[3] which is notable— among many other things—for its vivid evocation of the lifelong fascination which the Gothic held for Shelley, and which can still be felt at work in the sombre passages of his last poem, 'The Triumph of Life'. It is in keeping with this leaning that, while at Syon House Academy, he should have fastened on the productions of the Minerva Press which published and circulated many Gothic novels in the first decade of the nineteenth century. The year 1809 saw Shelley collaborating with his cousin Thomas Medwin in what Medwin described as 'the commencement of a wild and extravagant romance'.[4] This work was subsequently abandoned in favour of 'The Wandering Jew', an important early poem which has only recently been admitted to the Shelley canon since Medwin had claimed that he and Shelley had collaborated in this work.[5] Elsewhere, however, in the foreword to his own poem on the same legend—*Ahasuerus, The Wanderer* (1823)—Medwin explained that the earlier poem had been a 'juvenile production of Shelley alone.'[6] This is an important matter since, as we shall see, Shelley's interest in the Gothic and in the Wandering Jew went hand in hand with each other.

The two collections of poetry which Shelley produced in 1810—*Original Poetry by Victor and Cazire* and *Posthumous Fragments of Margaret Nicholson*—both contain a high proportion of Gothic materials, the former even reprinting 'St. Edmund's Eve' verbatim from Lewis's *Tales of Terror*. Vampires, the Banshee, and an array of spectres all figure prominently, and the morality of these poems is equally conventional. Deeds of dishonour must be purged by death even if the guilt has passed down to a later generation. 'Ghasta or, The Avenging Demon!!!' manages to combine the theme of guilt with that of the Wandering Jew. A stranger meets a weary warrior at an inn and learns that he is being tormented by a female ghost. The stranger offers to help and summons the ghost through an incantation. From her he learns that the warrior had wronged her and as punishment he reveals the brand on his brow. Horror-stricken, 'the warrior sank convulsed in death' and there the poem ends.[7] The influence of Monk Lewis is quite evident in Shelley's explanatory note that he had taken the idea of the poem from 'a few unconnected German stanzas'. Substantially the same device is used in his note on

Ahasuerus for *Queen Mab* which, he claims, was again a translation from the German.[8]

Not surprisingly, several critics have noted clear debts to earlier Gothic novels in *Zastrozzi*.[9] These parallels are misleading if they suggest that Shelley is simply repeating themes, however. He filters out the supernatural and any extensive treatment of oppression at the hands of family or Church such as we find in the fiction of Lewis or Mrs. Radcliffe. Instead the narrative centres on one Verezzi, a passive individual who is torn between the sexual attractions of Matilda and the ethereal and moral qualities of Julia. The narrative, in other words, dramatizes a conflict between sexuality and conscience. Partly from sheer weakness Verezzi is unable to reconcile these rival claims and, during a climactic scene where the two female characters finally confront each other, he stabs himself to death. *Zastrozzi* is a lurid and sensational work where violence spreads into the texture of the language itself. Everything focuses on the central psychological conflict to which description, narrative continuity, and even rudimentary explanation are sacrificed. Throughout this work sexuality is constantly associated with evil and wickedness, to the extent that a psychiatrist has used this text as evidence for the disturbed state of Shelley's adolescent psyche.[10] Suffice it to say here that *Zastrozzi* attempts fewer things than *St. Irvyne* and that its interest is limited accordingly.

*St. Irvyne; Or, The Rosicrucian*, was published in January 1811, and from the very beginning shows clear differences from *Zastrozzi*. The latter opened with action (the abduction of the hero) whereas *St. Irvyne* presents an apocalyptic thunder-storm:

> Red thunder-clouds, borne on the wings of the midnight whirlwind, floated, at fits, athwart the crimson-coloured orbit of the moon; the rising fierceness of the blast sighed through the stunted shrubs, which, bending before its violence, inclined towards the rocks whereon they grew:[11]

Shelley brilliantly evokes lurid shifts in light, the movement of the clouds, the change from gale to torrential downpour, and rising hubbub of the storm. This scene looks forward to Shelley's descriptive interest in natural change in his later poetry. The storm mirrors the inner turmoil of the central character Wolfstein through metaphorical hints in words like 'fits', 'fierceness', and 'sighs'; and thereby follows the method of *Zastrozzi*. There are, however, two significant differences. The description here is much fuller and more precise than in the earlier romance, and also it inflates Wolfstein's mental conflict to cosmic proportions as if his emotions will tear apart the very fabric of nature. Verbal references to the 'gulf' yawning before him on the mountainside where he has reclined, and to the 'darkness visible' of the cave where he is taken both make gestures towards Miltonic grandeur, and indeed a quotation from *Paradise Lost* forms the epigraph to chapter III.

An early fragment entitled 'Sadak the Wanderer' and dated conjecturally at about the same time as *St. Irvyne* opens in a similar way. Sadak, obviously an alternative form of the Wandering Jew, has made his way to a mountain-top to find relief from endless suffering. As with Wolfstein, his position throws his isolation into maximum prominence. The poet urges Sadak to plunge from the precipice, braving death in a transcendent but self-destructive gesture. Wolfstein by contrast collapses into unconsciousness. At this point Shelley introduces a brief humanizing element when some monks discover his body, but almost immediately a group of bandits attack them and capture Wolfstein.[12] Impressed by his lofty defiance of their threats, the bandits invite Wolfstein to join them, which he proceeds to do. In theory he has now become a bandit; in fact Shelley glosses over his activities with the gang and emphasizes how much of a brooding solitary Wolfstein is. We actually see him wandering alone in the Alps, meditating on his lot, and when an Italian Count appears on the scene, Wolfstein takes no part in the attack on him and his companions. Instead he joins the narrator in disapproving of the slaughter and limits his activity to contemplating the 'light symmetrical figure' of one Megalena de Metastasio who is captured (p. 174). In other words we must distinguish Wolfstein from the conventional evaluation of the bandits as 'a gang of lawless and desperate villains' (p. 175).

It seems then as if Wolfstein is a morally positive figure, but later in the narrative Shelley explains that he has had to abandon his German estate for 'an event too dreadful for narration' (p. 186). So he is at the same time guilty, a morally ambiguous figure, neither blameless or conventionally responsible for wrong-doing and at times Shelley appears to stress his majesty and nobility of stature in order to reconcile these ambiguities. He is, in other words, preoccupied mainly by Wolfstein's style, by the aristocratic indifference which he shows to his fate at the hands of the bandits. This emphasis is quite in keeping with Shelley's praise for impressive central characters in Thomas Hogg's novel, *Memoirs of Count Alexy Haimatoff* (1814), and Godwin's *Mandeville* (1817).[13] Wolfstein's notional guilt is partly a device to increase his isolation and is soon forgotten once events have gathered momentum. The very fact that Shelley concentrates on his isolation and on his temperament rather than on his guilt resembles a similar emphasis in the early poems using the Wandering Jew. In 'Ghasta' he becomes an agent of retribution and in 'The Wandering Jew's Soliliquy' (from the Esdaile MS.) he rails against the tyrant who condemned him to endless suffering. In each case the original cause of the wanderer's predicament has been erased or forgotten.

Fascinated by Megalena, Wolfstein learns with dismay that the bandit chief, Cavigni, intends to make her his wife, and decides to murder him. This decision shows that Wolfstein is no Verezzi, since the latter did not initiate any actions to speak of. Wolfstein takes on the stature of a Romantic hero when he longs for what he calls 'liberty' but this does not mean simply freedom from the bandits. He has in mind the more idealized notion of freedom from the conventional moral restraints of society, whereby his love for Megalena supplies enough justification for murdering Cavigni. His first attempt fails. His second is made while the bandits are feasting together, and is anticipated by the recital of a German ballad—and here Shelley is again drawing on Lewis's *Tales of Terror*—about a monk bewailing the death of his loved one.[14] In a frenzy he breaks open her coffin. Her skeleton, 'which dripp'd with the chill dew of hell' (p. 192), rises and the monk collapses in an embrace which signals his death. Wolfstein in the meantime slips poison into Cavigni's cup and the bandit chief falls to the ground in convulsions. With apparently suicidal bravado Wolfstein tells the bandits that he has poisoned him whereupon, contrary to the reader's expectations, another high-ranking bandit called Ginotti intercedes on his behalf, giving him a night's grace in which to escape. Wolfstein takes this opportunity and he and Megalena set off for Genoa.

By this point in the narrative it should be evident that Shelley has internalized the action far less than in *Zastrozzi*. There is comparatively more attention paid to setting, the action is fuller and contains more characters and it also has a more obvious consistency in terms of simple adventure. But Shelley still conceives of the action in mainly dramatic terms. In *Zastrozzi*, the narrative focuses its drama on pairs of characters: conflict between Verezzi and Matilda during the central portion of the narrative, and between Matilda and Julia at the climax. Similarly Wolfstein pits himself against Cavigni and then, more importantly, against Ginotti.

Like Wolfstein and Megalena, Ginotti has no antecedents. All three characters are given a purely dramatic identity. We know nothing of their origins or history, but only pay attention to their actions. Ginotti is a figure of mystery, reserved and gloomy, an object of fear to the other bandits. The first time that Wolfstein tries to poison Cavigni Ginotti dashes his cup from his mouth at the crucial moment. He seems, in other words, to know that the drink was poisoned. At the second attempt he 'intentionally' averts his gaze from Wolfstein so that he can again put poison in the cup. These mysterious actions give Ginotti a powerful psychological hold over Wolfstein; indeed he literally has the power of life or death when the former admits killing Cavigni. Inevitably Wolfstein recognizes that he is a lesser being: 'from the gaze of Ginotti Wolfstein's soul shrank, enhorrored, in confessed inferiority' (p. 195). So, at the very point where Wolfstein feels that he is beginning to achieve freedom, ironically he falls under the spell of Ginotti.

As the narrative progresses this hold strengthens. When Wolfstein and Megalena are fleeing to Genoa, a stranger appears at their inn and proves to be none other than Ginotti who forces Wolfstein to swear a solemn oath that he will discharge his obligation to the other. Ironically Ginotti states that he has conferred 'benefits' on Wolfstein, but the latter's temporary exhilaration at escape gives way quickly to a constant anxiety and even fear about his own autonomy. In Genoa Wolfstein goes to a party and sees in the crowd—of course Ginotti. As he grows bored with Megalena he takes to gambling and at the tables sees again Ginotti. Obviously Shelley is presenting a mysterious relationship between the two men, one which is closer than average social contact would make possible.

Clearly the sudden reappearances of Ginotti outrage our sense of probability and only become acceptable because Shelley minimizes the density of the narrative generally. He shows particular impatience with transitions, for example. Again and again he dismisses the various journeys in *St. Irvyne* as irrelevant periods between episodes charged with drama. Indeed the narratives of both of his prose romances take on a serial quality from passing rapidly from scene to scene as if we were witnessing a play. Thus we move rapidly from Wolfstein's poisoning to a brief soliloquy ('soliloquize' is a recurring term for thinking aloud in this work); then he meets Megalena to plan their flight and the scene shifts yet again to Breno where Ginotti catches up with them. Shelley's impatience with circumstantiality certainly gives the narrative a rapid pace but it leads him into difficulties of fact later in the narrative.

Ginotti can best be described as Wolfstein's *doppelgänger* or double, and the two figures thus represent different parts of the same self. Take, for example, the parallels between them. Both are of arresting stature and both have imperious eyes. Both are solitaries and both have temporary and fortuitous contact with the bandits. Also Ginotti steps to the forefront of the action just at the point where Wolfstein commits murder. Shelley hints at privileged knowledge of Wolfstein's plans as if Ginotti has gained some kind of access to his very mind. Wolfstein thus feels specific fear from Ginotti's knowledge of his murder, and a more general and dizzying fear that Ginotti may be controlling his every action. This increases in their brief confrontation at the party, and increases again when they meet at the gaming tables. Here Wolfstein determines to pursue Ginotti and unravel the mystery surrounding him. He follows him out into the streets but loses him. Returning to his house he half-notices, out of the corner of his eye, that one of the chairmen is very tall. Just as they arrive at his door the chairman reveals himself as Ginotti. Wolfstein's reaction is characteristic: 'as if hell had yawned at the feet of the hapless Wolfstein, as if some spectre of the night had blasted his straining eyeball, so did he stand transfixed' (p. 213). This description takes us back to the opening of the romance where

Wolfstein was standing on the brink of a precipice. Fear and the desire for oblivion smothered his contemplated suicide which came to nothing. But the image recurs again and again in the narrative to reflect Wolfstein's vertiginous terror at being helpless to control his own actions. It is interesting that Shelley preserves a Gothic vocabulary (the 'spectre' in the quotation above) without ever specifying one particular meaning. The gulf and pit have obvious connotations of Hell and this figure thus relates to the question of blasphemy raised later in the romance. At the beginning we saw a storm where Wolfstein's ego, as it were, filled all natural space. The pit emblematizes the opposite possibility— the fall of the self down to annihilation. For Shelley is working here with extreme opposites: man against God, total power against annihilation, etc. There is virtually no social middle ground, at least in the first half of the work. After he sees Ginotti at the party Wolfstein dreams of being pursued towards the brink of a precipice by an evil force. At the last minute Ginotti rushes forward to save him. Ginotti has, in other words, become internalized into a figure of dream. This helps to explain why he disappears temporarily into the night on their subsequent meeting, and why he seems to hover, literally and metaphysically, just on the edge of Wolfstein's vision. Hence, in the passage quoted above, Wolfstein's eyeball could be straining with the effort to see as well as from terror, and it is interesting that Ginotti's power, like that of the Ancient Mariner, is concentrated in his eyes. This is why Wolfstein is 'transfixed'.

Partly we could say that Ginotti becomes a personification of Wolfstein's conscience. After another death—this time in Genoa—he flees yet again with Megalena, and as epigraph to Chapter VIII Shelley uses a brief quotation from 'The Wandering Jew' which describes a paroxysm of fear. The key lines are as follows:

> The strange gaze of his meteor eye,
> Which, frenzied, and rolling dreadfully,
>     Glar'd with hideous gleam,
> Would chill like the spectre gaze of Death,
>     As, conjur'd by feverish dream,
> He seems o'er the sick man's couch to stand,
> And shakes the fell lance in his skeleton hand.[15]

Paulo, the wanderer of this poem, has the same proud gaze as Wolfstein and here, as in *St. Irvyne*, Shelley tries to pack emotion into the eyes. Also similar is the equivocation over Gothic vocabulary. Death produces, but only metaphorically, a 'spectre gaze' and the double analogy ('like . . . as . . .') keeps the impression carefully ambiguous, perhaps the product of fever. In 'The Wandering Jew' there is no clear narrative line partly because Shelley evidently could not decide on a unified subject. The opening is anti-monastic in that Paulo makes off with a novice just on the verge of taking her vows; then the subject takes on a brief philosophical dimension when the two discuss mortality; a long retrospective description of how Paulo fell under the curse then follows, and the last canto deals with the jealously of a rival for the girl's charms. Paulo's fear then is awkwardly isolated whereas in *St. Irvyne* the epigraph fits into Wolfstein's mounting panic. It is Ginotti's pursuit which gives as strong an impetus to these chapters as does Falkland's pursuit in *The Adventures of Caleb Williams* (1794).

In so far as he becomes a temporary personification of Wolfstein's conscience, Ginotti resembles a more famous example of the *doppelgänger*, Poe's William Wilson. In Poe's story Wilson feels dogged by his double, without even the notional justification supplied by the murder of Cavigni. Like Wolfstein he becomes a profligate and a gambler, and is exposed by his double as a cheat. He tries to escape but without success and expresses his desperation in rhetoric which is quite similar to Shelley's:

> *I fled in vain.* My evil destiny pursued me as if in exultation, and proved, indeed, that the exercise of its mysterious dominion had as yet only begun . . . . From his inscrutable tyranny did I at length flee, panic-stricken, as from a pestilence; and to the very ends of the earth *I fled in vain.* (Poe's emphasis).[16]

Wilson's fear of his double is articulated in terms of absolute control; his double becomes his destiny. Similarly Ginotti takes the place formerly occupied by God in Wolfstein's mind. He too becomes an embodiment of fatality, pursuing his victim as if for retribution or as if directing him towards a preordained end.

Also, like Wilson's double, Ginotti too is 'inscrutable' and described in the vocabulary of power. He exercises 'empire' over Wolfstein's soul, for example, and demonstrates a preternatural ability to track him down wherever he goes. D. G. Halliburton has argued ingeniously that Wolfstein wants God to act against him in order to relieve his sufferings without incurring the guilt of suicide; and in order to erase his doubts about God's existence.[17] The latter certainty is denied him by the emergence of Ginotti since he appears to possess knowledge and powers reserved for God. At times he thus seems to Wolfstein an agent of retribution, but Shelley carefully maintains a margin of mystery which prevents attributing any categorical identity to Ginotti.

In a recent survey of the double in fiction Claire Rosenfield has suggested:

> . . . the novelist who consciously or unconsciously exploits psychological doubles may either juxtapose or duplicate two characters; the one representing the socially acceptable or conventional personality, the other externalizing the free, uninhibited, often criminal self.[18]

This proposition would fit a later work like *Dr. Jekyll and Mr. Hyde* much better than *St. Irvyne*, because in the latter there is little contrast between social and non-social areas of the self. Dr. Jekyll consistently personifies social moderation, while Mr. Hyde equally consistently personifies archaic violent impulses. However, we note similarities between Ginotti and Wolfstein at one point, differences at another. The relation of the one to the other takes on interest because it is constantly dynamic, constantly changing. As Ginotti gains a stronger and stronger hold over Wolfstein he penetrates apparently into every area of his mind.

By contrast the love between Wolfstein and Megalena is banal and perfunctory. Megalena gives her love and then her body to Wolfstein without the suspicion of a struggle, overwhelmed by his grandiose claim that after 'the earth is dissolved away' they will both exist 'in eternal, indivisible . . . union' (p. 205). Verezzi makes a similar profession of love, as does Paulo in 'The Wandering Jew'. In each case the declaration grows out of Shelley's platonic concept of the union between kindred spirits which will survive the passage of time.[19] In *Zastrozzi* the rapid reversals of events as well as the basic passivity of Verezzi's character undermine his declaration, while Paulo's love is doomed by his general fate. In *St. Irvyne* the main interest centres on the mysterious connection between Ginotti and Wolfstein and this jostles the love-theme well to one side. Chapter IV, for instance, inserts a rather gratuitous episode which revolves around an aristocratic maiden called Olympia and which led one critic to speculate that it had been designed exclusively to 'increase the reader's contempt and abhorrence of the sex'.[20] Olympia is seized with a passion for Wolfstein and commits suicide when her feelings are not returned. Everything happens with characteristic Shelleyan speed, the main point of the episode being to drive the fugitives from Genoa to a castle in Bohemia where Ginotti finally reveals his identity.

In its retrospective method and general style Ginotti's narrative draws on Canto III of 'The Wandering Jew' where Paulo describes his suffering from his insult to Christ up to the present day. As his narrative progresses Paulo emerges as a figure with privileged insight:

> I pierce with intellectual eye,
> Into each hidden mystery;
> I penetrate the fertile womb
> Of nature; I produce to light
> The secrets of the teeming earth . . .[21]

God's curse on him has by now shaded into a positive benefit since it has transformed him into a seer. Here the transcendental impulse towards hidden knowledge finds sexual expression as if the mind's penetration fertilizes unseen areas of life. Paulo's pride in his own activity shifts him clearly from a villain into a hero who braves his fate with images of apocalyptic destruction. In *St. Irvyne* Shelley replaces an original act of sin (against Christ) with a psychological impulse. Ginotti tells Wolfstein that from his earliest youth he had been driven by curiosity, 'a desire of unveiling the latent mysteries of Nature' (p. 270); whilst Wolfstein, also a wanderer, has committed some nameless deed in the past. Whereas the first epigraph from 'The Wandering Jew' referred to Wolfstein, now a quotation from Canto III heads the chapter which contains Ginotti's narrative. The lines compare the wanderer to a 'scathed' pine-tree which has been struck by lightning, but which remains 'majestic even in death'.[22] Not only is Ginotti now linked with the Wandering Jew, but Shelley has cut out in his epigraph any direct reference to the religious origin of the legend, so that the image now suggests a quasi-heroic resistance to the forces of adversity. This modification of the legend now looks forward to the reappearance of Ahasuerus in Canto VII of *Queen Mab* where his mockery of Christ is justified by a preamble which shows God as a malicious tyrant. Ahasuerus's curse again changes into a privilege since it gives him a unique insight into the corrupting effects of Christianity over a vast stretch of time. The blasted tree image (this time of an oak) reappears to encapsulate Ahasuerus's fortitude in his suffering.[23]

As the religious dimension to the legend is gradually revised, so Shelley reduces the importance of the supernatural. In 'The Wandering Jew' Paulo demonstrates his magical powers by drawing a circle around him. There follows soft music, bright lights and unusual perfumes, in the midst of which appears a 'youthful female form'. She tries to seduce Paulo into signing away his soul in blood on a scroll, but he refuses and collapses unconscious in the tumult which follows.[24] Ginotti undergoes a similar trial, but with fewer pyrotechnics. His experiments in natural philosophy have led him to an impasse and he contemplates suicide. The sound of a convent bell brings him back to humanity and he weeps tears of relief, once again repeating Wolfstein's experiences at the beginning of the romance.[25] But then, falling asleep, he has a terrifying dream. First he seems lifted into the clouds where 'dark forms' move; as he gazes on them the stars blaze with unnatural brightness and soothing music wafts on his ear. As the music reaches a climax he sees 'a form of most exact and superior symmetry' (p. 274) who invites him to submit. When Ginotti refuses the form suddenly reverses into a gigantic and terrifying monster who drags him to the brink of a precipice and forces him to acknowledge his dominion over him. Shelley carefully avoids specifying that the horrific apparition is the Devil and leaves both forms visually vague so as to insist that their impact on Ginotti cannot be adequately explained. Above all, the whole experience is cast within a dream and suggests that Shelley is now moving away from a conventional notion of either magic or Faustian temptation, as demonstrated in 'The Wandering Jew', towards a more psychological conception of devils and apparitions.

Dreams in general play an important role in *St. Irvyne* for they reinforce characters' vulnerability to impressions beyond their control. Thus Wolfstein dreams of Ginotti's powerful hold over him just as Eloise unconsciously admits the sexual fascination which Nempere stimulates through dream. In both cases Shelley manages to convey a loss of control over central areas of the self without ever damaging our awareness that this process is taking place below the level of conscious articulation in either character. In *Zastrozzi* Shelley had already experimented with the evocation of dream-like states. At the opening of the romance Verezzi is seized from an inn during an unnaturally deep sleep and conveyed to a cavern where he is held captive. The continuous darkness blurs the distinction between night and day so that after his release he is not sure whether or not he had been suffering from a hallucination. Indeed one of the few successful aspects of *Zastrozzi* is the way Shelley keeps the narrative poised on the borderline between nightmare and waking. Shelley's interest in dreams is further confirmed by the fact that in 1815 he began to compile a catalogue of dreams with the aim of discovering what elements they possessed in common. This short-lived project helps to explain why dreams should figure prominently in *St. Irvyne*.

Eight or nine years after the publication of *St. Irvyne* Shelley articulated some of the implications of this development away from conventional Gothic in his early writings. The 'Essay on the Devil and Devils' (composed in 1819 or 1820) takes up a sceptical stance towards its subject, but makes an important opening statement:

> The Manichaean philosophy respecting the origin and government of the world, if not true, is at least an hypothesis conformable to the experience of actual facts. To suppose that the world was created and is superintended by two spirits of a balanced power and opposite dispositions is simply a personification of the struggle which we experience within ourselves, and which we perceive in the operations of external things as they affect us, between good and evil . . . .

The vulgar are all Manichaeans—all that remains of the popular superstition is mere machinery and accompaniment.[26]

Throughout the essay Shelley adopts a sarcastic attitude towards the role of the Devil within Christianity and, as in the passage quoted, rejects conventional religious belief while leaving the door open to transcendental categories like evil. In effect he detaches Manichaean dualism from Christianity and applies it to the struggle between good and evil which he sees as central to human life. If we apply this notion to Shelley's fiction it helps to explain his preference for dramatic engagements between pairs of antagonists. Verezzi's struggle with Matilda is presented partly as innocence being pitted against evil; Wolfstein's relation to Ginotti is more complex, but certainly, as far as Wolfstein is concerned, Ginotti personifies evil power. In Ginotti's dream we witness a particularly violent struggle when the evil form grasps his neck in a grip of iron. All the way through the romance the narrative keeps this sense of struggle in one form or another, and alternates between internal and external action in a way which parallels Shelley's description in the essay. Acts of physical violence constantly give way to dream; but, although Ginotti describes his apparitions as 'phantoms' or 'forms', they do not lack physical force.

Ginotti's quest for knowledge anticipates that of a rather more famous fictional hero—Mary Shelley's Victor Frankenstein. Both are driven on by an ambition to gain intellectual control over Nature. Both dabble in metaphysics. Ginotti denies the First Cause (one of the traditional arguments for God's existence); Frankenstein is searching for a 'final cause'. Both become obsessed with their studies at the expense of their humanity, and both are hunting for the elixir of life. Ginotti is trying, by an act of intellectual will, to overcome his own mortality, while Frankenstein is searching for the 'cause of generation and mortality'.[27] Despite their intellectual ambitions neither man can achieve his goal unaided. Ginotti must submit to an evil power, and Frankenstein must accept the rather more prosaic assistance of the university lecturers at Ingolstadt. In both cases secret ultimate knowledge is at stake, and the search is moralized as carrying a dreadful cost, in the one case the loss of redemption, in the other the subsequent loss of family. It is impossible to know what part Shelley played in the composition of *Frankenstein* (which was published seven years after *St. Irvyne*), but the presence of biographical parallels between himself and the hero and the fact that he wrote the preface to the first edition in the guise of the author suggests *some* involvement at least. *Frankenstein* further reduces the supernatural elements in the search for the principle of life and, by so doing, puts itself within the development of Shelley's thought from 'The Wandering Jew' to the 'Essay on the Devil'. Shelley confirms this in his 1818 preface where he insists that *Frankenstein* is no 'mere tale of spectres and enchantments'.[28] Since he was gradually casting off the influence of his early reading in the Gothic through the 1810s, his distinction here seems to be more than a conventional plea of novelty.

Although Shelley was turning away from conventional supernaturalism in *St. Irvyne*, he still preserved mystery as an important element in the narrative; and in November 1810 he wrote to his publisher to explain the secondary title of the romance: 'What I mean as "Rosicrucian" is the elixir of eternal life which Ginotti had obtained. Mr. Godwin's Romance of St. Leon, turns upon that superstition; I enveloped it in mystery for the greater excitement of interest'.[29] Godwin's Caleb Williams may lie equally behind both Ginotti and Frankenstein in his guiding impulse, although it does not lead him in a Faustian direction: 'the spring of action which perhaps more than any other, characterized the whole train of my life, was curiosity . . .'[30] *St. Leon* (1799) is an extended parable on the search for happiness where curiosity figures as part of the eponymous protagonist's motivation. A mysterious stranger comes to St. Leon's home whose appearance should by now be familiar:

> His eye-beam sat upon your countenance and seemed to look through you. You wished to escape its penetrating power, but you had not the strength to move. I began to feel as if it were some mysterious and superior being in human form, and not a mortal, with whom I was concerned.[31]

St. Leon's sense of helplessness anticipates Wolfstein's perception of Ginotti's uncanny powers, and he yields to the stranger's offer of secret knowledge. The reader is tantalizingly denied details of the elixir because, as St. Leon explains, 'into that I am forbidden to enter. My design in writing this narrative . . . is not to teach the art of which I am in possession, but to describe the adventures it produced to me'.[32] This focuses one of the main differences between Shelley's and Godwin's use of the legend. Godwin is concerned with consequences, and so the possession of the elixir starts a long train of events in motion which reflect variously on greed, happiness, the nature of society, etc. In *St. Irvyne* the elixir is communicated towards the end of the narrative dealing with Wolfstein. It changes his relation to Ginotti since it dissipates suggestions of malevolence, and seems to introduce a new narrative (Wolfstein's use of the elixir) just at the point where it ends. These differences indicate that Floyd Stovall is grossly exaggerating when he claims that '*St. Irvyne* was largely modelled after Godwin's *St. Leon*'.[33] In a letter to Godwin of 1812 Shelley admitted 'I had indeed read *St. Leon* before I wrote *St. Irvyne*, but the reasoning had *then* made little impression . . .'[34] This is certainly true because it would be difficult to imagine a starker contrast between Shelley's frenetic narrative and Godwin's patient and exhaustive examination of society. The rhythm of *St. Leon* is of the application and collapse of philanthropic schemes and with each collapse pessimism becomes more and more difficult to resist. Shelley's field of action is either sexual or metaphysical, but certainly not social.

At the conclusion to the romance Wolfstein goes to keep his appointment with Ginotti in the ruined abbey of St. Irvyne. To his horror he discovers Megalena's body expiring without any visible cause. On the stroke of midnight Ginotti appears and asks Wolfstein to deny God's existence. When Wolfstein refuses Ginotti is struck down by lightning, only his eyes gleaming luridly with a light symbolic of eternal torment. Wolfstein is also destroyed, 'blackened in terrible convulsions', but at least with the consolation of having saved his soul. Shelley points the moral in no uncertain terms:

> . . . let remorse and repentance expiate the offences which arise from the delusion of the passions, and let endless life be sought from Him who alone can give an eternity of happiness. (p. 298)

This sententious conclusion makes the general moral perspective

of *St. Irvyne* sound far more definite than it really is. Throughout
the romance Shelley has hinted at a transcendental horror which
can be reached through excess of ambition and passion; but he
has generally refused to attach a categorically religious meaning
to it. Secondly, the ending is, to put it mildly, abrupt. Wolfstein's
initiation into ultimate mysteries seems to introduce a new
impetus into the narrative, but just at this point Shelley cuts it off.
It may be that Shelley has briefly adopted a narrative stance
similar to the Abbé Barruel's grandiose denunciations in his
*Memoirs, Illustrating the History of Jacobinism* (1798). Shelley
obtained a copy of this translation in his first term at Oxford (i.e.
October 1810) and although the timing would be very close (*St.
Irvyne* was completed at least by November 1810), this work may
have influenced the romance.[35] Barruel surveys eighteenth
century freemasonry and the Illuminati movement, and,
interestingly in this context, includes some discussion of
Rosicrucianism. He adopts a harshly condemnatory tone towards
figures like Weishaupt (the founder of the Illuminati) whom he
presents as a moral profligate as well as a blasphemous over-
reacher. Barruel's stance is at least consistent, whereas it is
strange for Shelley to pose as a defender of religion at the very
point where he was planning the essay 'The Necessity of Atheism'
(begun that Christmas).

It is difficult to avoid the suspicion that Shelley wanted to
dispose of his characters as speedily as possible. Megalena had
become an encumbrance to the narrative anyway, and if
Wolfstein had successfully applied his secret knowledge it might
have drawn out the action at considerable length. Accordingly
Shelley presents the achievement of this knowledge as self-
destructive. We have already seen the irony of Ginotti, the
embodiment of power, submitting to an evil force. Now he and
Wolfstein are destroyed, Ginotti to everlasting torment. If this
were all, we could simply say that the conclusion was lurid and
abrupt. But there are other problems, and to unravel them we
need to go back to chapter VII of *St. Irvyne*.[36]

Here Shelley suspends the story of Wolfstein and begins a
second narrative centering on one Eloise de St. Irvyne, who, we
are told at the end of the book, is Wolfstein's sister.[37] From this
point on Shelley alternates chapters on each of the two narrative
strands. His purpose seems to have been a kind of doubling,

which we have already met in the relation of Wolfstein to Ginotti. Other parallels exist in the romance. Megalena's father is, like Wolfstein, 'a solitary wanderer on the face of the earth' (p. 184); Megalena composes poetry spontaneously as does Eloise; Olympia's imperious will resembles that of Wolfstein at the beginning of the narrative. Eloise and Wolfstein both dream of losing themselves to a powerful superior being. In short every character seems to echo or resemble another. George Levine has noted similar doublings in *Frankenstein* and argues that the inter-relationship between characters

> suggests how deeply incestuous and Oedipal the relationships are. It suggests, too, how close to the surface of this world are motives derived not from external experience, but from emotional and psychic energies beneath the surface of things.[38]

Levine's comment is apt since such connections in *St. Irvyne* are indeed 'beneath the surface of things' and for this reason are mysteriously complicated. Take, for example, the verbal parallels between Megalena's first impression of Wolfstein and Eloise's similar impression of Nempere (who is subsequently identified as Ginotti under another name). Megalena's reaction is as follows:

> His countenance . . . was engaging and beautiful; not that beauty which may be freely acknowledged, but inwardly confessed by every beholder with sensations penetrating and resistless . . . (p. 178)

Eloise perceives Nempere in almost identical terms:

> His countenance of excessive beauty even, but dark, emanated with an expression of superhuman loveliness; not that grace which may freely be admired, but acknowledged in the inmost soul by sensations mysterious, and before unexperienced. (p. 238)

In both cases Shelley demonstrates a desire to penetrate surfaces. Both passages dismiss a conventional beauty which resides in mere appearance and attempt to penetrate 'inwardly' to the 'inmost' areas of the self. Both descriptions carry clear sexual undertones (the penetration of secret parts of the self by exciting sensations) which extend in incestuous directions as we trace the connections between the characters. In the first we see Wolfstein through Megalena's eyes but, since the dominant perspective is Wolfstein's, it is almost as if he is watching the impression he is making. Later in the narrative Ginotti/Nempere becomes an obstacle to their sexual pleasure and disrupts their relationship. Eloise is not simply a sister of Wolfstein, but his female duplication insofar as she too falls under the power of Ginotti/Nempere. She retraces her brother's narrative in more sexual terms and subsequently has a child by Nempere. The danger in this kind of analysis would be to reduce all aspects of the narrative to incest. A. P. Antippas comes close to doing this in his examination of *St. Irvyne*. The parallels are, as he admits, sometimes crude, and could partly be explained simply as efforts on Shelley's part to bind the two narrative strands together. But Shelley's use of sexual nuance and of other more cryptic connections implies a deeper set of relations, even though these relations never come to light completely. The presence of incest in the romance need not be surprising since Shelley dealt with the subject tentatively in 'Rosalind and Helen' and explicitly in *The Cenci*. In *St. Irvyne* it is essential that the connection between characters should remain mysterious and Antippas relates this interestingly to the battle between Good and Evil:

> Evil and Good are neither figured forth distinctly nor defined clearly and appear as parallel shifting forms who are specter-shadow impostures of each other—each striving to authenticate itself at the expense of the others. These projections may also certainly be considered spatially distinct, objectified impersonations of the author's own ethical debate . . .[39]

This proposition helpfully modifies Shelley's own statement about the Manichaean struggle between Good and Evil, since Antippas moves away from a conflict between clearly identified adversaries to authorial projections who relate dramatically to each other but whose identity retains a blurred edge since it is continually shifting. This is precisely how the characters relate to each other in *St. Irvyne*. They are constantly moving nearer to each other or drawing away as fresh resemblances arise.

*St. Irvyne* thus becomes a considerably more intricate work to read than *Zastrozzi*. In the earlier romance Shelley focuses our attention throughout on Verezzi and establishes a perspective which brings the reader as close as possible to total identification with the protagonist. Witness the description of how he regains consciousness after one of his swoons:

> The soul of Verezzi was filled with irresistible disgust, as, recovering, he found himself in Matilda's arms. His whole frame trembled with chilly horror, and he could scarcely withold himself from again fainting.[40]

Shelley tries to pack the emotional force of the passage into key nouns like 'disgust' and 'horror', a crude enough tactic and one which precludes any sort of critical distancing on the reader's part. In *St. Irvyne*, on the other hand, Shelley begins to make use of extensive narrative comment which ironizes the passions of Wolfstein and Megalena. This sets up a clear distinction between an external narrative perspective and Wolfstein's own internal one. Once analogies and parallels begin to multiply the number of perspectives increases proportionately. The reader constantly has to pause and note similarities between characters and even between passages of description which has the overall effect of creating uncertainty. Once again every character seems to be an echo of another. The borders of identity blur and the linear thrust of the narrative slows down as the reader is taken up more and more with spatial cross-references. This is yet another reason why the assertive certainty of Shelley's moralizing conclusion does not ring true. In *Zastrozzi* the sensational, exclamatory language more or less forces the reader to wallow in the protagonist's horrors. In *St. Irvyne*, by contrast, Shelley has brought his predilection for the sensational under a firmer control. This is borne out by the opening storm-description, for instance. As the romance bends even farther away from the Gothic so its narrative language becomes more restrained. This is quite in keeping with Shelley's use of doubles and parallelism since it asks the reader to think more consistently about the narrative.

Shelley's 'Essay on Love' which D. L. Clark dates at 1814–15, offers an alternative, less sexual or moral interpretation of the use of doubles in *St. Irvyne*.[41] In this essay Shelley broadens the concept of love to include a 'powerful attraction towards all that we conceive, or fear, or hope beyond ourselves'. Shelley argues that each individual posits a miniature image of himself which he strives to externalize, and he gives the name of 'anti-type' to this projected self-image:

> The discovery of its anti-type; the meeting with an understanding capable of clearly estimating our own; an imagination which should enter into and seize upon the subtle and delicate peculiarities which we have delighted to cherish and unfold in secret; . . . this is the invisible and unaittainable [*sic*] point to which Love tends . . .[42]

While this absolute union might be impossible in life it could happen inside fiction, and in a sense helps to explain the changing relationship between Wolfstein and Ginotti. Wolfstein's stature diminishes as he recognizes his own impulse towards power and freedom in Ginotti. It does not matter that this perception causes terror in Wolfstein since Shelley includes fear as one of the emotions aroused by the anti-type. As Ginotti takes over Wolfstein's self the point where self and anti-type can meet comes nearer and nearer until the final union is achieved when Ginotti transfers his secret knowledge to Wolfstein. The main difference between the romance and the essay is that, whereas in the latter the point of ultimate union is an ideal towards which the self strives, in the romance the union proves to be self-destructive.

It is appropriate for Eloise to enter the romance when she does since love, which forms—theoretically, at least—an important theme in *St. Irvyne*, has lapsed into the background. Megalena fascinates Wolfstein to the extent that he convinces her to give in to him sexually, which she does, exclaiming 'prejudice avaunt!' At this stage Ginotti has hardly begun to exert his power over Wolfstein whose apotheosis about their love looks forward to an ideal point in the future as if it is within his reach. In fact his enthusiasm for Megalena proves to be short-lived. Partly this is due to Ginotti progressively monopolizing Wolfstein's attentions; partly Shelley makes it into a moral issue: 'Possession, which, when unassisted by real, intellectual love, clogs man, increases the ardent, uncontrollable passions of women even to madness' (p. 208). This kind of sententious narrative comment occurs with increasing—and irritating—frequency in the sections devoted to

Eloise, and always with some finger-wagging moral about the nature of love or innocence. Interestingly Shelley still attributes passion to women more than men just as he did in *Zastrozzi*. Indeed Megalena changes as did Matilda in the earlier romance, from a figure of beauty to a rather jaded socialite who no longer attracts Wolfstein. Olympia replaces Matilda's passion in her sexual advances to him, which diverges from the most predictable sequence of events, namely that Wolfstein would transfer his attentions to her. After Olympia's suicide, Wolfstein and Megalena flee to Bohemia and the theme of love lapses.

Shelley's narrative comments confine themselves mainly to the love-theme in *St. Irvyne*, and give him an opportunity to moralize with all the authority of an eighteen-year-old on the transience of lust and the vulnerability of innocence. Unfortunately these comments cut little ice with the *Anti-Jacobin Review* which pronounced the book 'impious and blasphemous' because of its sexual immorality, and offered salutary advice for its author: 'as to this Oxford gentleman' (Shelley had judiciously attributed the authorship to a 'Gentleman of the University of Oxford'), 'we recommend him to the care of his tutor, who, after a proper *jobation* for past folly, would do well, by *imposition*, to forbid him the use of his pen, until he shall have taken his *bachelor's degree*'.[43] Unfortunately or fortunately for Shelley the university had anticipated the reviewer's advice by expelling him in the preceding year for his pamphlet on atheism.

The introduction of Eloise into Shelley's romance not only revives their love-theme but radically changes the narrative. It seems now that Shelley is trying to insert a novel of sensibility into his romance, and this is borne out by the numerous parallels with *The Mysteries of Udolpho*. Eloise leaves her home with her mother who is on the verge of death, just as Emily leaves La Vallée with her father. Both suffer accidents to their carriage on the journey. Similarly, later in the narrative Eloise goes to a pavilion with one of her lovers which recalls Emily's fishing-house where she finds traces of her lover-to-be Valencourt. Shelley now pays slightly more attention to the landscape in order to evoke scenes associated with Eloise but the result is flat and stylized compared with the dynamic description of a storm in the opening pages. Now he uses hand-me-down Augustan phraseology like 'the mild beams of Hesper' or 'the solemn umbrage of the pine-trees'; and, in place of violent passion and fear, as befits a character who personifies 'sensibility and excellence', he concentrates now on melancholy, the sense of loss, gratitude, and happiness. In other words Shelley readjusts the proportions of the narrative away from melodrama, but with a corresponding loss of energy.

On her journey with her mother from St. Irvyne, the family home, Eloise meets a tall and impressive stranger who is identified later as Nempere and later still as Ginotti. She has a strange feeling of *déjà-vu*, which might be explained non-realistically by her repeating her brother's actions. When her mother dies Nempere arranges a meeting with her and offers his services as a friend. The gullible Eloise accepts, but then discovers that he has something rather more intimate in mind. There follows a discussion about the ethics of free love (paralleling that between Wolfstein and Megalena); Eloise eventually gives in, and at this point her resemblance to Mrs. Radcliffe's heroine vanishes. She submits so readily because Nempere has already begun to dominate her dreams and to possess 'resistless empire' over her. From the very beginning he has exerted a strong sexual fascination over her. Then Eloise is rescued from the grips of the dastardly Nempere by an English aristocrat called Mountfort. He proves to be a true friend, a rake with a heart of gold, and carries her away to a *cottage ornée* where she can give birth to Nempere's child. This she does and the child promptly disappears into thin air for we hear no more about it. In the meantime Eloise has formed an acquaintance with one Fitzeustace, an Irish friend of Mountfort's an acquaintance which rapidly develops into love. Mountfort arrives at the cottage one evening to announce that he has killed Nempere and must flee the country. This leaves the field clear for Eloise and Fitzeustace to declare undying love to each other and to depart for England (not Ireland) once Fitzeustace has persuaded her to marry him in order to satisfy the conscience of his father, who, it seems, is a stickler for this kind of thing. And that is the last we hear of Eloise.

The sections of *St. Irvyne* dealing with Eloise show a carelessness about detail which is both more noticeable and more disruptive than in the chapters relating to Wolfstein. Chapter VII opens with Eloise returning to her family home after years of absence. Shelley then begins a retrospective narrative which will gradually curve back towards this point. But it never does since she leaves for England with the admiring Fitzeustace. The most glaring discrepancy relates to Wolfstein and Ginotti/Nempere. Twice within the text we are told that Eloise's brother (i.e. Wolfstein) has died, and yet he is struck down again in the ruined abbey. Also, if Mountfort killed Ginotti/Nempere in Geneva, how could he die later with Wolfstein? Halliburton suggests that. he appears as a spirit, but Shelley's publisher Stockdale evidently took a more literal approach to these problems.[44] In November, 1810 we find Shelley writing:

> Ginotti, as you will see did *not* die by Wolfstein's hand, but by the influence of that natural magic which when the secret was imparted to the latter, destroyed him.—Moun[t]fort, being a character of inferior import, I did not think it necessary to state the catastrophe *of* him, as at best it could be but uninteresting. Eloise and Fitzeustace, are married and happy I suppose, and Megalena dies by the same means as Wolfstein.—I do not myself see any other explanation that is required.

Stockdale apparently did not agree, because five days later Shelley added:

> . . . on a re-examination you will perceive that Mountfort physically did kill Ginotti, which must appear from the latter's paleness.[45]

His explanation is still unconvincing. It is impossible to avoid the conclusion that Shelley had lost interest in *St. Irvyne* during composition. It began as a Gothic exploration of the theme of power, the way in which Ginotti came to exercise dominion over Wolfstein. In these early stages Shelley's main debt is probably to Matthew Lewis. Then, around the middle of the romance, he tried to bend the narrative in two different directions; Eloise's chapters are a pastiche of the novel of sensibility seasoned with some theoretical discussion of free love. The Wolfstein narrative centres originally on a wanderer-figure, and Ginotti shifts in the middle of the romance from a social outcast to a Faustian seeker after forbidden knowledge. Perhaps Shelley found that he had neither the patience nor the interest to pursue either of these narratives and so he disposed of Eloise through the time-honoured device of a happy marriage, and Wolfstein and Ginotti by the more unusual but no less effective means of divine intervention.

Probably a decisive influence in this shift of interest away from the Gothic was Shelley's discovery of Godwin's work. At least Shelley himself thought so for he wrote to Godwin in 1812 as follows

> From a reader I became [a] writer of Romances; before the age of seventeen I had published two 'St. Irvyne' and 'Zastrozzi' each of which tho quite uncharacteristic of me as now I am, yet serve to mark the state of my mind at the period of their composition . . . it is now a period of more than two years since first I saw your inestimable book on 'Political Justice'; it opened to my mind fresh and more extensive views, it materially influenced my character, and I rose from its perusal a wiser and better man.—I was no longer a votary of Romance; till then I had existed in an ideal world; now I found that in this universe of ours was enough to excite the interest of the heart, enough to employ the discussions of Reason.[46]

Shelley carries flattering exaggeration to such lengths that it seems as if a positive revolution took place in his thought. From romance he turns to realism; from the ideal world to the world of reason. Shelley requested a copy of *Political Justice* from Stockdale in November 1810 but *St. Leon* had already been exerting its influence on *St. Irvyne* (probably in the latter stages of composition) although, as Shelley admitted, its philosophical reasoning had made only a superficial impression on him.[47] Fired with enthusiasm, the convert to Reason began a Godwinian novel—to be called 'Hubert Cauvin'—where he was to analyse the state of French society before the Revolution.[48] Shelley worked on this during January 1812, and then abandoned it, probably in the bustle of his political activities in Ireland. This was to be the fate of Shelley's other fictional projects. After 1810 he was to devote his main energies to poetry and the fragments of prose fiction which survive only give us tantalizing glimpses of his shifts in interest.

'Hubert Cauvin' has disappeared, but several chapters survive of 'The Assassins' which he wrote during 1814. Perhaps the influence of Godwin can still be discerned in the quasi-philosophical scope of this work. The first two extant chapters describe the attempts of the Assassins to form a utopian community based on knowledge and truth. Shelley presents them as moral heroes for their refusal to temporize with the city authorities of Jerusalem, from where they flee. The first two chapters lay the theoretical ground-work for a fragment of narrative which describes how a young man called Albedir (one of the Assassins, presumably) takes an old man (once again a wanderer) into his family. One problem in the fragment is that Shelley begins by discussing a community but can only embody a family in the narrative proper. Perhaps this disparity led him to abandon the work.

Shelley's last important fragment grew out of his enthusiasm for Rome. 'The Coliseum' was begun in 1818 under the impetus of his and Mary's first impressions of Italy. An old man and a girl are sitting in the Coliseum when they meet a youth dressed in the classical style, a kind of animated status or *genius loci*. The youth sternly tries to direct the attention of the others to the artistic beauties of the place whereupon the girl tells him that the old man is blind. Stricken by remorse, the youth repeats Albedir's gesture of compassion in 'The Assassins', and a discussion begins about beauty. The fragment thus concentrates initially on compassion or love for others and secondarily on imaginative responses to the place, a contrast being established between the youth's physical vision and the old man's 'inner sight'—his capacity to create mental images from what he hears. Love also figures prominently in a prose piece of 1820; 'Una Favola' is an unfinished Petrarchan narrative which Shelley wrote in Italian. This piece repeats themes from 'Alastor', especially that of a youth wandering in search of a perfect female form.[49]

Even as early as April 1810 we can find signs of scepticism towards the Gothic in Shelley's writings. In that month he sent a letter to Edward Graham where he burlesques the paraphernalia of out-worn settings and themes of Gothic fiction:

> Stalk along the road towards them [the trees at Clapham school]—and mind and keep yourself concealed as my mother brings a bloodstained stiletto whic[h] she purposes to make you bathe in the life blood of her enemy. Never mind the Death-demons, and skeletons dripping with the

putrefaction of the grave, that occasionally may blast your straining eyeball.[50]

Unfortunately this refreshingly tongue-in-cheek attitude towards cliché does not extend into *Zastrozzi*, which was published two months later, but it is important to note that Shelley's impatience with the conventionally supernatural led him in a psychological direction. Even at his most sensational he seems more interested in the workings of the mind than in simply evoking horror. In that respect Shelley's romances take their place within a broader shift in taste which was taking place within the Gothic mode away from clichéd settings like ruined castles to internalized landscapes which focus attention on the mind. Coleridge's categorical statement in his essay 'Dreams and Apparitions' makes this shift explicit: 'the fact really is, as to apparitions, that the terror produces the image instead of the contrary'.[51] Coleridge's own evocation of dream in 'The Ancient Mariner', Godwin's depiction of persecution and paranoia in *Caleb Williams*, and the dramatization of guilt in *Frankenstein* provide three famous examples of this change.

Although Shelley rejected conventional representations of the supernatural in fiction, ghosts as such retained a fascination for him. While he and Mary were staying in Geneva in 1816 they had the famous series of discussions with Byron and Matthew Lewis which resulted in *Frankenstein*. Shelley temporarily took over Mary's journal to copy down a series of ghost stories which Lewis related, and commented on their conversations:

> We talk of Ghosts; neither Lord Byron nor Monk G. Lewis seem to believe in them; and they both agree, in the very face of reason that none could believe in ghosts without also believing in God. I do not think that all the persons who profess to discredit these visitations really discredit them, or, if they do in the daylight, are not admonished by the approach of loneliness and midnight to think more respectably of the world of shadows.[52]

In view of Shelley's gradual discarding of the supernatural several years earlier, it is interesting that he still keeps an open mind on the existence of ghosts. He was still interested enough to take part in the general composition of ghost stories suggested by

Byron. According to Mary, Shelley began a narrative 'founded on the experience of early youth'.[53] We know nothing more about this story, neither how far Shelley progressed with it nor what became of any manuscript. However Shelley's biographer, Walter Peck, has identified a story as the poet's which appeared in *The Indicator* in 1820.

This piece, entitled 'A True Story', is cast in an autobiographical mode and describes events which happened to the narrator when he was a young boy. The fact that he suffered from ill-health and went for solitary walks hints at biographical parallels with Shelley; and this suggests in turn, that the story may be a reworking of the piece which he originally began in 1816. The evidence is inconclusive and anyway it is more interesting to see how Shelley handles a mysterious subject in narrative. The boy clearly is a solitary and one evening stays out later than usual. The woodland scene is still, but then comes the apparition:

> From this reverie I was suddenly startled by the sight of a tall slender female, who was standing by me, looking sorrowfully and steadily in my face. She was dressed in white, from head to foot, in a fashion that I had never seen before; her garments were unusually long and flowing, and rustled as she glided through the low shrubs near me, as if they were made of the richest silk. My heart beat as if I was dying, and I knew not that I could have stirred from the spot: but she seemed so very mild and beautiful, I did not attempt it. Her pale brown hair was braided round her head, but there were some locks that strayed upon her neck; and altogether, she looked like a love picture but not like a living woman. I closed my eyes forcibly with my hands, and when I looked again she had vanished.[54]

Compared with the melodramatic language of Shelley's early romances, this description pays comparatively little attention to the boy's reactions and controls the visual image with remarkable precision. There is a certain ambiguity about the figure which is caused partly by the lack of transitions. She appears 'suddenly' in the middle of the boy's reverie and vanishes just as abruptly when he closes his eyes. Accordingly the reader is uncertain whether or not she is a product of the boy's imagination, which is glanced at when she is compared to a picture. Shelley cleverly balances realistic detail (the few stray locks of hair) against her attenuated movement (she *glides* rather than walks), which helps to preserve the margin of uncertainty. On later evenings the boy senses the woman again and even gets some slight recognition from her (she 'looked sweetly at me'), but then catches a fever. During his illness he learns that the woman is in fact real and has lost her reason after having been disappointed in love. The reader too is disappointed to receive such a banal rationalization of the boy's experience. Briefly Shelley manages to create the sort of poised ambiguity we have come to expect of later writers like Henry James, but then the story collapses into cumbersome explanations.

Shelley's 1812 letter to Godwin makes it sound as if his interest in the Gothic, the supernatural and the legend of the Wandering Jew—all implied in his term 'romance'—disappeared as soon as he read *Political Justice*. Such is not the case. Scepticism towards the supernatural is already shown in the letter to Graham quoted earlier, in the brief discussion of spirits in 'The Wandering Jew' and in the psychological level of action in *Zastrozzi*. *St. Irvyne* carries this process a stage further by comparatively toning down the narrative language, excluding the religious origins of the wanderer-figure, and attenuating the Gothic down to similes and metaphors. On her mother's death Shelley describes Eloise's apprehension as 'the indefinable terror of one who dreads to behold some phantom' (p. 245). This captures her new sense of vulnerability and her fear and fascination with Nempere who hovers on the edge of her consciousness. Similarly in 'The Assassins', which has a more chastened language and more philosophical pretensions, Shelley dismisses the perverse, vile and vicious—i.e. the moral obstacles to the sect's formation—as 'shapes of some unholy vision, moulded by the spirit of Evil.'[55] It is quite appropriate to the Assassins' millenarian zeal to get away from evil that Shelley should reduce their obstacles to mere phantasms which can easily be swept away. The Wandering Jew reappears in as late a work as *Hellas* (first published 1822) in a similar role to that in *Queen Mab*. Once again he is a sage whose eye 'pierces/the Present, and the Past, and the To-Come'.[56] Similarly 'A True Story' confirms that Shelley retained an interest in mystery and a Gothic vocabulary long after he had stopped trying to imitate figures like Monk Lewis and Mrs. Radcliffe. The comparison of autumnal leaves to 'ghosts from an enchanter fleeing' in the 'Ode to the West Wind' is only the most famous example of a kind of imagery which spreads throughout Shelley's mature poetry.

# Addendum

## Chronology of Shelley's Prose Fiction

| | |
|---|---|
| Winter, 1809–10 | An 'extravagant romance' ('The Nightmare') begun with Thomas Medwin. |
| June, 1810 | *Zastrozzi, A Romance* published by Wilkie and Robinson. Probably written in the first half of 1809. |
| December, 1810 | Shelley planning a novel 'to convey metaphysical and political opinions'. |
| January, 1811 | *St. Irvyne; Or, The Rosicrucian: A Romance* published by J. J. Stockdale. Probably written in 1810. |
| January, 1812 | 'Hubert Cauvin'—a Godwinian novel on the French Revolution—begun and abandoned. |
| August, 1814 | Shelley begins 'The Assassins'—four chapters written—the work abandoned in September. |
| August, 1816 | Shelley takes over Mary's journal and copies down ghost stories told by Lewis. Shelley begins a narrative based on 'experiences of early youth', and has discussions with Mary about *Frankenstein.* |
| [1818 | *Frankenstein* published, with preface by Shelley.] |
| November, 1818 | Shelley begins 'The Coliseum'—subsequently abandoned. |
| 1820 | 'Una Favola' begun, but unfinished. |
| July, 1820 | 'A True Story' published in *The Indicator.* |

## NOTES

1. F. R. Leavis, *Revaluation* (Harmondsworth, 1964), 188.
2. Walter Edwin Peck, *Shelley. His Life and Works* 2 vols. (London, 1927), i. 30.
3. Richard Holmes, *Shelley. The Pursuit* (London, 1976), 24–5.
4. Thomas Medwin, *The Life of Percy Bysshe Shelley* ed. H. Buxton Forman (London, 1913), 39.
5. The authorship question is discussed by S. G. Andrews in his 'Shelley, Medwin, and "The Wandering Jew" ', *Keats-Shelley Journal* 20 (1971), 78–86.
6. Thomas Medwin, *Ahasuerus, The Wanderer* (London, 1823), vii.

7. *The Complete Poetical Works of Percy Bysshe Shelley* ed. Neville Rogers (Oxford, 1972), i. 62. This is the only edition of Shelley's poetry, hereafter referred to as *Rogers*, to print the full text of 'The Wandering Jew'.

8. Shelley's Note 14 is entitled 'Ahasuerus, rise!' and purports to be the 'translation of part of some German work'.

9. See, for example, A. B. Young, 'Shelley and M. G. Lewis', *Modern Language Review*, i (1906), 322–324; and A. M. D. Hughes, 'Shelley's *Zastrozzi* and *St. Irvyne*', *Modern Language Review*, vii (1912), 54–63.

10. Eustace Chesser, *Shelley and Zastrozzi: Self-Revelation of a Neurotic* (London, 1965).

11. Harry Buxton Forman, ed., *The Works of Percy Bysshe Shelley in Verse and Prose* 8 vols. (London, 1880), v. 165. Subsequent page-references to *St. Irvyne* are to this edition and are incorporated into the text.

12. This episode (in the third paragraph of *St. Irvyne*) is a pastiche of the opening lines of the poem entitled 'The Stranger' from Lewis's *Tales of Terror*.

13. *Critical Review* 4th series, vii (December, 1814), 368; 'Remarks on *Mandeville* and Mr. Godwin', *Works* vii. 5–6.

14. Poe uses a similar device in 'The Fall of the House of Usher' where the reading of a legendary tale is synchronized with mounting drama in the narrative proper.

15. *Rogers*, 197 (ll.445–51). The full epigraph consists of ll.435, 443–51.

16. Edgar Allan Poe, *Selected Tales* ed. Kenneth Graham (London, 1967), 141.

17. D. G. Halliburton, 'Shelley's "Gothic" Novels', *Keats-Shelley Journal* (1967) xvi. 45.

18. Claire Rosenfield, 'The Shadow Within: The Conscious and Unconscious Use of the Double', *Daedalus* (Spring, 1963), 328.

19. For an early statement of this concept *v.* 'Fragment' (''Tis midnight now—athwart the murky air') ll.42–45.

20. *Anti-Jacobin Review*, xli (January, 1812), 71.

21. *Rogers*, 208–209 (ll.799–803).

22. Ibid. 208 (ll.780, 782–790 form the epigraph to Chapter X of *St. Irvyne*).

23. This image appears in *Queen Mab* VII. 259–66.

24. *Rogers*, 211–14 (ll.881–995).

25. Cf. Victorio's identical experience at the beginning of Canto IV of 'The Wandering Jew': *Rogers*, 218–19 (ll.1120–70).

26. *Works*, vi. 383, 384.

27. Mary Shelley, *Frankenstein* ed. M. K. Joseph, Oxford English Novels (London, 1969), 36, 40, 52.

28. *Frankenstein*, 13.

29. *Letters* (Oxford, 1964) i. 25.

30. William Godwin, *Caleb Williams* ed. David McCracken, Oxford English Novels (London, 1970), 4.

31. William Godwin, *St. Leon. A Tale of the Sixteenth Century* 3rd edn. 4 vols. (London, 1816) ii. 34.

32. Ibid. *St. Leon* ii. 98.

33. Floyd Stovall, *Desire and Restraint in Shelley* (Durham, N.C., 1931), 8.

34. *Letters*, i. 231.

35. Holmes, op. cit., 53. In July, 1785 an Illuminatus called Lanz was struck by lightning and killed while on a mission. This might conceivably have suggested the ending of *St. Irvyne* to Shelley (Neal Wilgus, *The Illuminoids. Secret Societies and Political Paranoia* (London, 1980), 19.

36. *St. Irvyne* has no Chapters V or VI, just as *Zastrozzi* has no Chapter VII.

37. St. Irvyne, Eloise's family home, was the name of an estate near Field Place which Shelley had commemorated in poem dated 1805—'To St. Irvyne—To Harriet'.

38. George Levine, '*Frankenstein* and the tradition of Realism', *Novel*, vii. No. 1 (Fall, 1973), 20.

39. A. P. Antippas, 'The Structure of Shelley's *St. Irvyne*: Parallelism and the Gothic Mode of Evil', *Tulane Studies in English*, xviii. (1970), 67.

40. *Works*, v. 68.

41. *Clark*, 169.

42. *Works*, vi. 267–68, 269.

43. *Anti-Jacobin Review*, op. cit., 70, 71.

44. Halliburton, op. cit., 44.

45. *Letters*, i. 20, 21.

46. Ibid., i. 227–28.

47. Ibid., i. 21.

48. Ibid., i. 218, 229.

49. On the connection between 'Una Favola' and 'The Triumph of Life' see below,

50. *Letters*, i. 10.

51. Samuel Taylor Coleridge, *Miscellanies, Aesthetic and Literary*, ed. T. Ashe (London, 1885), 165.

52. Frederick L. Jones ed., *Mary Shelley's Journal* (Norman, Oklahoma, 1947), 57.

53. *Frankenstein*, 7.

54. Peck, op. cit., i. 6. Peck reprints the full text of the story.

55. *Works*, vi. 232.

56. *Hellas*, ll.147–48.

# The Shelleyan Psycho-Drama: 'Julian and Maddalo'

## VINCENT NEWEY

While it would be surprising now to find anything like Browning's almost religious enthusiasm for Shelley's sublime perceptions of 'Power and Love in the absolute, and of Beauty and Good', his response to the more discreet creativity of 'Julian and Maddalo' seems as typical of our own time as of the mid-nineteenth century, both in its comparative reticence and its confident assertion of the work's thorough 'objectivity':

> I would rather consider Shelley's poetry as a sublime fragmentary essay towards a presentment of the correspondency of the universe to Deity, of the natural to the spiritual . . . than . . . appraise the worth of many detachable portions which might be acknowledged as utterly perfect in a lower moral point of view, under the mere conditions of art. It would be easy to take my stand on successful instances of objectivity in Shelley: there is the unrivalled *Cenci*; there is the *Julian and Maddalo* too . . .[1]

At least Browning offers elsewhere in the 'Essay on Shelley' a good working definition of the 'objective' poet, who seeks 'to reproduce things external (whether the phenomena of the scenic universe, or the manifested action of the human heart and brain) with an immediate reference . . . to the common eye and apprehension of his fellow men'.[2] Harold Bloom is less helpful, though equally certain about the specific nature of 'Julian and Maddalo': a triumph in 'the middle style', it introduces 'another Shelley, a master of the urbane'—except, that is, in the effusive rhetoric of the maniac's soliloquy, which is an expendable 'excrescence'.[3] To Donald Davie, whom Bloom's comments clearly echo, the maniac's speech finally proves acceptable because it does have a certain dramatic propriety as the 'tiresome and unpoetic' ravings of a lunatic within a controlled narrative that admirably upholds the virtues of civilized conversation, of 'purity' and 'urbanity'. We come away from Davie's statements with the firm impression that by thus distancing the 'incoherency' of his habitual 'sublime pretensions' in the form of a madman's imagined reflections, and by resisting this dominant side of his poetic personality in favour of 'lean and bare prosaic language', Shelley produces in 'Julian and Maddalo' an essentially and responsibly anti-Shelleyan poem.[4] In Davie's view the 'objectivity' is at once a strength and a salvation.

The following essay will be concerned only incidentally with challenging or developing such existing attitudes to 'Julian and Maddalo'. It springs, rather, from a desire to confront anew three very basic questions. Wherein exactly does the art of 'Julian and Maddalo' consist? Precisely what kind of poem is it? Does it possess any special literary-historical significance? In general, however, there has been an evident failure among critics to recognize not only the complexity of the poem as a whole, including the section on the maniac, but also one obvious generic feature—its two-sidedness. For subjective impulses are no less present in 'Julian and Maddalo' than a command of objectivity, the reproduction of things external. Not that the poem is a flawed hybrid. As in so much Romantic poetry, above all that of Wordsworth and Coleridge, inwardness—confession and self-revelation—combines with an urge towards the dramatic; the two are inseparable, and only in theory is there any contradiction. It is in this characteristic that my analysis will centre.

\*      \*      \*      \*

We may usefully begin with reference to two possible approaches which, though in themselves dead-ends, do signal more fruitful directions. By itself biography will merely provide a superficial gloss to particular portions of the poem. As Donald Reiman points out, the maniac's speech reflects Shelley's recent interest in the love and madness of Tasso and comes finally to bear the influence of his estrangement from Mary Shelley after the death of their son at Rome in June 1819.[5] It is certain, too, that 'Julian and Maddalo' demonstrates a change in Shelley's relationship with Byron (Maddalo) by centralizing his proud, passionate pessimism at the expense of the outright idealization which in 'Lines written among the Euganean Hills' had made him the saviour-poet, potential redeemer of a degenerate civilization.[6] These simple facts do little to advance our essential understanding of what is, after all, a self-justifying poetic creation with a life independent of exterior circumstance; but they help nevertheless to bring into focus at least one salient facet of that creation. Its autonomous life *is* bound up with Shelley's emotional and mental existence in precise ways: his pre-occupation with the legend of Tasso, enchained genius, is part of a larger personal concern with the singular condition of the Poet that finds ample expression in 'Julian and Maddalo', while the shift in attitude towards Byron relates to an advance in self-awareness—a reassessment of an earlier idealism—which 'Julian and Maddalo' consistently registers and puts forth. The creation is, whatever else, a landscape of the creating mind.

The same conclusion emerges if we try to see the poem as a statement of ideas. Certainly it is 'philosophic' in the sense that it interprets life and attitudes to life (those of Julian and Maddalo), but not in the more limited sense so often applicable to Shelley. It is not an ideological work, either in the manner of *Queen Mab*, where poetry supplies the dress of socio-political convictions, or the less direct promulgatory didacticism of *Prometheus Unbound* in which the mythopoeic imagination yields a world of 'beautiful idealisms of moral excellence' in the service of the same millenarian radicalism.[7] In other words, 'Julian and Maddalo' has no part to play in that project so dear to Romanticism, and to Blake and Shelley in particular, of creating a secular scripture, a *logos* whereby the human spirit might be renewed so as to be able once again to 'love, and admire, and trust, and hope, and endure'.[8] ('Scripture' seems all the more apt when we consider that Shelley's, or Blake's, principled distrust of custom and elevation of man's inward potentialities gives fresh frameworks for belief while appearing to deny them: *Prometheus Unbound* is the exact radical counterpart of the conservative *Excursion* which rests its hopes on the revivification of orthodox religious tradition.) In 'Julian and Maddalo' ideals and idealism, the

optimistic creed of freedom and man's perfectibility represented
in the young Julian, are made to look severely inadequate as a
response to the human condition. By 'The Shelleyan Psycho-
drama' is meant in the final analysis not so much a 'drama of
Shelley's mind' as an impersonal 'drama of mind' anticipating
not only the form of the Victorian dramatic monologue but also
the psychological empiricism and moral relativism which Robert
Langbaum has so convincingly shown to be its underlying
principle and ultimate goal.[9] The 'idea' of 'Julian and Maddalo'
is the rejection of ideas in favour of sympathetic insight into 'being',
philosophic speculation and views in favour of the imaginative
embrace of experience. That is the message of the narrative itself
and of the dialectical interplay of character—the opposition
between Julian and Maddalo—that takes place within it. At the
same time, however, this Julian whose ideological stance
constitutes the negative side of the dialectic is so obviously an
authorial self-portrait that the poem must be seen in part as a
process of self-criticism, a personal comment on the personal
credal optimism that informs *Queen Mab* and *Prometheus Unbound*.

Julian is presented from the first as one who views the world
and being-in-the-world in straightforward intellectual terms—
the simple Godwinian 'ameliorist' passionately attached, as the
prose Preface says, 'to those philosophical notions which assert
the power of man over his own mind, and the immense
improvements of which, by the extinction of certain moral
superstitions, human society may yet be susceptible'.[10] What he
says in the body of the poem merely fills out this preliminary
impression. To Maddalo's sombre account of our helpless
confinement to a life of suffering and frustration, where thought
and desire gather round the rent heart and pray, as madmen do,
for they know not what, till death

> severeth
> Our memory from itself, and us from all
> We sought and yet were baffled! . . . (ll.128–30)

his friend opposes an eager sense of man's capacity for redeeming
his earthly state through a right application of the will so as to
throw off alike the leaden laws of Custom and the manacles
forged for the mind by the mind's own weakness:

                    . . . it is our will
That thus enchains us to permitted ill—
We might be otherwise—we might be all
We dream of happy, high, majestical.
Where is the love, beauty and truth we seek
But in our mind? . . .
                              . . . We know
That we have power over ourselves to do
And suffer—what, we know not till we try;
But something nobler than to live and die—. . .
                    (ll.170–75, 184–87)

Thus, the maniac's predicament, in which Maddalo reads the
extent of human vulnerability, suggests to Julian a flawed
personality and lack of wisdom, 'a want of that true theory
still,/Which seeks a "soul of goodness" in things ill'—'this is not
destiny/But man's own wilful ill' (ll.202–11).

This portrait of the young enthusiast is an unmistakable
image, if on a greatly reduced scale, of the poet of *Queen Mab*. It is
as though Shelley were looking back through the wrong end of a
telescope, contemplating a sober miniature of the self who had
proclaimed the Godwinian faith in the inner light of reason and
virtue, chronicler of the corruptness of 'this thorny wilderness'
and celebrant of that secular inward and social paradise, 'happy
Earth! reality of Heaven', attainable through the action of
'resolute mind, . . . lofty, pure and unsubdued'.[11] It would be
oversubtle to see the difference between the poetic flights of *Queen
Mab* and Julian's earnest theorizing as an attempt to throw the
former into relief and so validate them. Rather, it is a means of
putting the utopian philosophy of the earlier poem, and indeed
all philosophizing, firmly in its place—of exposing its naivety.
The 'innocent' Shelley of *Queen Mab* is everywhere viewed with
detachment by the 'experienced' Shelley of 'Julian and
Maddalo'—with some respect to be sure (for the speech quoted
above has the ring of decent, honest zeal), but also with a degree
of humour, conspicuous even in the simple portrait of the Preface
itself—which concludes on the deadpan remark that 'Julian is
rather serious'. Whereas Maddalo's warning to Julian of the
dangers of blasphemy as they travel to the madhouse by gondola,
'. . . if you can't swim/Beware of Providence', is perhaps a joke

against Providence as much as against the latter's notorious
atheism, many of his witty, frank interjections do place heterodox
idealism in a pointedly searching light. 'You talk Utopia', his
sharp retort to his companion's dreams of man's possible 'happy,
high, majestical' state, for example, is no less effective in
challenging the validity of 'aspiring theories', by emphasizing
their purely speculative nature, than is his account of man's
tragic destiny, our baffled confinement, in response to the
emblematic potential of the gathering of 'lost souls' at the
asylum.

But we do not have to rely entirely on the Preface and
Maddalo's opinions for evidence of Shelley's sceptical
relationship with abstract idealism. The action of the narrated
drama, the story itself, also underlines its limitations. We shall
come to the broader significance of the maniac's predicament
later, but there can be no doubt that, for one thing, the very fact
of his inconsolable despair punches a massive hole in Julian's
theory of 'the power of man over his own mind'. The mysterious
spectacle of actual suffering and psychic disorder is a lesson to
Julian, and a lesson to us all; it is the acid test of experience before
which untried philosophical notions must fail, dissolving into
ineffectual pity and wonderment. All Julian—and for that
matter, Maddalo—can do after penetrating the secret desert
places of a mind that longs for the perverse refuge of the grave as
an escape from the prison-house of endless oneiric confusion ('. . .
quick and dark/The grave is yawning . . .', ll.505ff.) is to weep
(1.516) and acknowledge the weakness of even the noblest spirits
(when they trace his condition back to a self-violating 'blot of
falsehood' incurred in the service of love by a heart which
flourished only 'in the light of all-beholding truth').[12] The
impression of human helplessness which emerges so powerfully
from the sustained image of the maniac's own frantic mental
circlings is thus extended to take in Julian himself—all the more
completely when his subsequent plan to reclaim the sad sufferer
from his dark estate by patient care comes to nothing:

> this was all
> Accomplished not; such dreams of baseless good
> Oft come and go in crowds or solitude
> And leave no trace . . . (ll.577–80)

For all his idealism, whether intellectual or the emotional kind displayed in the 'deep tenderness' he feels towards the maniac, Julian is himself a prisoner of circumstance, time, and the limits of human capacity. He has to leave Venice, 'urged by [his] affairs' (l.582); and on his return years later he learns that the maniac's history proved to the very end 'a mournful tale'. That this painful news comes from Maddalo's daughter strikes a last decisive blow at such hopeful faith in human happiness as Julian had asserted in the debate with Maddalo: the same 'lovely child' he had used as an *exemplum* of ontological bliss, a being 'blithe, innocent and free' in contrast to the state of wilful subjection to 'sick thoughts' (ll.166ff.), has herself necessarily grown to an anxious knowledge of suffering:

> if thine aged eyes disdain to wet
> Those wrinkled cheeks with youth's remembered tears,
> Ask me no more . . . (ll.611–13)

The *exemplum* had always seemed of doubtful relevance to Julian's argued plea for comforting thoughts, since childhood is so obviously a privileged and temporary condition, but now, above all in that poignantly understated request for silence ('Ask me no more . . .'), we see exemplified directly the inevitability of pain. Julian's naive instance of human freedom has become a proof of human confinement. And even he has come in the end to recognise the ineluctable bleakness of existence. He comments finally, no longer upon 'how good may be made superior', but simply upon the world's coldness:

> she told me how
> All happened—but the cold world shall not know.
> (ll.616–17)

An act of self-criticism then, and also apparently a pessimistic account of the world and existence. Yet 'pessimism' of course will not really do to describe the vision of 'Julian and Maddalo', for it teaches us to take nourishment from theoretically negative conditions and preoccupations—loss, futility, the oppression of madness—so as to redeem perception and feeling comprehensively. Something of this will be already evident from what we have seen of the end of the poem. Shelley does not flinch from the fact of grief—'youth's remembered tears'—but feeds creatively upon it. Although his reference to 'the cold world' conspicuously lacks any such consolatory idea of man's ability to eradicate the coldness as accompanies the same phrase in *Queen Mab*,[13] he does not hopelessly reject the world but rather snatches affirmation from the jaws of denial by turning its harshness into a compelling mystery. This is a minor example of a typical and major effect. It is clear enough, however, that two selves are being constantly projected in 'Julian and Maddalo': the past self whose speculative idealism is questioned and a maturer self who accepts life for what it is and finds there his inspiration. The latter one could identify merely as the poet behind the poem. But he is present also in the 'I' of the narrator:

> I love all waste
> And solitary places; where we taste
> The pleasure of believing what we see
> Is boundless, as we wish our souls to be . . . (ll.14–17)

'The *pleasure* of believing', 'as we *wish*': in this reticent yet definite acknowledgement of the gulf dividing desire and actuality, pleasurable illusion and reality, we register an experienced voice and outlook that contrasts vividly with the younger Julian's eager declarations of the boundlessness of the soul. While the invention of a character, 'Julian', makes it impossible for the reader to assume a straightforward act of personal reflection, as we do in 'Mont Blanc' or 'Tintern Abbey' or 'Frost at Midnight', neither are we offered an entirely objective fiction like Browning's 'Andrea Del Sarto' or 'Bishop Blougram's Apology', where the poet's presence is limited to artistic traits and (some would say) philosophic preferences.[14] Julian the narrator is a persona of Shelley at times barely distinguishable from the 'I' of the poet, and in the implied difference between narrator and his former self is expressed the maturity which finds fuller articulation through the vision and values of Shelley's poem as a whole.

The disposition of 'psychopoeic' energies\* is therefore

---

\* I coin the word 'psychopoeic' by analogy with and in opposition to 'mythopoeic'. We are in desperate need of a critical term to signify creative activity that centres in and makes manifest, not shared patterns of human experience, action or belief, but individual psychological processes, impulses and goals—the life and landscape of the conscious and unconscious mind.

discernible in 'Julian and Maddalo' in both the criticism of self and the related establishment of a poetic identity committed to anti-philosophic and life-embracing vision. This vision, as it is expressed across the poem (and not just in the cumulative emphasis on confinement, failure and suffering), is itself not altogether new in Shelley, however, since it consists of essentially the same interplay of dark and bright apprehensions that had been present in his poetry almost from the start. In *Queen Mab* the claims of evil and ruin upon Shelley's imagination had been outflanked by mytho-philosophic incantations of the paradisal state of perfected sensibility when 'the human being stands . . . Immortal upon earth',[15] but there is in 'Hymn to Intellectual Beauty', 'Mont Blanc', and 'Lines written among the Euganean Hills' a more even balance of delight and desolation, mountings of a spirit in touch with 'awful loveliness' and fallings-back into a consciousness of this 'dim vast vale of tears, vacant and desolate'. As Harold Bloom points out,[16] Shelley is equally the poet of radiant ascent and of intense dereliction—of the shadow that consumes Alastor or that is so powerfully announced at the beginning of 'The Two Spirits', the lyrical-allegorical counterpart of the debate between optimistic and pessimistic views of human destiny which takes place in the conversation of Julian and Maddalo:

> O Thou, who plumed with strong desire
> Wouldst float above the earth, beware!
> A Shadow tracks thy flight of fire—
>     Night is coming! ('The Two Spirits', ll. 1–4)

But it is not this debate that I have in mind when talking of the interplay within the vision of 'Julian and Maddalo'. Julian's cerebral optimism is too much called in doubt to provide an effective polarity to the 'dark' impressions of man's condition which emerge in general from the action and events of the poem. For the 'bright' side of 'Julian and Maddalo' we must go to the moments of pure well-being, the epiphanic experiences, imaged in certain of the narrator's recollections—which are of course expressions of the lyrical Shelley, the Shelley of imaginative flight, though subdued to the less aspiring mood, and willing engagement with the familiar world, characteristic of this poem.

The passages in question are shot through with suggestions of the speaker's—that is, both the poet's and the narrator's—active sense of the freedom and singular joy to be found in the presence of nature. In the very first paragraph, for example, the verb 'love', so often a dead metaphor, draws a vital authenticity from the excited, expansive rhythms and perceptual clarity of the description of natural phenomena:

>                 . . . I love all waste
> And solitary places; where we taste
> The pleasure of believing what we see
> Is boundless . . .
>              . . . I love
> To ride as then I rode; for the winds drove
> The living spray along the sunny air
> Into our faces; the blue heavens were bare,
> Stripped to their depths by the awakening North;
> And, from the waves, sound like delight broke forth
> Harmonizing with solitude, and sent
> Into our hearts aerial merriment . . .
> So, as we rode, we talked; and the swift thought,
> Winging itself with laughter, lingered not,
> But flew from brain to brain . . . (ll.14–17, 20–30)

There is much more to this than 'the adoption, from prose or careful conversation, of a vocabulary of natural description'; and neither—to query Donald Davie's other main comment—does Shelley's observance of the logic of spoken usage preclude a figurative dimension.[17] The natural description is itself of a particular kind, operating as it does to show forth, 'figure', the self-contained dynamic life of the non-human world. The previous lines have already brought this life into focus: that the salt ooze 'breeds' weeds and thistles from 'earth's embrace' amply signifies the strange harmonies of nature's generative processes; the verbs—'breaks', 'ever-shifting', 'makes'—suggest endless activity beneath apparent stasis; the few stark details—the weeds, the sand, the lone fisher, one dwarf tree . . .—evoke a sense of both the timeless and the temporal, the primeval and present, a landscape visited by man for work and pleasure (fisher and narrator) but immutable and untouched by civilization. And nature's autonomous energies are similarly emblematized in the active verbal forms ('drove', 'awakening', 'broke forth, harmonizing' . . .) and unelaborate, perfectly *natural* epithets ('sunny', 'blue', 'bare') of the quoted passage. Yet what is ultimately depicted is not simply the independent life of nature but a reciprocal interaction between self and nature: the winds drove the spray 'into our faces', while the waves' sound 'sent', as if on purpose, 'into our hearts aerial merriment', provoking a correspondent inward wave of pleasure which leads on in turn to the release of mental energies akin to those of nature itself as the 'swift thought, Winging . . . flew from brain to brain'. This reciprocity is mirrored, moreover, in the speakers's present relation to nature; the experiences offered by her have fostered a love for her, issuing in that enthusiasm and respect embodied in the poetic-perceptual act of description.

The account of the sunset over Venice is more densely metaphoric and nearer to the 'transcendent' Shelley of 'Mont Blanc' and other lyrics. If the emotions and poetic spirit may find liberation in waste and solitary places, how much more is to be expected from an evening of extraordinary splendour and beauty. The initial expression of joy in nature— 'Oh!/How beautiful is sunset, when the glow/Of Heaven descends . . .' (ll.54–56)—is fulfilled, after a brief pause for reflection, in a spontaneous act of creation-in-recollection, a sustained process of imaginative activity that yields a sublime vision of universal Power and Harmony. Nature, Art, and Civilization unite in a mighty *discordia concors*, a spectacle of eternal order within endless movement, difference, and change. Mountains, seas, and vineyards 'encircle' the towers of cities, so that the works of man lie intimately in the bosom of nature—an integral yet distinct part of a greater Nature (ll.58–59). The 'flood' stands between 'the city and the shore', separating but also linking the human and non-human worlds; 'paved with the image of the sky', it connects earth with heaven (ll.66–67). Mountains *tower* around the sun; Earth and Sea dissolve into 'one lake of fire'; hills become a 'clump of peaked isles'; the temples and the palaces of the City are like 'fabrics of enchantment piled to Heaven', informed as it were by the same magic as nature, and providing a ladder on which the aspiring spirit might climb to the summit of aspiration. Above all, nature displays its perfect workmanship—an Art beyond art, though akin to it:

half the sky
Was roofed with clouds of rich emblazonry
Dark purple at the zenith, which still grew
Down the steep West into a wondrous hue
Brighter than burning gold . . . (ll.70–74)

As in the earlier passage, the verbs—'grew' is a good example—
point everywhere to an organic, inwardly generated power and
order. There is no idea whatsoever of an Artificer Divine such as
we find in eighteenth century nature poetry, whether 'deist'
(Thomson) or Christian (Cowper), or even of the presiding Spirit
evoked often enough by Wordsworth whose dealings with
nature, although in practice 'unmediated', are still linked
philosophically to traditional concepts of a numinous Deity.[18]
Nor is there, of course, any didactic aim, like that of the 'later'
Wordsworth's own conservative religious meditation upon 'An
Evening of Extraordinary Splendour and Beauty', which
transforms the effulgent landscape into a deliberate inspirational
*logos* in the mode of Puritan emblematic readings of the Creation,
interpreting its gradations as 'a glorious scale' leading men's
thoughts upwards to Heaven and downwards to their 'frail
mortality'.[19] Shelley's lines possess nothing of the religious or the
moral. They celebrate Nature's magnificence and harmonies for
their own sakes—a self-justifying triumph of autonomous
energies.

Having said that, however, it needs stressing that we are also
aware of an effort of perception. The references to analogy and
appearance—'appeared', 'as if', 'as from', 'did seem'—signalize
overtly what the architectural terminology and disposition of
perspective more continuously imply: a receptive and
constructive self, circumscribing the unencompassable ('roofing'
the sky, making of it a temple or palace), structuring as it soars
upwards to the zenith of nature's manifest structure, weaving
pattern out of offered pattern, 'growing' downwards in unison
with the sweep of intensifying colour that 'still grew/Down the
steep West'. The poetry is once again a record of mutual give and
take, reciprocity. The imagination bounds nature without
binding her down; and, vice versa, the life and forms of the
external world set limits to the imagination even as they rouse it
to act, thus precluding just those dangers that we shall see imaged

in the condition of the maniac, of self-absorption and visionary confusion. We witness not only the 'bright eternity' of natural process but a 'bright' ontological state, the state of stable and creative 'being'.

Typically of 'Julian and Maddalo' these passages operate on a number of interrelated levels, of which the descriptive level is only the most obvious. They have, in the first place, a narrative and dramatic function, in that they help to characterize Julian the narrator and supply a setting for both the story of his encounter with the maniac and the story of the maniac himself, the tale-within-a-tale. Their subjective-confessional dimension is hardly less evident. While the portrait of the young Julian involves a criticism of self, these epiphanic episodes incorporate self-assertion, Shelley's allegiance to the brighter side of his imaginative impulses. More than this, they constitute one side of a dialogue of the mind with itself, at the other extreme of which stand the subterranean fears and tragic self-awareness articulated in the maniac episode; as a register of Shelley's own capacity for outgoing creativity they represent something that was at this time under particularly acute pressure, reflected not only in his preoccupation with the oppression of madness but also in the solipsistic pessimism of 'Stanzas written in Dejection'— 'Alas! I have nor hope nor health,/Nor peace within nor calm around'.

Before unlocking the secrets of the asylum-cell, however, it is worth pausing to say that 'Julian and Maddalo' is also in its own way powerfully 'philosophic', if by 'philosophic' we understand a meaning virtually opposite from 'the holding to and communication of ideas'. To underline its confessional ingredients is not to deny its status as a rich canvas of universal truths. Whatever their precise needs and compulsions, Shelley's mind and imagination produce generalized images of experience and being, each of them a message about human potentiality or human limitation. The sections we have just considered are no exception: a psychological act—an affirmation of personal well-being and continuing creative capacity within an overall context of self-assessment and self-doubt—yields a poetic landscape celebrative of *man's*, the individual's, ability to escape the prison-house of self into the unselfconscious joy of communing with a benign and active universe. In talking of this effect of generalization, I am concerned as much with the emblematic quality of Shelley's style as with an inevitable result of the narrative-dramatic mode. At one point the text offers a direct incentive to symbolic interpretaion, when Maddalo insists upon a metaphoric, and humanized, 'reading' of the madhouse and its belfrey tower, as a representation of man's impotent and mortal state: 'And this must be the *emblem* and the *sign*/Of what should be eternal and divine . . .' (ll.121–22, italics mine). He goes on, as we know, to take the bell as an image of the soul, which hangs desolate beneath the indifferent light of heaven and summons us to pray like baffled maniacs for we know not what, and the sunset as an emblem of 'the night of death' that 'severeth' us, defeated, from our desires and pointless endeavour. But this formal invitation to a poetic response to reality simply endorses a habit already enforced—or reinforced—by 'Julian and Maddalo' in the kinetic *exempla* of unfettered 'being'. Indeed, because we have met with these *exempla* we are able to push the response beyond the limits to which Maddalo leads us, and to discover in the 'windowless . . . pile' a hell-on-earth of sense-deprivation where the individual, everlastingly screened off from external stimuli, is denied the secular salvation of ennobling interchange with Nature. In their conjunction of figurative amplification and comment on existence Maddalo's lines on the madhouse epitomize a central procedure of the whole poem. Moreover, they are characteristic too in their 'relativity'—the fact that, whatever Maddalo's designs with regard to Julian, they make no claims on us as a statement of *absolute* truth about life, but are rather a report on it. The positive thrust of the poetry of 'Julian and Maddalo' corresponds to the negative thrust of its undermining of ideological philosophy: it validates, and involves us in, different ways of experiencing, seeing, and interpreting the world without allowing total precedence to any.

The maniac episode itself is the least easily decipherable of the tableaux of experiential and ontological states. Reiman suggests a biographical source for some parts—'emotional lines that probably reflect [Shelley's] own estrangement from Mary Shelley'.[20] But 'the personal' is present in a less narrow form than that, for beyond the self-portraiture in Shelley's conception of the young Julian lies the self-portraiture in his conception of the

madman, the fated idealist who shares the radical sensibility of
the poet of *Queen Mab* yet has the one tragic flaw of over-
sensitivity, too brittle a heart—

> he seemed hurt,
> Even as a man with his peculiar wrong,
> To hear but of the oppression of the strong . . .
>                                   (ll.237–39)

There are times, to be sure, when the maniac does seem to be a
mouthpiece for Shelley's own immediate feelings of despair and
resentment, especially in the long bitter complaint of cruel
mistreatment by an unfeeling lover:

> *Me*—who am as a nerve o'er which do creep
> The else unfelt oppressions of this earth . . .
>                    . . . that thou on me
> Should'st rain these plagues of blistering agony . . .
>                                   (ll.449–50, 52–53)

The figure is much more, however, a poet's vision of what he
might become—an embodiment of deep-rooted fears and fancies
involving a sense, not only of the vulnerability of a sensitive spirit,
but of the precariousness of the imaginative temper itself.
Wordsworth had given direct expression to his feeling for the
dangers inherent in the singular privilege of poethood: 'We Poets
in our youth begin in gladness;/But thereof come in the end
despondency and madness' ('Resolution and Independence').
Shelley's anxiety is at once more covert and more revealed. It
springs to life as a personification, a shadowy form living out an
agony of relentless mental turmoil and extravagant urges, a
travesty of creative being. In him, for example, the imagination
at its height engenders inverted perceptions of immortality—
perversions indeed of Shelley's own concept of the 'time-
destroying infiniteness' of pure, 'perfected' thought. For all the
maniac can envision is an eternity of pain, a 'living-death of
agonies' like those of a worm:

> As the slow shadows of the pointed grass
> Mark the eternal periods, his pangs pass
> Slow, ever-moving,—making moments be
> As mine seem—each an immortality! (ll.416–19)

His state is itself the terrible opposite of that prophesied by

Shelley in *Queen Mab* and elsewhere as the inheritance of the man perfect in 'virtue and talent', whose inner sanctity and power of exalted thought will 'gift/With self-enshrined eternity'.[21] His is not 'the paradise' but 'the hell' within, the hell (as he puts it in one of his many images of confinement) of a 'pent mind'. He is an outstanding instance of the psychological prisoner, perpetually 'communing with himself' (as Maddalo remarks, 1.269), destined always to repeat his woe without ever purging it, doomed to swing restlessly between the poles of reason and passion so that (for instance) his noble desire to set aside 'scorn or hate' collapses before bitter thoughts of personal wrong that burn the brain and '[blot] all things fair/And wise and good which time had written there' (ll.460ff.), and, most prominently of all, fuelling his despair with fantasies of its own breeding.

We are encouraged after the madman's rhapsody to see him as a type of the true poet, when Julian recalls that his language was 'high,/Such as in measure were called poetry' and remembers Maddalo's remark on how wretched men are 'cradled into poetry by wrong', learning in suffering 'what they teach in song' (ll.540–47). Maddalo is right of course; and, in view of Reiman's picture of Shelley's emotional distress at this time, Shelley's interest in so familiar a truth may represent a therapeutic search on his part for a conviction of pain's hidden profit. Nevertheless, though suffering may educate the soul and sharpen the senses, the condition imaged in the madman is more to be feared than sought after, especially by poets. It is essentially that state of enclosed, uncreative being which haunts the Romantic and pre-Romantic consciousness like a giant spectre, an outgrowth of the shadow-side of the self-centred imagination. The atrophied bard of Gray's *Elegy* ('drooping, woeful wan . . ./Or crazed with care'), Cowper's picture in 'Retirement' of the silent, fevered, self-communing melancholic with 'lips busy and eyes fixt . . .', the solipsistic poet of Wordsworth's 'Lines, left upon a Seat in a Yew-tree' always nurturing 'a morbid pleasure' in acts of gloomy contemplation, the vitiated self of Coleridge's 'Dejection Ode' in whom reciprocity with nature has been displaced by passionately unimpassioned grief—these are but a few of the plainer analogues to Shelley's waking vision of the imprisoned self, the poet buried above ground.[22] Section three of 'The Sensitive-Plant' enacts, in allegory, the sombre reverse of fruitful interchange between the powers of insatiable 'self' and inexhaustible 'world'—the view, that is, of nature as parasitic, with monstrous forms of 'spawn, weeds and filfth' battening on mind-space until its points of growth are changed to 'a blight of frozen glue'.[23] The maniac's predicament is one in which everything is parasitic except nature, from which he is in any case ineluctably cut off. We see him at once as under the spell of an *idée fixe* ('Some fancy *took him* and he would not bear removal', ll.251–52), and, in another very common convention of the *topos* of the afflicted poet, find psychic impasse mirrored in physical paralysis ('. . . his pale fingers twined/One with the other . . ./And he was muttering, and his lean limbs shook . . .', ll.273ff.).[24] As he speaks, he falls prey to the rapacious encroachments of experience, memory, imagination, and even language itself: remembrance of an idyllic past—

> . . . years long past, since thine eye kindled
> With soft fire under mine . . .

conspires with a sense of loss and imagined offence—

> Thou wilt tell
> With a grimace of hate how horrible
> It was to meet my love . . .

to provoke a curse upon the infection and torture of words—

> But from my lips the unwilling accents start
> And from my pen . . .
> . . . My sight
> Is dim to see that charactered in vain
> On this unfeeling leaf which burns the brain
> And eats into it . . . (ll.468–69, 460–62, 475–80)

As language thus becomes an instrument of torment rather than a privilege of the wise, so memory, Mother of the Muses out of which 'Julian and Maddalo' was itself born and source of 'vivifying virtue' to the Romantic mind at large, forms the embalming-cloth of moments of hideous pain—'Thou . . . / . . . cearedst my memory o'er them,—for I heard/And can forget not' (ll.432–34). The mind's space is the dwelling-place of grotesque dreams of self-abuse ('That, like some maniac monk, I had torn out/The nerves of manhood by their bleeding root'), the haunt of phantom-figures ('. . . pale Pain/My shadow, which will leave me not again'), the breeding-ground of garish oneiric confusions whereby 'tomb' and 'bridal bed', wedding festival and funeral, desire and revulsion, waking and dying, merge in an unstable kaleidoscope of images until the maniac, mercilessly visited from within, is at last mercifully 'left alone' (ll.383ff.). *His* imagination constructs merely the architecture of the grave, that last place of confinement whose 'roof shall cover/My limbs with dust and worms under and over . . .' (ll.506–7).

The maniac is then both a persona of the wounded Shelley and a surfacing or exteriorization of the darker currents of his mind and imagination, of that same preoccupation with doomed creativity which haunted him as early as *Alastor* and as late as 'The Triumph of Life' (the maniac's fate, which is for the mind to move endlessly inward, is the mirror-image of Alastor's where it travels eternally outwards). That this preoccupation is a prominent Romantic *topos* makes it no less of a psychological reality in Shelley. Just as his belief in the 'immortality' of the inspired 'man of virtue and talent' who outlives the priest-ridden slave reflects a personal hope,[25] so his pictures of the living death of uncreative selfhood articulate personal fear; and, more than this, the fear, the dark imaginings, the gloomy self-consciousness, are themselves potentially an abyss that might destroy him. But it is an abyss of course that Shelley does not fall into in 'Julian and Maddalo'. He looks into it from the outside, and with a great deal of curiosity.

There could in fact be no more spectacular example of the paradox generally present in the Romantic concern with non-being, dereliction, confinement—the sheer energy and inventiveness with which these states are realized. To recall just one of our previous references, Coleridge wrote what is arguably his most vigorous poem out of the embrace of a 'drowsy, stifled, unimpassioned grief'. With the maniac's speech and environment, however, we enter a more ornamented and melodramatic world of imprisonment, nearer to 'The Ancient Mariner' or Byron's 'Prisoner of Chillon' than to 'Dejection: an Ode'. The shaping of grand edifying significances ('How vain are words . . .', 'Those who inflict must suffer . . .') and the constant agile aestheticism of the imagery ('Month after month . . . to bear this load/And as a jade urged by the whip . . .', 'As the slow

shadows of the pointed grass/Mark the eternal periods'), indeed
the whole metaphoric amplication of the subject, elevate the life
and lessons of ultimate aloneness and stress, the madhouse and
madness. The veil of the pent mind is removed to reveal a strange
beauty, and an array of defamiliarized general truths of which
the following heightened, almost Shakespearean, conception of
the workings of scorn and hate is a fair representation:

> Yet think not though subdued—and I may well
> Say that I am subdued—that the full Hell
> Within me would infect the untainted breast
> Of sacred nature with its own unrest;
> As some perverted beings think to find
> In scorn or hate a medicine for the mind
> Which scorn or hate have wounded—o how vain!
> The dagger heals not but may rend again . . .
>                                    (ll.350–57)

There is much nobility and much sense in this madness.

Such passages as this give a strong sense of the ambiguity of
Shelley's Romantic vision of confinement and isolation—the
view of 'prison' as at once holy place and place of deprivation. As
Victor Brombert puts it in a general essay on the theme, 'the
locked-in individual in his solipsistic "recreation" learns how to
enter into dialogue with the self',[26] which in the case of Shelley's
maniac means the discovery of private strength as well as
personal vulnerability, the desire though 'subdued' to keep the
purer self untainted, or the heroism of patriotic sacrifice and
sacrifice in friendship's cause—

> I am prepared: in truth with no proud joy
> To do or suffer aught, as when a boy
> I did devote to justice and to love
> My nature . . . (ll.379–82)

The potential of suffering and sequestration is thus continually
implied, as a pathway to self-knowledge. They are, too, a source
of that passionate language which is one of the languages of
poetry—'Strong passion expresses itself in metaphor borrowed
from objects alike remote or near, and casts over all the shadow of
its own greatness'.[27] Even for Shelley's 'sad meek' sufferer
confinement opens the door to poetic utterance, bearing out

Victor Hugo's contention that '*Un poète est un monde enfermé dans un homme*'. Up to a point his is the exalted state which, in Leopardi's imaginary dialogue between Tasso and his '*genio familiare*', renovates the spirit ('*ringiovanisce l'animo*') and galvanizes the imagination, the '*virtu di favellare*'.[28]

But only up to a point. The negative aspects of his condition are in the end more apparent than its privileges. Poet though he is, he achieves no such triumph as Byron's Tasso in whom 'prisoned solitude' breeds 'wings wherewith to overfly/The narrow circus of my dungeon wall,/And [free] the Holy Sepulchre from thrall'.[29] As we saw at length earlier, he is not so much a beneficiary of the imagination as a victim of it and not so much an *exemplum* of 'the eternal spirit of the chainless mind' (Byron, 'Sonnet on Chillon') as an everlasting cautionary spectacle of psychic arrestment and non-progression. In comparison with the spiritual victories of Byron's Tasso and prisoner of Chillon, or for that matter of Shelley's own Prometheus whose enchainment is the prelude to a great renewal, the worst aspect of the maniac's fate is indeed the inability to 'break out' inwardly—to affirm the ultimate freedom of the soul. As Brombert reminds us, carceral imagery always suggests a threshold, the possibility of a passage; but this prisoner never passes from torment to peace(he weeps even in his dreams [ll.513–14]), from the inside to the beyond except to imagine the perverse refuge of the 'grave' and its 'oblivion', or from despair to that mysterious joy which Hugo von Hoffmansthal associates with the eternal secret of human bondage—'*das ewige Geheimnis der Verkettung alles Irdischen*'.[30] As a testing-ground of inner purity and noble instincts the asylum does, we know, yield some gains, yet even these are compromised by the maniac's perpetual reversal into self-regarding thought: the self-abnegating idealism referred to above soon gives way to a wish for death and a passive acceptance of a passive confinement ('Heap on me soon, o grave, thy welcome dust!/Till then the dungeon may demand its prey . . .'), while later the approach to pure selflessness ('Here I cast away/All human passions, all revenge, all pride . . .') turns out to be a way to yearnings for a final end to an unbearable despair ('. . . the air/Closes upon my accents, as despair/Upon my heart—let death upon despair'). These are the maniac's last words, how he dreams death will come; a fatal smothering is the *telos* to which his burdened consciousness is irredeemably pulled.

Yet whatever the negations imaged in his condition, the madhouse is to everyone else—Julian, Maddalo, the poet Shelley, the reader—truly a 'holy place' visited for both instruction and the strange pleasure that comes from contemplating the forbidden corners of the heart. Shelley himself does not glorify the oppression of madness as he glorifies the archetypal Promethean bondage, but he does wring from it a potent poetic landscape and a study in experience, as well as afterwards a lesson in human sympathy—

> . . . we
> Wept without shame in his society. (ll.515–16)

Shelley's redeeming of perception and feeling in 'Julian and Maddalo' is nowhere more apparent than in the fact that he gives amplitude to constriction and value to failure and helplessness, a value expressed no less in the feelingly understated pathos of the image of the pitying onlookers than in his final respect for the humanity of the object of their pity. It is surprising that he should find no place in Brombert's excellent documenting of the poetization of confinement in Romantic, and pre-Romantic, literature—a psycho-historical event which W. B. Carnochan is surely right to describe as a salient reflection of, and saving reaction to, the great crisis of change during the Enlightenment from an anthropocentric universe to a sense of endless space of which man occupies a small and insignificant corner.[31] 'Julian and Maddalo' participates in none of Romanticism's most audacious 'answers' to the challenge of science and mechanistic philosophy, seemingly bent upon robbing the world of divinity and value; it does not, like *Prometheus Unbound* and the great lyrics, make claims for the god-likeness of man and the spirituality of the place he inhabits, removing God from his heaven and situating him familiarly in nature and the human mind. But it offers the no less important salvation of imaginative acceptance—the creative embrace of limitation and despair, the reaches of our shut-in state.

To talk of 'imaginative acceptance' and 'creative embrace' is to suggest a notable objectivity in Shelley's relation to life and experience, the responsiveness-in-detachment of the narrative-dramatic artist. This is not at odds with my earlier emphasis on the subjectivity of the work, though it may appear so. A dialogue of the mind with itself can also be a dialogue with the world, out of which springs a 'criticism of life'. Shelley in fact had at least one powerful model of personal-impersonal narrative before him in Book One of *The Excursion*, with which he seems to have been especially familiar.[32] Jonathan Wordsworth offers a fine analysis of the tale of Margaret and the Ruined Cottage as a noble tragedy of love, loss, and decline, a triumph of negative capability in which Wordsworth feels powerfully for passions not his own.[33] As I have argued at length elsewhere,[34] however, 'The Ruined Cottage' is manifestly rooted in self-consciousness, with the authorial self being projected in three separate directions: the youthful Poet who is schooled by the Pedlar's account of Margaret's suffering from immaturity to a necessary sense of 'all that is endured'; the Pedlar, Wordsworth's ideal of the mature Poet who is sympathetic yet steadfast in the face of man's adversity—an ideal he has in a sense already achieved in writing the poem; more obliquely, Margaret whose 'madness', which involves subjection to the imagination ('. . . evermore her eye/Was busy in the distance, shaping things . . .'), represents a danger that Wordsworth always feared and often felt the immediate need to overcome. The categories have their fairly exact counterparts in 'Julian and Maddalo': Julian, the past self who has been transcended and who had to confront suffering on the road to maturity; Maddalo, touchstone of experienced insight; the maniac who is both a 'threshold' within a retrospective drama of personal maturation and an emergence of the shadow side of the mature consciousness itself, a mirror of those fears and fancies which can never be entirely put to rest. Neither poem is simply a record of the past but rather a reconstruction whereby the poet establishes a present identity, charting his journey from innocence to experience and at the same time confirming that change through the critical perspectives he throws upon his former self and through the view he now takes of life. Shelley's present identity, like Wordsworth's, is based in stoical acceptance of a 'cold world' where dreams go unaccomplished and there is little of transcendent worth, where man is eternally impotent and shut in—a stoicism which is, however, amply compensated not only by a sense of the ontological freedom repeatedly available to the individual in the presence of Nature but also by a realization of the opportunities offered up to the imagination from the cold world itself.[35]

One way of putting it would be to say that Shelley's personal discovery in 'Julian and Maddalo' is the discovery of impersonality—a fourth self that incorporates, controls, and goes beyond all the 'identities' located within the poem, the wise, sceptical, poetic Maddalo as well as the maniac-victim of the tyranny of memory and imagination. So complete is this discovery, and so thorough his dramatization of the materials and orientations of his consciousness, that the poem can consistently stand as an instance of Browning's 'objectivity', the reproduction of 'things external . . . the manifested action of the human heart and brain'; it may be read, in other words, as an achieved dramatic monologue. Indeed, the incentives of the text are all in this direction. The 'depersonalizing' effects of the Preface, which I have mentioned before, cannot be overstressed, guiding the reader, as they do, to approach the work as a study in character and points of view: 'Count Maddalo is a Venetian nobleman . . . a person of the most consummate genius . . . But it is his weakness to be proud . . .'; 'Julian is an Englishman of good family . . . for ever speculating how good may be made superior . . .'; in the maniac's exclamations 'will perhaps be found sufficient comment for the text of every heart'. We are conditioned to respond to personality—what the figures in the poem are, how they feel, what they think. Donald Davie praises the conversational style on the grounds that it 'civilizes the reader', but while such a view is perfect in relation to (say) Cowper's *The Task*, where the cultured sobriety is itself a manifestation of the moral standards the poet is upholding in his attacks on the contemporary debasement of all life and literature, it seems of doubtful relevance to a context in which 'the familiar style' functions, not as the exemplary voice of an educated and educating spokesman, but as a flexible means of specifying and differentiating the speaker behind the words. During their debate Julian and Maddalo do, it is true, share the cultivated tone which Davie designates 'the habit of gentlemen', yet the lean and bare prosaic language which he sees as the basis of this 'urbanity' belongs almost all to the former, and is in fact a register of his *limitations*. The wry prefatory comment that 'Julian is rather serious' has its practical extension in the dry, unmellowed rhetoric of his speeches, where what there is of metaphor and the language of feeling is merely the plain dress and slender embellishment of preconceived logic ('See/This lovely child, blithe, innocent and free . . .', '. . . those who try may find/How strong the chains are which our spirit bind;/Brittle perchance as straw . . .'). Maddalo on the other hand, though no less a master of civilized argument, is distinguished by that imaginative relationship with the world which can transform the madhouse into a hell of lost souls and in turn make of that hell a 'heaven of sacred silence' when the madman plays his music (ll.259-61). It is the absence of imagination that provides the fullest measure of Julian's immaturity, and his progress from debater to narrator involves primarily a shift from words and theories to articulate imaginative responses, a creative sympathy with everything from the peculiar life of waste and solitary places to the anguish of a lunatic.

As further evidence of this sympathy we might take his present view of Maddalo's daughter, which contrasts perfectly with his former mechanical image of the representative 'lovely child':

> A lovelier toy sweet Nature never made,
> A serious, subtle, wild, yet gentle being,
> Graceful without design and unforeseeing,
> With eyes—oh speak not of her eyes!—which seem
> Twin mirrors of Italian Heaven, yet gleam
> With such deep meaning, as we never see
> But in the human countenance . . . (ll.144-50)

He goes on to describe how he had nursed her when she first came to 'this bleak world', and how she still remembered him, 'Less changed than she was by six months or so'. In his sense, now, of the child's complex beauty and individuality, in the playful, consciously overstated metaphoric comparisons which yet do nothing to undermine the force of his genuine delight in this 'miracle' of Nature, in his simple gratitude for the pleasures to be found in 'this bleak world', we perceive a Julian 'much changed', a Julian 'humanized'. Or, again, there is the fact that, just previously, his reconstruction of the Venetian landscape takes a richly sober colouring from a renewed sense of mortality prompted by the memory of Maddalo's elegiac vision of 'the night of death'—so that the description expresses a matured

sensibility, a mind attuned to the still sad music both of nature
and humanity:

> The churches, ships, and palaces were seen
> Huddled in gloom;—into the purple sea
> The orange hues of heaven sunk silently.
> We hardly spoke . . . (ll.136–39)

He has become, like Maddalo, a man and a poet—so much like
Maddalo, indeed, that he even displays the same healthy, witty
scepticism about intellectual speculation in his early mock-epic
comparison between their serious talk along the Lido and the
high dispute that Milton's devils 'held within the dales of
Hell/Concerning God, freewill and destiny' (ll.41–42), while at
the same time sharing his friend's capacity for poetizing physical
reality, notably in his transmutation of the madhouse into an
underworld of ghostly presences ('Long tangled locks flung
wildly forth') presided over by the maniac, whose words are so
precious and pregnant with forbidden truth that the elements
conspire to drown them:

> the loud and gusty storm
> Hissed through the window, and we stood behind
> Stealing his accents from the envious wind. (ll.295–97)

But the poem is the more convincing as an account of the
development of a personality because it signalizes continuity as
well as change. For something of the old Julian survives. The
narrator who, remembering how he argued with Maddalo
'against despondency', asks 'for ever still/Is it not wise to make
the best of ill' (ll.46–47) remains the idealist, committed to the
view that 'it is our will that . . . chains us to permitted ill'. How far
committed however? That his sense of man's ability to cope with
'ill' is now cast in the form of a questioning aside, and that he talks
of a *wise* course of action rather than a revolution of the heart,
indicates the same modification of outlook as his previous casual
admission that spiritual freedom is an illusion, a hope of the
imprisoned—'boundless, as we *wish* our souls to be'. There is no
naivety about this Julian. He knows the world for what it is, and
can even speak of his own hopes of curing the maniac as 'an idle
thought' (l.567). All the same, he is no cynic cut off from the
demands of humanity and the promptings of human nature; he

still values the 'deep tenderness' he felt towards the maniac, observing that 'The man who were not [moved by the madman's suffering], must have lacked a touch/Of human nature' (ll.518–19). But his monologue proves him capable of finding value everywhere, in nature and in life. If he is an exemplary figure, it is surely more because of this than on account of his 'urbanity'.

We have covered some of this ground before when considering the confessional bias of 'Julian and Maddalo': Julian the narrator is a persona of Shelley, and his perspectives are an affirmation of Shelley's own maturity. My immediate concern, however, has been to show that for all its very real subjective content the poem does construct a coherent objective 'character'. The elements of setting, situation and action further increase the effect of objectivity, supplying as it were the secondary features of an impersonal poetic drama. It is essential to acknowledge, though, that these are wholly subservient to the interest of personality, experience, and 'being'. Although made admirably present to us, the Venetian landscape is not important for itself or simply for locating a series of narrative incidents, but operates as an aspect of psychological and ontological events, whether of intercourse with nature or such milder acts of 'fond remembrance' as when Julian recalls the delights of the city—'. . . books are there,/Pictures, and casts from all those statues fair/Which were twin-born with poetry . . .' (ll.554–56). It is a *locus* in the narrator's unfolding mind, a spot revisited above all for the sake of the formative experience that took place there. 'Julian and Maddalo' is less a tale than a psycho-drama involving recollection of two other psycho-dramas—the confrontation with the maniac's giant agony and the drama enacted in the mind of the maniac himself (where narrative, the history of his love-affair, is similarly of subordinate significance).

Now this sounds very much like the effect aimed at by Wordsworth in the *Lyrical Ballads*: 'the feeling therein developed gives importance to the action and situation, and not the action and situation to the feeling'.[36] And 'Julian and Maddalo' comes near to the *Ballads* not only in its general experiential and psychological emphasis, but also in the fact that it seems to be a 'composite' of kinds of poems prominent in that collection—the 'debate' represented by 'Expostulation and Reply' (which, incidentally, elevates feeling and imagination over bookish learning), the dramatic monologues like 'The Female Vagrant' and 'The Mad Mother' where a character displays and explains a present state of mind through contemplation of a 'sad history', and the more personal drama of maturation of 'Tintern Abbey'. 'The Ruined Cottage' is a still closer analogue of course, not least because it combines the three types—debate, monologue, and confession—in a single structure.

But there are significant parellels from the next, as well as the previous, generation. Joseph-Antoine Milsand, reviewing Browning's *Men and Women* in 1856, found that the poet

> . . . sympathizes equally with both kinds of inspiration, . . . and partly without his knowing it, his constant effort has been to reconcile and combine them, in order to find a way of being, not in turn but simultaneously, lyric and dramatic, subjective and pictorial . . . [He] would have us conceive the inner significance of things by making us see their exteriors.[37]

Here Milsand uses 'subjective' in the sense of referring to the interior life and meaning, 'the inner significance', of characters and situations, rather than that of relating to the author's own consciousness or capacities, the creating mind and imagination. Both senses are applicable to 'Julian and Maddalo', as they are to Browning's earlier work—*Pauline, Paracelsus,* and *Sordello*—which, despite the superficial accuracy of the poet's contention that his writings were 'always dramatic in principle, and so many utterances of so many imaginary persons', J. S. Mill quite properly thought to be possessed of conspicuously 'intense and morbid self-consciousness'.[38] When saying of these poems, in 1863, that 'My stress lay on the incidents in the development of a soul: little else is worth study . . . others may one day think so',[39] Browning apparently forgets that the soul in question is transparently his own and that others before him had thought little else than the subject in question to be worth study—not only the Wordsworth of 'Tintern Abbey' and *The Prelude*, or the Keats whose preoccupation with 'soul-making' took him at last to the initiatory shrine of Moneta in one of the great Romantic allegories of maturation, but also the Shelley of *Alastor* and 'Julian and Maddalo' itself. But it is *Alastor*, much more than any other piece, that provides the model for Browning's autobiographical soul-histories—those introspective-external-ized expressions of the passionately idealistic and endlessly self-absorbed Shelleyan seeker after truth. 'Julian and Maddalo' is in its effects and procedures altogether more tautly and sharply impersonalized, more 'subjective and pictorial' in Milsand's sense. As I suggested earlier, no sensitive reading can exclude the constant apprehension of Shelley's complex personal presence within and behind the poem, whereas 'Andrea del Sarto', 'Fra Lippo Lippi', 'Cleon' and the rest are notable, especially after *Paracelsus* and *Sordello*, for the absence of any manifest authorial self-contemplation or psychological confession, whatever the extent of Browning's own involvement in the ideas and situations of his characters. Nevertheless, 'Julian and Maddalo' takes us to the very verge of that dedicated anatomizing of individual experience and personality, the deliberate psychological empiricism, which, as Robert Langbaum above all argues so forcefully, constitutes the most positive poetic endeavour of the nineteenth century (parallel of course to the probably more primary trends of the novel), finding a perfected expression in the Victorian dramatic monologue but forming the centre of a wider 'distinctively modern tradition' grounded in the assumptions that 'the poem exists not to imitate or describe life but to make it manifest', that 'we know the poem through sentience, and the poem's meaning is the sentience which it calls into awareness', that poetry should make its statement not as an idea 'but as an experience ... the genuine experience of an identifiable person'.[40]

For Langbaum, the Victorian dramatic monologue represents the 'objectification' of the Romantic subjective lyric as represented by 'Tintern Abbey' or 'Frost at Midnight', 'a form imitating not nature or an order of ideas about nature but the structure of experience itself: a poetry of experience';[41] but in Shelley's poem an objectification has already taken place. So it has in 'The Female Vagrant' or 'The Mad Mother'. 'Julian and Maddalo', however, is closer to the Victorian model simply because it *is* more elaborately dramatic—more developed in its presentation of the consciousness of an individualized speaker. Pound's description of his own poetry—'I catch the character I happen to be interested in at the moment he interests me, usually a moment of song, self-analysis . . . And the rest of the play would bore me . . .'—may imply the influence of the brief dramatic lyric, and indeed the drama itself, as much as that of the dramatic monologue and so casts doubt perhaps on Langbaum's implicit claims for the latter's primacy within the development of his 'distinctively modern tradition' (which takes in Yeats, Pound, and, above all, Eliot).[42] Nevertheless, inasmuch as the monologue has importance, 'Julian and Maddalo', to my knowledge its first mature manifestation, significantly shares in it.

Finally, there is one paramount feature of Langbaum's 'poetry of experience' which is of particular usefulness in assessing the nature of our overall response to 'Julian and Maddalo'. This is his view that the 'poetry of experience' is also a 'poetry of sympathy', so much so in Browning that our moral judgement of the Duke in 'My Last Duchess', or of the worldly Bishop Blougram, or the ignobly vulnerable Andrea del Sarto, is decisively outflanked by the thoroughness with which we are made to understand them, to (in M. W. MacCallum's phrase) appreciate 'facts from within'.[43] I am sure that moral evaluation is actually a more persistent effect of Browning's monologues than Langbaum would allow, for who would wish to act like this Duke or be like Andrea? Are they not in the end both instances of 'sickness' which as human beings we resist and judge? Yet Langbaum is fundamentally right about our relation to character and action in Browning and his successors—a certain dramatic understanding that implies a certain dramatic sympathy; and what he is seeing is an extension of a specifically Romantic contribution to literature, whereby *Einfühlung* becomes the primary way of knowing, and meaning is derived from the poetic material itself rather than from any external, publicly accepted orders of ideas or values. 'Julian and Maddalo' participates as firmly in this contribution as any subjective lyric, where the person speaking commands all our intimate assent to the triumphs and the failures of his perceptions and intellect, or as any sympathetic revelation of the condition and feelings of 'low' characters. The young Julian's speculative idealism is certainly judged—not, however, according to absolute standards of 'right' or 'wrong' but as a limitation to be overcome through experience, during, that is, the process of personal growth which is inferred from the perspectives and character of the narrator. The narrator is exemplary in his

*211399*

capacities—which themselves include sympathetic feelings and a sympathetic imagination—and not in conduct, behaviour seen in social or moralistic terms. But especially we have the poem's view of the maniac, cast always in the language of sympathy and of a desire to understand:

> we
> Wept without shame in his society . . .
>
>              his was some *dreadful* ill
> Wrought on him boldly . . .
>              some *deadly* change in love . . .
>              it were a *grief* indeed
> If he had changed one unsustaining reed
> For all that such a man might else adorn.
>                     (ll.515ff., italics mine)

It is as if the Augustan theme of *quantum mutatus ab illo,* as examplified in Pope's portrait of Villiers in 'On the Use of Riches' or Johnson's *exempla* in *The Vanity of Human Wishes,* has shed all its moralistic weight and been transmuted (as in Wordsworth's picture of the changed Simon Lee or Michael) into a lesson in the unaccountable sadness, the 'grief', of things. The maniac is never criticized or recoiled from; the emphasis falls on a tender compulsion to know his condition, to study 'all the beatings of his heart/With zeal, as men study some stubborn art/For their own good' and 'by patience find/An entrance to the caverns of his mind' (ll.570–73). We are invited to take (with Julian) the role of psychologist, not moralist—which is the role that Romantic, and post-Romantic, poetry characteristically would have us assume, whether we read it as authorial confession or a reproduction of things external. Though there may be no cure for the riven heart, we none the less contemplate it zealously—and for our 'own good'.

Our own good? Indeed, 'Julian and Maddalo' does in a sense have a strong moral thrust, for its lessons are truly lessons in humanity, in capacity and incapacity, opportunity and impossibility, the brightness and the darkness of 'being'. Locke, encoding the philosophic implications of Newtonian physics, contends that the world of our ordinary perceptions is largely illusory, that the only objective reality consists of particles of matter moving in space; he leaves us a world without aesthetic or spiritual significance.[44] Against this, the Romantic protests by an appeal to his own insight into 'the life of things'. To him it is *matter* which is illusory, a mere concept, while 'the life of things'—what his perceptions, imagination, and feelings reveal to him—is the true reality. Nature and human nature thus become everywhere a repository of potential value, one's capacity for tapping it being the touchstone, the standard, of well-being. 'Julian and Maddalo' sees into 'the life of things', and teaches us to see into them, no less than Shelley's 'transcendent' lyrics, but in a manner that asks us to look more intensely at their familiar face instead of pursuing the distant ideal beyond it; it gives a model for a poetry of experience and a model for experiencing the world. In many ways it appears a poem *sui generis* among Shelley's writings, having little more in common with his other poems in the so-called 'familiar style'—the Prioresque 'Letter to Maria Gisborne' or the Blakeian 'Sensitive Plant'—than with those texts like *Prometheus Unbound* in which he tried to re-establish a collective faith on revolutionary principles, a new myth of universal redemption, an unorthodox religious orthodoxy; little more, that is, except, in the case of 'Letter to Maria Gisborne', the successful poetization of personal consciousness and 'ordinary' life, the inner and outer landscapes. In the 'Letter' Shelley of course takes simple refuge in the relaxed contemplation of the 'magical' powers of his imagination and in an earthly paradise of friendship and fun, while 'Julian and Maddalo' displays a keener consciousness both of self and the human condition, closer to the tragic sensibility and anxious introspection of 'The Triumph of Life'. But all three poems are, despite their differences, dramatizations of mental process, of the mind in the act of exploring both its own and the world's confines, situating significance *there* and not in any inviolable system of belief. 'Julian and Maddalo' is more representative of Shelley than it might at first seem—and more representative, too, of his Romanticism and his modernity.

## NOTES

1. 'Essay on Shelley' (1852), in Hugh Sykes Davies, *The Poets and their Critics* (London, 1962), ii. 172.

2. I am indebted for this point to the comments on Browning's Essay in *Browning: Selected Poems* ed. Kenneth Allott, (Oxford, 1967), Introduction,

32–33. This edition reprints the relevant sections of the 'Essay' as an appendix; op. cit., 191–96.

3. *Shelley: Selected Poetry and Prose* (Signet Classics, New York, 1966), Introduction, xvii.

4. *Purity of Diction in English Verse* (London, 1967), 141–44.

5. *Shelley's Poetry and Prose*, ed. Donald H. Reiman and Stuart R. Powers (New York, 1977),112, n.1 (hereafter *Poetry and Prose*). Quotations from 'Julian and Maddalo' follow the text of this edition, which is based on the version of the poem in the author's manuscript in The Pierpont Morgan Library. All other references are to *Poetical Works*.

6. See 'Lines written among the Euganean Hills', ll.167–205.

7. Shelley, Preface to *Prometheus Unbound, Poetical Works*, 207.

8. Ibid., 207.

9. Robert Langbaum, *The Poetry of Experience* (London, 1957; Penguin Books edn., 1974), passim.

10. *Poetry and Prose*, 113.

11. See especially Section III, ll.118ff. and Section VIII, ll.198ff. of *Queen Mab*.

12. See ll.529ff.

13. Particularly the ability to rise above the seductions, influences and conditions of this world by dint of

> . . . consciousness of good, . . .
> . . . a life of resolute good,
> Unalterable will, quenchless desire
> Of universal happiness, the heart
> That beats with it in unison, the brain,
> Whose ever wakeful wisdom toils . . . (*Queen Mab*, Section V, ll. 223ff.)

This triumph of the inner man—which is of course Godwin's idea of 'perfected sensibility'—is said by Shelley to be a 'nobler glory' that solaces 'all human care' and 'deserts not virtue in the dungeon's gloom' (loc. cit., ll.214–17); but the very same qualities of mind cannot console or save the maniac of 'Julian and Maddalo' in his dungeon, which virtually overthrows Shelley's earlier optimistic theory and makes the maniac an example of the wakeness, even the futility, of the Goodwinian 'inner light'. This is very much in keeping with the anti-speculative 'realism', and self-criticism, of the poem; the old philosophy falls before an imaginative commitment to the evidences of life and experience.

14. Even Langbaum, chief exponent of the dramatic and relativist Browning, admits that the poet can have an axe to grind (*Poetry of Experience*, 93); but there is nothing in Browning's monologues like the personal and psychological presence of Shelley in 'Julian and Maddalo'.

15. See in particular, *Queen Mab*, Section VIII, 198–238, to which Shelley appended his famous note asserting the perfectibility of the human sensibility and, therefore, the possibility of virtual (not literal) immortality: 'Time is our consciousness of the succession of ideas in our mind . . . . If, therefore, the human mind . . . should become conscious of an infinite number of ideas in a minute, that minute would be eternity . . . . sensibility is perfectible . . . .' *Poetical Works*, 825; see also, *Poetry and Prose*, 62.

16. Op. cit., xi–xiii.

17. *Purity of Diction*, 142.

18. For example, Richard E. Brantley's *Wordsworth's 'Natural Methodism'* (New Haven, 1975), though it maddeningly overstates the case, shows convincingly enough that Wordsworth continues Evangelical concepts of God's presence in the Creation.

19. See especially 'Composed upon an Evening of Extraordinary Splendour . . .', Section III, where, in a sustained Biblical reference, Wordsworth transforms the 'ridges' of the sky into a Jacob's ladder inviting us 'heavenward'. This is firmly within the tradition of Puritan 'occasional' meditation and meditation on nature as practised by, say, Joseph Hall or Edmund Bury, or, in the eighteenth century, Cowper and James Hervey.

20. *Poetry and Prose*, 112, n.1.

21. See n.15 above.

22. See Gray's *Elegy*, ll.101–8; Cowper, *Retirement*, ll.279ff.; Wordsworth, 'Lines, left upon a Seat . . .', ll.24–44. To these must be added Keats's picture of the poet in the revised *Hyperion*, the 'dreaming thing,/A fever of thyself'.

23. *Sensitive-Plant*, iii. 78–81.

24. The convention referred to is present of course in all the examples specified above, n.22. The Romantic and pre-Romantic preoccupation with psychic arrestment, the curse of an *idée fixe*, and the dangers of imagination extends often to the treatment of characters: e.g. Cowper's Paralytic (*Task*, i. 472–90), Coleridge's Ancient Mariner, Wordsworth's Margaret, Michael or shepherd in 'Last of the Flock' (all three of whom fall prey to fast-rooted obsession ironically springing, as in the maniac, from love, the noblest of emotions), Keats's Isabella etc.

25. '. . . the life of a man of virtue and talent, who should die in his thirtieth year, is, with regard to his own feelings, longer than that of a miserable priest-ridden slave, who dreams out a century of dulness' (Shelley's note on human perfectibility; see n.15 above). Shelley died in his thirtieth year.

26. 'The Happy Prison: A Recurring Romantic Metaphor', in *Romanticism: Vistas, Instances, Continuities*, ed. David Thorburn and Geoffrey Hartman (Ithaca, 1973), 69.

27. Shelley, Letter to Leigh Hunt, 15 August 1819; *Letters*, ii. 108.

28. Victor Hugo, *La Legende des Siècles* (Paris: Garnier, 1962), poem XLVII, 629. Leopardi's dialogue is quoted in Victor Brombert, op. cit., 69.

29. Byron, *The Lament of Tasso*, ll. 20ff.

30. Hugo von Hoffmansthal, *Die Frau ohne Schatten*, quoted in Brombert, op. cit., 67.

31. W. B. Carnochan, *Confinement and Flight* (Berkeley, 1977), chap. 1.

32. The Preface to *Alastor*, for instance, closes with a quotation from it.

33. See Jonathan Wordsworth, *The Music of Humanity* (London, 1969).

34. 'The Steadfast Self: an Aspect of Wordsworth', in *Literature of the Romantic Period*, ed. R. T. Davies and Bernard Beatty (Liverpool University Press, 1976), 36–55.

35. The correspondences between Shelley's poem and Wordsworth's could be multiplied, but their investigation must await another occasion. It is worth emphasizing here, however, that Shelley's respect for Julian's tender feelings

towards the maniac matches precisely Wordsworth's view of the Poet's 'love' for Margaret and blessing of her 'in the impotence of grief'—though neither poet flinches from the facts of suffering sorrow and despair, or fails to seek in them a food for his imagination.

36. Wordsworth, Preface to *Lyrical Ballads; Wordsworth and Coleridge: Lyrical Ballads 1805*, ed. Derek Roper (London, 1968), 24.

37. Joseph-Antoine Milsand, review of *Men and Women* in *Revue Contemporaine*, September 1856; quoted in Langbaum, *Poetry of Experience*, 75.

38. See Langbaum, op. cit., 74.

39. Dedication of 1863 edition of *Sordello* to Milsand; *The Poetical Works of Robert Browning*, ed. A. Birrell (London, 1908), i. 115.

40. *Poetry of Experience*, 28–29, 40, 231–32, and passim.

41. Ibid., 40.

42. Pound to William Carlos Williams, 21 October 1908, *Letters 1907–1941*, ed. D. D. Paige (London, 1951), 36. An appraisal of Langbaum's version of 'modern tradition' is, needless to say, beyond the scope of this essay; but it is undoubtedly accurate in stressing the experiential, psychological and amoral emphases of poetry since the Enlightenment—amoral, that is, in its appeal to the 'sentience' of the individual (both speakers and readers) rather than to any corporate moral ideals. The poems of Wordsworth and Browning, with their individualized speakers and objects, are essentially of the same 'tradition' as the symbolist poems of Yeats and Eliot with their archetypal speakers and objects, because 'since the archetype is a psychological concept designed precisely to elude the rationalistic concept of the type, the archetypal perception is no less psychological and no less empiric than the individualized perception' (*Poetry of Experience*, 231–32).

43. M. W. MacCallum, 'The Dramatic Monologue in the Victorian Period', *Proceedings of the British Academy 1924–1925*, 276.

44. *Poetry of Experience*, 14–15. Cf. Carnochan on 'epistemological prisons': '. . . they are, so to speak, an abstracted image of the desire to break out and to make contact with the world beyond self . . . . Who suffers willingly the deprivation that follows from the Lockean version of mind as screened off from reality and the external world, receiving only shadowy projections of things as they are? . . . some believe that good fences do make good neighbours. It is another thing to be cut off from the fulfilment of questions answered and curiosities appeased' (*Confinement and Flight*, 7).

# Speech and Silence
# in *The Cenci*

## MICHAEL WORTON

When examining *The Cenci*, one is immediately confronted by a paradox: as a play, it is flawed and it differs from the main thrust of Shelley's work,[1] yet it has exerted an enormous influence on the development of European theatre. On the thematic level, Shelley's tragedy studies the problems of identity and personal morality, and its relentless presentation of Beatrice's search for moral certainty prefigures the Existentialist preoccupation with self-knowledge and self-justification. Shelley's legacy in this domain is to be found in Alberto Moravia's *Beatrice Cenci*,[2] a true drama of Existentialism, focussing essentially on boredom (which signifies the incapacity for living to which both Beatrice and Cenci are prey), which is undoubtedly influenced by Shelley's anti-social vision which perceives the 'absurd' relationship between the individual and his environment. On the theatrical level, *The Cenci* is of primordial importance, since it inspired the only major play by Antonin Artaud. In 1935, the French actor-director, founder of the Theatre of Cruelty and perhaps the most important single figure in the history of twentieth-century stage-craft, chose Shelley's tragedy as the basis for his play, *Les Cenci*,[3] in which he put into practice his theories which have since influenced Ionesco, Beckett, Genet, Peter Brook, Jerzy Grotowski, and the Living Theatre of New York. Artaud wished to create a new, 'physical', language, capable of communicating more than conventional language, and it is significant that he chose to adapt Shelley's play, since the fundamental modernity of *The Cenci* lies in its analysis of the efficacy of language, a facet of the play which has hitherto escaped critical scrutiny.

Long considered a mere closet-drama, *The Cenci* has, in recent years, benefited from renewed critical attention as its themes and structures have been examined from a modern rather than a purely Romantic stand-point. The play has been the subject of a comprehensive monograph[4] and penetrating studies have been made of Shelley's perversion of Christian theology,[5] of his conception of moral responsibility,[6] of the allegedly faulty structure of the tragedy,[7] of the function of the minor characters,[8] of the image structures[9] and of its relationship with the theatre.[10] The most exciting development in *Cenci* studies would seem to be that Shelley is now beginning to be considered not only as a poet-dramatist but as a *playwright*, as a writer aware of the necessary confrontation between audience and stage. Earl R. Wasserman sees the goal of the play as 'a creative moral insight by the audience, an insight to which the play can only provoke and guide the audience by a true representation of human nature and its experiences',[11] and Joseph W. Donohue, while holding that *The Cenci* is 'the best and finest example of poetic drama in the Romantic age',[12] believes that the main weakness of the tragedy lies in Shelley's *elitist* attitude towards his audience: 'A playwright can hardly present a successful tragedy to an audience for which he feels nothing but contempt'.[13] Now Shelley was undoubtedly aware that his highly individualistic system of ethics differed from the generally accepted attitudes of his time, but his Preface reveals to us that he does not seek to impose his own philosophies on his audience: 'I . . . have sought to avoid the error of making [the characters] actuated by my own conceptions of right or wrong, false or true . . .'[14] He intends rather to lead his audience to self-analysis: 'The highest moral purpose aimed at in the highest species of the drama is the teaching of the human heart, through its sympathies and antipathies, the knowledge of itself' (p. 276). Shelley's correspondence reveals clearly to us that he considered *The Cenci* as a new departure for him (though he often stresses that he preferred *Prometheus Unbound*): his intent, as he declared in a letter to Charles Ollier, was to reach a wider audience than he had hitherto touched: '*Cenci* is written for the multitude and ought to sell well'.[15]

As he tells us in the Preface, his prime concern is to communicate the *passion* of Beatrice in 'the familiar language of men' (p. 278), 'in such language and action as would bring it home to their hearts' (p. 276). A linguistic preoccupation, then, characterizes the Preface and, by extension, the audience will be drawn to a consciousness not only of the narration of events but to the nature of this narration. Having deliberately chosen an 'eminently fearful and monstrous' story (p. 276), the poet insists that:

> The person who would treat such a subject must increase the ideal, and diminish the actual horror of the events, so that the pleasure which arises from the poetry which exists in these tempestuous sufferings and crimes may mitigate the pain of the contemplation of the moral deformity from which they spring. (p. 276)

Here is the essential paradox of the play: there is a consistent and deliberate refusal by the playwright to *name* the catalysing action within the tragedy, although he will discuss it openly in his Preface as well as in his correspondence. The veiling of the incestuous rape is usually explained by the restrictions imposed by contemporary theatrical conventions which certainly preoccupied Shelley, as he admits in a letter to Thomas Love Peacock in July 1819:

> . . . my principal doubt as to whether it would succeed as an acting play hangs entirely on the question as to whether any such a thing as incest in this shape however treated wd. [sic] be admitted on the stage—I think however it will form no objection, considering first that the facts are matter of history, and secondly the peculiar delicacy with which I have treated it—[16]

In a letter to Maria Gisborne of 16 November 1819, he writes, however, of Calderon and affirms: 'Incest is like many other *incorrect* things a very poetical circumstance. It may be the excess of love or hate'.[17] The poet understands, then, that incest both is a potent subject and may be mentioned in a literary work.

The fact that the incestuous rape occurs off-stage and is only mentioned by implication must be considered within a pattern of *reporting* which structures the play. All the major events are, in fact, reported rather than presented: this insistence upon indirect presentation of actions is, one might submit, more than a simple adherence to the conventions of classical theatre, since it directs the audience's attention to an awareness of its own dependence upon language as a purveyor of truth.

In *A Defence of Poetry* we find the following definition of language: '. . . language is arbitrarily produced by the imagination and has relation to thoughts alone; but all other materials, instruments, and conditions of art have relations among each other which limit and interpose between conception and expression.'[18] Modern theories of language would certainly challenge this affirmation, but it is important to note that Shelley was concerned with the barriers separating 'conception' and 'expression', since all theatre, even the so-called 'closet-drama', has extra-linguistic qualities which permit communication (and expression) to be effected in non-verbal ways. If language is impotent to give satisfactory form to thought, that is to say, if conception and expression become incompatible, the inner self will find itself in conflict with the social self and therefore with the social system which depends on communication. A character incapable of full self-expression will thus become, almost inevitably, a rebel, will be forced to find expression in a non-verbal way—in action.

The opening line of the tragedy, 'That matter of the murder is hushed up', creates immediately a world external to that of the text and simultaneously establishes Cenci as a criminal. Here Shelley's villain would seem to exemplify Donohue's theory of the Romantic dramatic character type who 'must reflect in advance the results of deeds yet undone. Paradoxically, the character's identity is shaped from the first by what is, with regard to the play, only a potentiality'.[19] This powerful line, however, has a further function: it posits the existence of an action but provides no details of the murder and so reduces its reality, while conversely unleashing the connotational possibilities of the word 'murder'. From the very beginning of the play, it is suggested to the audience that evil exists in some unnamed way and that crimes may therefore be excluded from the conscious, 'real', world if a cloak of silence is thrown over them. Shelley elects, in *The Cenci*, to communicate through implication rather than through explication, through connotation rather than through denotation, since he is more interested in the violence of emotion and its concomitant expression (or lack of expression) than in physical violence.

Beatrice never articulates the crime committed against her by

her father, for fear that she would give it greater reality by
bringing it into the conscious world:

> Yet speak it not:
> For then if this be truth, that other too
> Must be a truth, a firm enduring truth,
> Linked with each lasting circumstance of life,
> Never to change, never to pass away. (III.i,59–63)

> I have talked some wild words, but will no more. (III.i,66)

She has earlier articulated her distress in a rare example of
empathic imagery in Shelley's work,[20] but she realizes that to
*name* the crime would be to accept a fact which she refuses at this
point to acknowledge. The verbal formulation of the nature of
the crime, far from having a beneficial therapeutic effect, would
demand an intellectual structuring of her emotions which remain
uncodifiable. Her refusal to name the rape would seem then to
fulfil two purposes: (1) it is an attempt to exclude the rape from
the 'real' world (as with the murder Cenci committed), and (2) it
exonerates her from the necessity to confront consciously her own
anguished state.

Later in the scene, when Lucretia attempts to obtain
confirmation of her fears, Beatrice asks:

> What are the words which you would have me speak?
> I, who can feign no image in my mind
> Of that which has transformed me: I, whose thought
> Is like a ghost shrouded and folded up
> In its own formless horror: of all words,
> That minister to mortal intercourse,
> Which wouldst thou hear? For there is none to tell
> My misery . . . (III.i,107–14)

Language is clearly posited as an inadequate means of expressing
violent inner emotions: it suffices only for 'mortal intercourse'.
She returns to this theme in her dialogue with Orsino
(III.i,141–142, 154–157), but remains unable to name the
crime, just as she is unable to name the punishment. She is the
first character to speak of death but this is a wild resolve on
suicide which her religious scruples forbid her to commit. Just as

her anguish is inexpressible, her conception of a punishment is formless—'What is this undistinguishable mist/Of thoughts, which rise, like shadow after shadow,/Darkening each other?' (III.i,170–172). Orsino insidiously draws Beatrice into self-anatomy and towards verbalization of her thoughts, but it is still left to Lucretia to articulate explicitly the thought: 'You think we should devise/His death?' (III.i,226–227).

Beatrice's inability to speak coherently of her sufferings indicates that language cannot codify extreme emotion, and the playwright reveals, through the mouth of Orsino, that it is through non-verbal communication that Beatrice initiates the plot to assassinate Cenci:

> She interrupted us, and with a look
> Which told before she spoke it, he must die, . . .
>
> (III.i,360–61)

A further example of non-verbal communication is to be found in the manner employed to signal Giacomo's complicity in the murder:

> *Beatrice:* . . . yet kiss me; I shall know
> That then thou hast consented to his death.
>
> (III.i,385–86)

Much use is made in this play of the 'penetrating look'—this is a stock device of the Romantic theatre, as of melodrama, but Shelley repeatedly insists that the gaze, a vehicle for 'inner' communication, precedes and even negates speech which, as the play progresses, is seen more and more as a means of social communication, incapable of expressing the essence of a character.

Of all the protagonists, Beatrice is most preoccupied with language and silence. In her first scene, she twice urges Orsino 'Speak to me not of love' (I.ii,9, 14), suggesting that she believes that if she eliminates the *word*, she will negate the *feeling*, yet when her own thoughts in vain demand expression, she implores him to 'speak but one word' (I.ii, 44) and 'Oh, speak!' (III.i, 151). The key to Beatrice's character is indeed to be found in Orsino's oft-quoted lines:

> . . . 'tis a trick of this same family
> To analyse their own and other minds.
> Such self-anatomy shall teach the will
> Dangerous secrets: for it tempts our powers,
> Knowing what must be thought, and may be done,
> Into the depth of darkest purposes. (II.ii,108–13)

'Self-anatomy' is possible only if there exists a linguistic system capable of codifying thought. Beatrice would seem in Acts I and II to accept, as Cenci does, that language dominates thoughts, and she refutes summarily Lucretia's accusation that she is mad: 'You see I am not mad: I speak to you' (II.i,34). However, the relationship between speech and madness is reversed by Beatrice in Act III: 'If I try to speak/I shall go mad' (III.i,85–6). This reversal can hardly be fortuitous; rather it indicates that a momentous event has revealed to her that the language of speech breaks down when faced with the necessity to express extreme emotion, since language serves only to structure thought. Beatrice, however, must not permit the 'formless horror' of her thoughts to be structured: only if they remain semi-conscious and incoherent can she retain her sanity.

Her suffering has awakened her to an awareness of the importance of a non-verbal language. As has already been noted, Orsino interpreted Beatrice's intention from her look before she articulated it verbally; when confronting Marzio after his confession, she alerts the Judges and the audience to the converse:

> I prithee mark
> His countenance: unlike bold calumny
> Which sometimes dares not speak the thing it looks,
> He dares not look the thing he speaks, but bends
> His gaze to the blind earth. (V.ii,82–86)[21]

Beatrice's gaze compels Marzio to examine the totality of his thoughts and moral judgments; this inevitably leads to his retraction of the confession and his withdrawal into silence:

> *Marzio:* My brain swims round . . . I cannot speak . . .
>        Take me away! Let her not look on me! (V.ii,88, 90)

Just as Beatrice cannot express her suffering and cannot later explain rationally her innocence, Marzio realizes the impotence of language and 'holding his breath, died' (V.ii,183).

In the prison as they await execution, Beatrice in her desire to comfort Lucretia and Giacomo, chooses no words of her own imagination but a song, 'some dull old thing,/Some outworn and unused monotony . . .' (V.iii,124–25), and even in this song, we are alerted to a language which transcends the purely verbal (V.iii,143–45). As Beatrice prepares for death, aware of the social opprobrium that will be attached to her name, she nonetheless insists that language, which is essentially a social instrument, does not necessarily convey truth, and she urges Bernardo to see beyond both temporal justice and social labelling (V.iv,145–54). She chooses to prepare for her death in the mechanical action of binding up the hair which had symbolically fallen loose after the rape: order has been restored to Beatrice, but this very order is possible only in a silence which cannot deceive as words do.

Beatrice's attitude to language alters after her rape; Count Cenci suffers no such violation and can therefore maintain his control over language—which he consciously manipulates in order to deceive. Lucretia highlights Cenci's perversion of the function of language when, in the banquet scene, she tries to comfort Beatrice who is terrified for her brothers: 'Fear not, Child,/He speaks too frankly' (I.iii,35–36). At the banquet, as in his self-revelation with Camillo, Cenci is being honest with himself but is also deliberately misleading his hearers: in both cases he is 'an artist, conscious of his every effect . . . aware of the slightest flaw in texture or technique and capable of its instant correction.'[22]

Cenci believes that there exists a causal, almost mystical, relationship between words and events—after all, his curses and prayers are answered in the deaths of his sons. However, in his first soliloquy, he consciously avoids articulating his thoughts:

> And yet I need not speak
> Though the heart triumphs with itself in words.
> O, thou most silent air, that shalt not hear
> What now I think! (I.i,138–41)

His self-imposed silence springs not from fear of discovery, but rather from an awareness that verbalization is not so much therapeutic as a means of determining one's actions. Like Beatrice later, he here wishes to maintain his thoughts 'formless' since, when they are expressed, actions are—or become—decided.

In this play whose generating force is a confrontation of wills, Shelley juxtaposes two major examples of the imposition of a will through gesture rather than through language: first, Cenci's silencing of the banquet guests and secondly, Beatrice's domination of the Count himself, which he describes thus:

> Then it was I whose inarticulate words
> Fell from my lips, and who with tottering steps
> Fled from your presence . . . (II.i,112–14)

Although the word 'inarticulate' might mislead here, one may suggest that Cenci's silences are what may be termed 'silences of repression', whether the silences are self-imposed or imposed by Beatrice, and that Beatrice herself is the character who most often experiences 'silences of inadequacy', when language breaks down completely. Indeed, for Cenci, language would appear to be a means of affirming his identity. He is, after all, a paradigm of authority with the Pope and God and believes that he can manipulate language as his tool, destroying all expected relationships with truth: just as the Pope can overlook his crime of murder, he can create a 'believed truth' with false words and convince Giacomo's wife that Giacomo had squandered her dowry (III.i,318–28), incidentally imposing on her a '*silent* scorn' for Giacomo's 'ardent truth'—here Shelley powerfully associates language with the figure of oppression.

The successful fulfilment of his unnatural curses on his sons drives Lucretia to beg him to retract his curses on Beatrice in Act IV—'For thine own sake unsay those dreadful words' (IV.i,137)—and his reply indicates his conviction that his words can cause events, but are also his slaves: 'Go, bid her come,/Before my words are chronicled in Heaven' (IV.i,158–59). The Count is a member of the sinister triumvirate (Cenci, the Pope, and God) who oppress the world and who have transformed language into a means of supporting their position. Beatrice is essentially innocent but she will be slandered for centuries; Cenci is essentially evil, he however is 'shielded by a father's holy name' (II.ii,73).

In his examination of the relationship between truth and language, Shelley obliges all his characters to question the function of speech and communication. Giacomo falls into self-imposed silence as Orsino seeks to manipulate him into murder, but the Prelate goads him on, asserting speciously:

> Fear not to speak your thought.
> Words are but holy as the deeds they cover. (II.ii,74–75)

Orsino tempts Giacomo into 'self-anatomy' and verbalization with the argument that words have no inner meaning or power but that *content* alone is important, although this attitude has already been refuted by Cenci in Act I. Like Beatrice, Giacomo fears the articulation of his thoughts:

> Ask me not what I think; the unwilling brain
> Feigns often what it would not; and we trust
> Imagination with such phantasies
> As the tongue dares not fashion into words,
> Which have no words, their horror makes them dim
> To the mind's eye. (II.ii,82–87)

Similarly in Act III, he breaks off a speech of revenge, aware that his words are carrying him away, anticipating Beatrice's ultimate rejection of human justice:

> God can understand and pardon,
> Why should I speak with man? (III.i,296–97)

If there are two kinds of silence in *The Cenci*—the silence of repression and the silence of inadequacy—there are also two kinds of verbal expression: (1) the act of speaking in order to communicate and (2) the act of self-expression, which falls inevitably into silence as language proves incapable of formulating thought. The opposition between the two modes is most clearly enunciated in Act II when Beatrice broods on suicide. Here Lucretia urges, 'Oh, talk not so, dear child!', and immediately continues:

> Tell me at once
> What did your father do or say to you?
> . . . Speak to me
> *Bernardo:*   Oh sister, sister, prithee, speak to us!
> (II.i,58–59, 61–62)

Throughout, a pattern is created by successive characters falling into silence and being subsequently encouraged to speak. Many of the characters conventionally equate speech with sanity and coherence. As I have already suggested, the effect of the rape on Beatrice is to alert her to the insufficiencies of language. She now understands that, by structuring thought, language fulfils a restrictive role and therefore functions as a support for a social system which the poet consistently presents as unacceptable: by transference, then, the spectators may be led to question the validity and functioning of speech within their own society.

Orsino, like Cenci, believes that he can manipulate language for his own ends, as he coaxes the Cenci family to verbalize their thoughts and thereby move towards action and their own perdition. However, even he has doubts as to whether he can escape the tyranny of language:

> Have I not the power to fly
> My own reproaches? Shall I be the slave
> Of . . . what? A word? which those of this false world
> Employ against each other, not themselves;
> As men wear daggers not for self-offence. (V.i,97–101)

Orsino realizes that words are used as social weapons rather than as a means of expression, but his last lines in the play betray his dread that he himself will be touched by the corrosive power of language:

> But if I am mistaken, where shall I
> Find the disguise to hide me from myself,
> As now I skulk from every other eye? (V.i,102–4)

Orsino knows the words of accusation that will be levelled at him in his absence and accepts, as he departs into silence, that their power is inescapable except in death.

*The Cenci* develops from a presentation of Beatrice locked in a combat of wills with her father into a portrayal of her confrontation with society; consequently, speech is examined initially as a vehicle for personal expression and later as a medium employed to effect a questionable justice. At her trial, Beatrice refuses to enter the linguistic world of human justice, since she sees no correspondence between her act and 'what men call a crime' (V.iii,84); she abandons even her denial of guilt, challenging her judges:

> Now do your will;
> No other pains shall force another word. (V.iii,88–89)

Despite her refusal to confess, it will be her very silence, her rejection of the validity of 'mortal intercourse', which will lead to her conviction.

On what grounds, then, is she convicted? Marzio's evidence is clearly the hub of the prosecution's case, but, in his presentation of this evidence, Shelley subtly analyses the relationship of language and silence. In Act IV, Marzio maintains a resolute silence and Savella decides to arrest the Cenci family on the basis of the letter found in Marzio's possession, asserting that: 'Their [the lines'] language is at least sincere' (IV.iv,89). Yet in what consists this 'sincerity'? The letter breaks off in a fashion analogous to the sudden silences which characterize the speeches of Beatrice and Giacomo and does no more than allude to the incestuous rape, as Lucretia affirms:

> It speaks of that strange horror
> Which never yet found utterance . . . (IV.iv,97–98)

This letter says nothing definite or explicit; in the absence of a confession from Beatrice, Savella can only 'conjecture' upon what Orsino himself has 'conjectured' from Beatrice's veiled words. Similarly, the Judges will accept Marzio's confession (after torture) because 'This sounds as bad as truth' (V.ii,19). As servants of the Pope and, by extension, paradigms of oppressive paternity, the Judges require a conviction, a verbal admission of guilt: this is extracted by torture but is nonetheless sufficient, despite the fact that Marzio recants his confession later. Cenci, another exemplar of tyranny, may 'unsay' his words, but Marzio is one of Shelley's oppressed victims and is therefore permitted no possibility of 'accepted' retraction.

The question of justice and the audience's response to it is undoubtedly central to the play, as Shelley makes clear in his Preface:

> It is in the restless and anatomizing casuistry with which
> men seek the justification of Beatrice, yet feel that she has

done what needs justification; it is in the superstitious horror with which they contemplate alike her wrongs and their revenge, that the dramatic character of what she did and suffered, consists. (pp. 276–77)

If justice exists in the world, Beatrice must be punished for the parricide she has committed, but, from the opening line of the play, the spectator finds himself in an ambiguous world where crimes, both legal and moral, can be concealed, where Cenci's indeterminate murder will be overlooked if he cedes land to the Pope. These two tyrannical figures, each with his own paternal role, are allied by their determined defence of the social structure which sustains them—and by their common desire for possession.[23] Shelley's desire to create dramatic irony is often cited as creating one of the least convincing moments of the play, the moment, that is, when he decides to have the Pope send Savella to the Castle of Petrella with a warrant for Cenci's death. A close reading of both the play and the Preface suggests however that this action has adequate motivation. The first scene is a virtuoso performance given by Cenci in order to divert Camillo from the purpose of his visit and to avoid explicit acquiescence to a demand which he seeks to circumvent:

> I must use
> Close husbandry, or gold, the old man's sword,
> Falls from my withered hand. (I.i,126–28)

Cenci clearly intends to keep his land: the Pope's decision would therefore seem to find its justification in revenge against a disobedient subject who has cut off a major source of income. The Preface reveals Shelley's view of Pope Clement and his cynical conception of the state of justice:

> ... the death of [the Pope's] victims can scarcely be accounted for by the love of justice. The Pope, among other motives for severity, probably felt that whoever killed the Count Cenci deprived his treasury of a certain and copious source of revenue. (p. 275)

The arrival of Savella would, then, be no mere contrived example of dramatic irony, but a means of undermining all notions of justice and of the sanctity of the Pope. Beatrice has, by her murder, both stemmed the flow of Cenci money into the Pope's coffers and, more importantly, attacked the oppressive scheme in which the three tyrants 'constitute a tacit hierarchy; each is plenipotentiary within his own sphere, concentric with the other two, and each serves his own interest with that of the others'.[24] Beatrice must be eliminated, but her execution is necessitated by the fact that in the world of *The Cenci*, parricide is more than a murder—it is a crime against the State.

Shelley thus devalues the notion of human justice before the trial scene itself, and, when the First Judge warns Marzio to 'Speak truth and the whole truth' (V.ii,4), the audience is conditioned to interpret this as a travesty of true justice. Marzio's last speech in the play gives the essential Shelleyan response to the Judge's command:

> Torture me as ye will:
> A keener pang has wrung a higher truth
> From my last breath. She is most innocent!
>
> (V.ii,163–65)

There are indeed no words to express the truth which transcends the narrow boundaries of human justice and the social systems they uphold: the inner and the external worlds are now revealed to be fundamentally incompatible.

The poet himself suffered from an inability to adapt completely to the social world, hence the preponderance in his writings of sympathetic, subjective images over sensorial, empathic images; and his predilection for intellectual, non-sensorial projection of himself into the object of his contemplation would explain further his exclusion from *The Cenci* of physical violence and his insistence upon the struggle between violent but formless emotion and a language which tyrannically attempts to codify the uncodifiable. Even the most committed of modern psychoanalytic critics may be reluctant to follow Herbert Read in his view of Shelley as a narcissistic, unconsciously homosexual neurotic, but would surely concur with his judgment that Shelley 'was not a *visuel*; he was a transcendalist, for whom words are never sufficient for the vision they must express'.[25] The very prolixity of *The Cenci* may, in fact, be more than the weakness it is customarily taken to be: it could even be seen as one of its main supports. As I have tried to show, all the characters are preoccupied with speech and silence. In the case of the main protagonist, Beatrice, we find that first a silence of repression is imposed upon her by her father's will (and his hierarchical power) and subsequently a silence of inadequacy is imposed by his physical assault. The rape drives Beatrice into an impotent mutism in which she strives to find a new language to express her feelings, finally breaking back into speech with the strikingly empathic imagery at the beginning of Act III. In the play, the silences of repression betoken an acceptance of the value and necessity of verbal communication and are followed by a return to speech, but the silences of inadequacy have a a more complex function: they are more than simply speechlessness, since in *The Cenci* the break-down of words represents the transition into deeds and leads subsequently to the ultimate silence of death. For a dramatist whose sole medium of expression is words, such a device as the suppression of words at moments of extreme emotional climax seems at once the most obvious and the most unexpected. The tragic flaw with which Shelley endows his Beatrice is her family's tendency constantly to 'analyse their own and other minds' (II.ii,109), since, when she is confronted by an action which she can neither comprehend nor describe, she resorts in desperation to a deed which runs counter to her natural goodness and innocence. From this point of view, Beatrice would seem to be an exemplar of the Romantic dramatic character who 'acts *for the moment* against [her] true nature and so elicits sympathy from all who observe [her] pathetic dilemma'.[26]

Shelley himself patently believed, as he affirmed in his Preface, that in order to create dramatic tension, one must create a moral dilemma in the minds of the audience. How is this dilemma resolved in the course of the play? Donohue suggests persuasively that Shelley intends his audience progressively to withdraw their sympathetic response to Beatrice: 'The detachment effected by the closing action of the play parallels Beatrice's own detachment, born of despair, which just precedes her execution.'[27] However, Beatrice's stance at the end of the play must be considered in the context of the linguistic preoccupations that mark the Preface and the play itself. Throughout *The Cenci*, the playwright situates the major events off-stage, thus obliging the audience to focus on the nature of the narration and to analyse these events according to the reports and (often highly subjective) descriptions given by the protagonists.

When it is remembered that Shelley insists in his Preface that the function of the drama is not to promulgate any creed but to lead the audience to self-awareness, one begins to grasp why the poet in fact offers no solution to the moral dilemma of Beatrice's guilt or innocence.[28] The essential problem is one of *justification*, yet Beatrice withdraws into silence, refusing to justify herself, for to speak would be to accept the constrictions of a socially determined language. Throughout *The Cenci*, at moments of tension and decision, the poet opposes silence and speech and then proceeds to spotlight this opposition, thereby creating a leit-motif which consistently accompanies and challenges the more obvious theme of moral justice. The function of this internal structuring of the play is to lead the spectator to question the validity of language *within* the play—and also consequentially the language *of* the play. By alerting his spectator to the insufficiencies of language, Shelley is able to demand from him, as he does from Beatrice, a greater dependence on the inner self, rather than on the judgement of a society which manipulates language to protect its own position—or even on the philosophies of a poet!

*The Cenci* is perhaps the most egalitarian of all Shelley's works, for, although 'written for the multitude', it is in no way patronizing but seeks to engender self-awareness on the part of the audience by the radically modern technique of calling itself into question. The tragedy has been attacked since its publication and its first performance,[29] but its position in the history of European theatre can now perhaps be better understood: through its concern with identity and moral issues, it has exercised an influence on the existentialist theatre, and, more importantly, through its concern with language and silence, it has encouraged, by way of Antonin Artaud's influential adaptation of 1935, the new 'revolutionary theatres' of the late twentieth century.

# Addendum

## *Three major foreign productions of*
## The Cenci

While this essay has not intended to present a stage history of *The Cenci*, it might be useful to mention three foreign productions which are landmarks in the development of modern theatre.

(1) On January 1, 1891, the Théâtre d'Art presented, as its second *spectacle*, a single performance of *The Cenci* in a translation by Félix Rabbe at the Théâtre Montparnasse, directed by Lugné-Poe. The Théâtre d'Art was a company founded in 1890 by the seventeen-year-old Symbolist poet Paul Fort in reaction against theatrical naturalism; it counted among its designers Bonnard and Vuillard and among its composers Debussy and Chausson and can be said to have laid the foundations for theatrical symbolism and expressionism. Although little is known of the actual staging, the critics praised the play, while deploring the standard of the acting.

(2) In October 1922, Karel and Josef Čapek presented *The Cenci* at the Municipal Theatre in Prague. This was a powerful expressionistic staging with a set comprised mainly of interchangeable red porphyry cubes and complicated lighting and projection effects. (Further information and three sketches of the stage designs may be found in *The Graphic*, CVI, December 9, 1922, p. 878.)

(3) On May 6, 1935, Antonin Artaud inaugurated his Theatre of Cruelty at the Théâtre des Folies-Wagram with *Les Cenci*, his adaptation of Shelley's and Stendhal's versions, in which he himself played the part of Cenci. While Artaud makes several textual changes, (i) combining Camillo and Savella into the one character, Camillo, (ii) condensing Shelley's Acts IV and V into one act, and (iii) cutting the Orsino/Giacomo scene and the interrogation of the suspects, on the whole he remains fairly close to Shelley's text, extracting from Stendhal's translation of the original manuscript only details of greater physical violence than Shelley chose to use (Stendhal's text 'Les Cenci' is to be found in his *Chroniques Italiennes*, vol. I (Paris, 1968), pp. 41–86). Artaud's

production put into practice the theories expounded in *Le Théâtre et son Double*, and incorporated strident electronic music (using the recently-invented *ondes Martinot*), expressionistic costumes by Balthus and highly structured movement patterns. While the full mise-en-scène remains unpublished, details of the banquet scene are to be found in *Cahiers Renaud-Barrault*, no. 51, November 1965. Artaud's production, considered a failure at the time, is a seminal work in the history of theatre, in that it initiates the concept of 'total theatre' and establishes the director as both visionary and puppet-master.

Furthermore, it is interesting to note that the revolutionary American stage designer, Robert Edmond Jones, was fascinated by *The Cenci* and designed it three times (although these designs were never used). His first designs (dating probably from 1910) were heavily expressionistic, the second (in 1913) were influenced by Gordon Craig and set out to reproduce in physical form the image-patterns of imprisonment in the play and the third (in 1916) used a silent 'chorus' and transformed the play into a ritual dance. These three sets of designs are, in a sense, a summary of stage design in the early twentieth-century and underline the modernity and versatility of *The Cenci*, which may well be seen as a work ahead of its time.

(Further details of productions may be found in Stuart Curran, *Shelley's Cenci: Scorpions ringed with fire*, Princeton, 1970.)

## NOTES

1. In his correspondence, the poet reveals that he intended *The Cenci* to differ from his other work. See the important letter of July [c.20], 1819 to Thomas Love Peacock, where he asserts: '. . . I have taken some pains to make my play fit for representation . . . . It is written without any of the peculiar feelings and opinions which characterize my other compositions . . .', *Letters* ii.102; the letter of 20 April 1820 to Thomas Jefferson Hogg where he writes: 'You will see that it is studiously written in a style very different from any other compositions . . .', *Letters* ii.186; the letter of 26 May 1820 to Leigh Hunt where he states: '. . . I wrote this thing partly to please those whom my other writings displeased', *Letters* ii. 200; the letter of 27 July 1820 to John Keats, where he reiterates that *The Cenci* was 'studiously composed in a different style', *Letters* ii. 221.

2. Originally published in *Botteghe Oscure* quaderno 16, 1955, pp. 363–461: reprinted with *La Mascherata* in *Opere complete di Alberto Moravia*, vol. X, *Teatro*, Milan, 1958. The relationship between the Moravia and the Shelley versions has hitherto passed virtually unnoticed (for a brief and suspect comparison of

the two versions, see Jane Cottrell, *Alberto Moravia*, New York, 1974, 128–129). Although there are certainly major differences, the insistence, in the Moravia text, on the importance—and the inadequacy—of speaking and telling and on the paradoxical relationship of guilt and innocence would seem to indicate a certain debt to Shelley. As suggested below, the confrontation of social justice and transcendental justice is central to Shelley's play; and this opposition, to which Shelley directs us in his Preface, is frequently articulated by Beatrice herself (notably IV.iv,111–113, V.ii, 151–57, V.iii,24–27, V.iv,145–149). The paradox of Beatrice as simultaneously guilty and innocent is wholly acceptable if, following Shelley, one accepts that the external and the inner worlds are hostile to each other; while Shelley's concern is moral rather than philosophical, his perception of this opposition is analogous to that of the Existentialists, whose definitions of the 'absurd' insist on a separation between the individual and his life and surroundings (see, for example, Albert Camus, *Essais*, Paris, 1965, 101, 108). Moravia's intention is clearly philosophical, but it is significant that he chooses to express his perception of the 'absurd' in the Shelleyan terms of guilt and innocence: '*Secondo la vostra giustizia voi potrete certamente dimostrare che io sono colpevole della morte di mio padre. Ma non potrete mai dimostrare che io non sia al tempo stesso innocente secondo un'altra giustizia che voi non potete né cognoscere né tanto meno amministrare*' (*Teatro*, 266, 'According to *your* justice you will certainly be able to prove I am guilty of my father's death. But you will never be able to prove that I am not at the same time innocent according to another justice—a justice which you can neither know nor, even less, administer', Alberto Moravia, *Beatrice Cenci*, translated Angus Davidson, London, 1965, 186).

3. The text of the play with variants is to be found in Antonin Artaud, *Oeuvres complètes*, vol. IV (Paris, 1978).

4. Stuart Curran, *Shelley's 'Cenci': scorpions ringed with fire* (Princeton, 1970).

5. See James Rieger, *The Mutiny within the Heresies of Percy Bysshe Shelley* (New York, 1967), 112–27.

6. James D. Wilson, 'Beatrice Cenci and Shelley's Vision of Moral Responsibility' in *Ariel*, vol. 9, no. 3 (1978), 75–89.

7. Charles L. Adams, 'The Structure of *The Cenci*', *Drama Survey*, 4 (1965), 139–48.

8. Joan Rees, 'Shelley's Orsino: Evil in *The Cenci*' in *The Keats–Shelley Memorial Bulletin*, no. 12 (1961), 3–6, and Paul Smith, 'Restless Casuistry: Shelley's Composition of The Cenci', *Keats–Shelley Journal*, vol. 13 (1964), 77–85.

9. Jean Perrin, *Les Structures de l'imaginaire shelleyen* (Grenoble, 1973).

10. Kenneth N. Cameron and Horst Frenz, 'The Stage History of Shelley's *The Cenci*' in *PMLA*, lx (1945), 1080–1105, Marcel Kessel and Bert States, '*The Cenci* as a Stage Play', *PMLA*, lxxv (1960), 147–9, and Curran, op. cit., 183–256.

11. Earl R. Wasserman, *Shelley. A Critical Reading* (Baltimore, 1971), 102.

12. Joseph W. Donohue, Jr., *Dramatic Character in the English Romantic Age* (Princeton, 1970), 161.

13. Donohue, op. cit., p. 181.

14. *Poetical Works*, 277. All subsequent references to the play and its Preface will be to this edition and will be included in the text.

15. *Letters* ii. 174. The letter is dated 6 March 1820. See also the letter of 13 March 1820 to Charles Ollier: 'My friends here have great hopes that the Cenci will succeed as a publication', *Letters* ii.178, and the letter of 1 May 1820 to Thomas Medwin: 'The people from England tell me it is liked', *Letters* ii. 189.

16. *Letters* ii. 102.

17. *Letters* ii. 154.

18. *Clark*, 279–80.

19. Joseph Donohue, 'Character, Genre and Ethos in Nineteenth Century British Drama', in *The Yearbook of English Studies*, vol. 9, 1979, 80–81.

20. See Richard Harter Fogle, *The Imagery of Keats and Shelley* (Chapel Hill, 1949), 177–83, for a consideration of the two examples of striking empathic imagery in *The Cenci*.

21. It is significant that the '*silent* air' which was not to hear Cenci's thoughts (Ii.140–41) is now replaced by the '*blind* earth', as visual communication supersedes verbal communication.

22. Curran, op. cit., 73.

23. Since the over-manipulative dissertation of Wilhelm Wagner, *Shelleys 'The Cenci', Analyse, Quellen und innerer Zusammehang mit des Dichters˙Ideen* (Rostock, 1903), some critics have tended to accept over-eagerly the identification of Cenci with Timothy Shelley. Rieger's interpretation is more persuasive, in that he places the 'triple entente' of Cenci, the Pope, and God in the context of Shelley's atheism and philosophical pre-occupations.

24. See Rieger, 115.

25. Herbert Read, *In Defence of Shelley and other Essays* (London, 1936), 23.

26. Donohue, *Dramatic Character in the English Romantic Age*, 184.

27. Donohue, op. cit., 181.

28. Shelley's play would, in fact, exemplify a definition of theatre formulated more than a century later by Jean-Paul Sartre: '*Le théâtre n'est fait ni pour la démonstration ni pour les solutions. Il se nourrit de questions et de problèmes*' (Interview in *Le Figaro*, 30 March 1948).

29. *The Cenci* was severely censured on its publication for the subversive nature of its anti-social vision, but reviewers conceded reluctantly or implicitly that it had merit as a play. For an excellent compilation of contemporary reviews, see Newman White, *The Unextinguished Hearth: Shelley and his Contemporary Critics* (Durham, N.C., 1938).

# Shelley's Magnanimity

## KENNETH MUIR

Shelley arrived in Italy in March 1818. His daughter Clara died in September on the day they arrived in Venice, and William died in the following June. Despite these bereavements and Mary's consequent resentment, and despite continued travelling—Este, Ferrara, Bologna, Rome, Naples, Rome again, Livorno, Leghorn, and Florence—this was Shelley's most productive period. His output included three plays, a translation of Euripides' *Cyclops*, three long poems, some of his finest lyrics, and the unfinished pamphlet, *A Philosophical View of Reform*. In this essay I shall concentrate on *Prometheus Unbound* and try to show how it is related to other works written between October 1818 and December 1819.

The 'Lines written in the Euganean Hills' may be seen as a kind of prologue to the works of the following months. There Shelley had contrasted the paradise of exiles, Italy, with the enslavement of the Italian people under a foreign government,

> Where the peasant heaps his grain
> In the garner of his foe. (ll.218–9)

He lamented that

> Force from force must ever flow,
> Or worse; but 'tis a bitter woe
> That love or reason cannot change
> The despot's rage, the slave's revenge. (ll.232–35)

At the end of the poem he expressed the forlorn hope that he and his friends would be able to build a bower 'Far from passion, pain and guilt', which

>          may even entice
> To our healing Paradise
> The polluting multitude;
> But their rage would be subdued
> By that clime divine and calm. (ll.354–58)

Shelley's beliefs when he arrived in Italy had hardly changed from those he had held five years before when he dedicated *Queen Mab* to the unfortunate Harriet. In that poem he had attacked the exploitation of labour and the corrupting effect of power:

> Power, like a desolating pestilence
> Pollutes whate'er it touches. (III.176–77)

And there, too, he had expressed the belief that with the abolition of the wielders of power—kings, priests, and statesmen—man, naturally good, would be governed by love, and enter a new golden age. In *The Revolt of Islam* Shelley explained the failure of the French Revolution by its use of violence. His hero, Laon, spares a tyrant's life, who repays this act of mercy by bringing in a foreign army to overthrow the revolution. This might seem to discredit Shelley's own theories; but he believed, despite the defeat of his cause and the martyrdom of Laon and Cythna, that their virtuous example would in the end convert others to virtue. Whereas Godwin had believed that men would become perfect through the exercise of reason, Shelley thought that a sudden conversion was necessary.

The Furies in *Prometheus Unbound* tempt the Titan to despair by showing him the state of the world, with its wars, its massacres, the corruption of the ideals of the reformers in the French Revolution,[1] the Crucifixion,[2] and the persecution in the name of Christ of

> The wise, the mild, the lofty and the just. (I.605)

The final temptation is the worst—the fear that things will never get any better:

> In each human heart terror survives
> The ravin it has gorged: the loftiest fear
> All that they would disdain to think were true:
> Hypocrisy and custom make their minds
> The fanes of many a worship, now outworn.
> They dare not devise good for man's estate
> And yet they know not that they do not dare.
> The good want power, but to weep barren tears.
> The powerful goodness want: worse need for them.
> The wise want love, and those who love want wisdom;
> And all best things are thus confused to ill. (I.618–28)

In 1819, when these lines were written, reformers had every reason to be despairing. After a long war, which had led finally to the defeat of Napoleon, the Congress of the victorious powers had tried to make Europe safe for reaction. In England the various laws which had been passed as wartime measures were not relaxed. Although there were pamphlets and demonstrations in support of parliamentary reform, there seemed to be no chance of anything practical being done. No one could foresee the Reform Bill of 1832. A century later, quoting these same lines in the autumn of 1919 after another great war, Maynard Keynes pointed out that men's ideals were at a low ebb.[3]

The Peterloo massacre—the dispersal by the yeomanry of an unarmed crowd—took place in August 1819; and Shelley heard of it a few weeks later. Instead of deepening his despair, the event prompted an outburst of feeling which found expression in some of his best and most direct political writing.

The first act of *Prometheus Unbound* containing the lines quoted above, was written in October 1818; the second and third acts were finished in the following spring. As at first planned, the play was complete. Then Shelley spent the summer in writing *The Cenci* which is indirectly political, for it is concerned with the use of violence in the face of intolerable wrongs. In September, on hearing of the Peterloo massacre, he wrote *The Mask of Anarchy* for a more popular readership than his two plays, though he should have known that no publisher was likely to run the risk of prosecution. Soon afterwards, he wrote a group of popular poems—a new National Anthem, hymning Liberty, a sonnet on the state of the nation (with a mad king, a corrupt government, and an oppressed people), 'Song to the Men of England', 'An Ode to the Asserters of Liberty' (as it was originally called),[4] the 'Lines written during the Castlereagh Administration', and the savage similes describing Sidmouth and Castlereagh. We know from a letter to Hunt, written in the following year, that Shelley was thinking of a volume of such poems:

> I wish to ask you if you know of any bookseller who would like to publish a little volume of *popular songs* wholly political and destined to awaken [and] direct the imagination of the reformers.[5]

In October 1819 Shelley was able to combine his passion for reforming the world with his love of nature in the 'Ode to the West Wind': the wind is a symbol of poetic and prophetic inspiration, and the poem is a dedication of the works of the previous months:

> by the incantation of this verse,
>
> Scatter, as from an unextinguished hearth,
> Ashes and sparks, my words among mankind!
> Be through my lips to unawakened Earth
>
> The trumpet of a prophecy! (ll.65–69)

One is reminded of the claim, at the end of *A Defence of Poetry*, that poets are

> the trumpets which sing to battle and feel not what they inspire; the influence which is moved not, but moves. Poets are the unacknowledged legislators of the world.[6]

Finally, at the end of the year, Shelley composed the most mature of his pamphlets, *A Philosophical View of Reform*. Despite its deliberately, and even disappointingly, moderate views, which were designed to appeal to all men of goodwill, it was not published until a century later.

(It should be added that in this brief summary of Shelley's extraordinary output during 1819 I have not mentioned either *Swellfoot the Tyrant*, that somewhat feeble burlesque, or *Peter Bell the Third*, which is a brilliant parody.[7] And of course any complete account would remind us that during this period Shelley also produced some of his best-known lyrics; along with 'Ode to the West Wind', 'An Exhortation', 'The Indian Serenade' and 'Love's Philosophy' are all of 1819.)

At first sight the popular poems appear not merely to demand a different kind of reader, but also to embody a different kind of message. Already in the first act of *Prometheus Unbound*, Shelley had prepared the way for a happy ending by making his hero retract his curse of Jupiter, and the moral is emphasized in the final speech of the play. The qualities necessary to save us from destruction are

> Gentleness, Virtue, Wisdom and Endurance;

and the 'spells' required for our salvation are

To suffer woes which Hope thinks infinite,
To forgive wrongs darker than death or night;
To defy power which seems omnipotent;
To love, and bear; to hope till Hope creates
From its own wreck the thing it contemplates.

                              (IV.562, 570–74)

The same attitude of passive endurance is apparently advocated
in *The Revolt of Islam* and in *The Mask of Anarchy*, though in that
poem, at least in the early stanzas, we are more impressed by the
poet's hatred of tyrants than by his advocacy of non-resistance.

I met Murder on the way—
He had a mask like Castlereagh—

. . . . . . . .

Next came Fraud, and he had on,
Like Eldon, an ermined gown;
His big tears, for he wept well,
Turned to mill-stones as they fell.

. . . . . . . .

Clothed with the Bible, as with light,
And the shadows of the night,
Like Sidmouth next, Hypocrisy
On a crocodile rode by. (5–6, 14–17, 22–25)

If we read *A Philosophical View of Reform*, we can see that Shelley
was not absolutely opposed to the use of force; and a passage from
that pamphlet, commenting on the Peterloo massacre, provides a
useful commentary on the poem:

If the majority are enlightened, united and impelled by a
uniform enthusiasm, and animated by a distinct and
powerful apprehension of their object, and full of confidence
in their undoubted power,—the struggle is merely nominal.

He goes on to say that the leader of a demonstration, a true
patriot (the italics are mine),

will exhort them peaceably to risk the danger and to expect
without resistance the onset of the cavalry, and wait with
folded arms the event of the fire of the artillery and receive
with unshrinking bosoms the bayonets of the charging
battalions. Men are every day persuaded to incur greater

perils for a less manifest advantage. And this, *not because resistance is not justifiable when all other means shall have failed*, but because in this instance temperance and courage would produce greater advantages than the most decisive victory. In the first place, the soldiers are men and Englishmen, and it is not to be believed that they would massacre an unresisting multitude of their countrymen drawn up in unarmed array before them and bearing in their looks the calm and deliberate resolution to perish rather than abandon the assertion of their rights . . . this unexpected reception would probably throw him back upon a recollection of the true nature of the measures of which he was made the instrument, and the enemy might be converted into an ally.[8]

Shelley's belief in the efficacy of non-resistance—not proved until the last years of the British Raj—was based on the willingness of ordinary people to risk, and even to court martyrdom, and on his conviction that English soldiers, unlike those of other nations, would be ashamed to slaughter unarmed civilians:

> With folded arms and steady eyes,
> And little fear, and less surprise,
> Look upon them as they slay,
> Till their rage has died away.
>
> Then they will return with shame
> To the place from which they came,
> And the blood thus shed will speak
> In hot blushes on their cheek. (ll.344–51)

Mary Shelley apologized for the poem, excusing it on the grounds that in writing for a popular audience Shelley inevitably produced inferior work. In actual fact the possibility of a wider audience—though the poem was not published in Shelley's lifetime—had the effect of purifying his style, stripping it of false poeticisms. But, as we have seen, the process of purification had begun earlier. The stanzas in which Shelley defines Liberty—not in abstractions, as he was tempted to do, but in concrete terms— are a pointer to Shelley's increasing maturity at the age of twenty-six. Liberty is Justice, Wisdom, Peace, Love, Patience, and Gentleness; it is lit by the lamps of Science, Poetry, and

Thought; but before all this Liberty is bread, clothes, fire, and food.

Soon after writing *The Mask of Anarchy*, Shelley told Leigh Hunt that the government was responsible for whatever violence took place:

> I fear that in England things will be carried violently by the rulers, and that they will not have learned to yield in time to the spirit of the age. The great thing to do is to hold the balance between popular impatience and tyrannical obstinacy; to inculcate with fervour both the right of resistance, and the duty of forbearance.[9]

Shelley's alternative, or parallel, political strategies were to convert people by reason (as Godwin had advocated) to convert them by courting martyrdom, and to use the power of the majority. He distinguished, of course, between the rulers who ordered a policy of repression and the soldiers who were merely carrying out orders. It could be argued, however, that although some of the shorter poems were designed to foster the love of liberty (for example the 'New National Anthem'), others would have had the effect of arousing hatred, not merely of oppression but of the individual oppressors, Sidmouth, Castlereagh, and Eldon. One powerful poem uses the image of abortion to characterize the England of 1819. 'Lines written during the Castlereagh Administration', first published by Medwin in the *Athenaeum* for 8 December 1832, begins with a reference to literal abortion,

> Corpses are cold in the tomb;
> Stones on the pavement are dumb;
> Abortions are dead in the womb . . . , (ll.1–3)

continues with a metaphorical statement about aborted liberty in England,

> The abortion with which *she* travaileth
>     Is Liberty, smitten to death . . . , (ll.9–10)

and he goes on to describe the oppressor in related terms,

>         sole lord and possessor
> Of her corpses, and clods, and abortions . . . (ll.14–15)

It is difficult to reconcile the forgiving attitude of Prometheus with the revulsion expressed in this poem, and still more difficult to reconcile it with the hatred apparent from the similes used to describe Sidmouth and Castlereagh in the four-stanza poem first published by Medwin in the *Athenaeum* a few months earlier (25 August 1832):

> As from their ancestral oak
>       Two empty ravens wind their clarion,
> Yell by yell, and croak for croak,
> When they scent the noonday smoke
>       Of fresh human carrion:-
>
> As two gibbering night-birds flit
>       From their bowers of deadly yew,
> Thro' the night to frighten it,
> When the moon is in a fit,
>       And the stars are none or few:-
>
> As a shark and dog-fish wait
>       Under an Atlantic isle,
> For the negro-ship, whose freight
>       Is the theme of their debate,
>   Wrinkling their red gills the while—
>
> Are ye, two vultures, sick for battle,
>       Two scorpions under one wet stone,
> Two bloodless wolves whose dry throats rattle,
> Two crows perched on the murrained cattle,
>       Two vipers tangled into one.

It is not, of course, certain that Shelley would ever have published these lines. Conservative historians in recent years have tried to show that Castlereagh was a good man; and they have deplored the intemperate attacks on him by Shelley and Byron. But Shelley attacked Castlereagh not as a man, but for his political acts, which if well-meaning, were nevertheless certainly oppressive and therefore immoral. It does not do to have both Poetry and History ranged against one.

In the 'Ode to the Asserters of Liberty', Shelley adopts a more forgiving tone. The people are urged to fight for freedom, to overcome revenge, pride and power, to hide their bloodstains beneath 'crownals of violet, ivy and pine', and to forget their injuries:

> Let not the pansy among them be;
> Ye were injured and that means memory. (ll. 30, 34–35)

Shelley thought that Satan, the defier of a tyrannical God, was the real hero of *Paradise Lost*, although his feelings of hatred, envy and revenge Shelley could only deplore:

> The character of Satan engenders in the mind a pernicious casuistry which leads us to weigh his faults with his wrongs, and to excuse the former because the latter exceed all measure . . . But Prometheus is, as it were, the type of the highest perfection of moral and intellectual nature, impelled by the purest and the truest motives to the best and noblest ends.[10]

It is doubtful whether spotless characters make satisfactory heroes of plays or novels, but it is easy to see why the creator of Laon was attracted to the victim of Jupiter's tyranny. What Shelley wanted, however, was a hero who was a rebel against secular and religious tyranny, yet without the evil apparent in Milton's Satan. He wanted, in fact, an idealized version of himself, or at least one who could act as his spokesman without incongruity.

Prometheus, the firebringer, the champion of man, the rebel against divine tyranny, was in some ways a suitable choice; but the Aeschylean story was unsatisfactory to a man of Shelley's convictions. At the end of *Prometheus Bound* Prometheus protests forcibly against the injustice of his punishment:

> It is no shame
> To suffer torture at the hands of foes . . .
> O Mother,
> O great Mother! O air that rollest light
> To all, both good and evil, thou behold'st
> How unjust are the pains which I endure![11]

In the lost sequel, *Prometheus Unbound*, the hero was released after he had warned Jupiter not to consummate his marriage with Thetis. Shelley, not unnaturally, was averse from a catastrophe so feeble as that of reconciling the Champion with the Oppressor of mankind.

The moral interest of the fable, he declared,

> which is so powerfully sustained by the sufferings and endurance of Prometheus, would be annihilated if we could conceive of him as unsaying his high language and quailing before his successful and perfidious adversary.[12]

Professor Wasserman in his second chapter on the play has described the alterations which Shelley was driven to make. The secret of Shelley's Prometheus cannot be that of Aeschylus's—the knowledge that if he married Thetis he would be overthrown by his offspring:

> the traditional secret, even though Prometheus were never to reveal it, implies that Jupiter could have been responsible for his own destruction or preservation by either marrying or eschewing Thetis, and this would deny that the moral burden is entirely Prometheus' . . . Shelley must place the moral burden entirely on Prometheus, and hence the 'secret' has no specific content.

The union of Jupiter and Thetis is 'a sterile rape'. Professor Wasserman goes on to suggest that

> Shelley's conception of the difference between the potential Prometheus and the received myth is of a piece with his view of the difference between the life and doctrines of Christ and the Church's perversion of them for the purpose of fabricating an institutional religion presided over by a tyrannical and arbitrary deity.[13]

Although Shelley was perfectly entitled to alter the myth to suit his beliefs and purposes, and although he obtained some effective ironies by the contrast between his reading and that of Aeschylus, the alterations were nevertheless damaging to the dramatic qualities of the story. Once Prometheus has retracted his curse of Jupiter, everything else in the remaining half of the play is an anti-climax. As Thetis is present, and as Jupiter is apparently expecting the arrival of his son by her, we are made to think that the marriage to Thetis is the cause of his downfall. The scene is singularly feeble, both in its conception and its

expression; there is no real conflict and the god's collapse comes
in the middle of a line:

> Detested prodigy!
> Even thus beneath the deep Titanian prisons
> I trample thee! thou lingerest? Mercy! Mercy!
>
> (III.i,61–63)

Although there is some splendid poetry in the later acts of the
play, as a drama it remains invertebrate.

'The task of *Prometheus Unbound*', said Carl Grabo,[14] was to fuse

> three diverse elements, revolutionary social philosophy,
> Platonism or neo-Platonism, and scientific speculation into
> a unified whole. He must reconcile materialism and
> idealism, physics and metaphysics, science and religion.

One can see that something like this was Shelley's aim, and one is
bound to admire his expression of these diverse elements, while
doubting whether the fusion really takes place. Some of the lyrics
in Act IV (as Whitehead and others have demonstrated)[15]
exhibit a remarkable grasp of scientific ideas, besides being
admirable as poetry; and the songs at the end of Act II—'Life of
Life! thy lips enkindle' and 'My soul is an enchanted boat'—are
two of Shelley's best. The passages in Act I which bring out the
tragic contrast between the teaching of Jesus and that of his
Churches, and the attacks on tyranny in the same act are moving
expressions of Shelley's social philosophy, going far beyond the
cautious arguments of *A Philosophical View of Reform*. The
description of the liberated world is Shelley's most captivating
Utopia. Some of the blank verse in Acts I and III shows us the
poet at the height of his powers. But, nevertheless, I believe that
many sympathetic readers, while admiring parts of *Prometheus
Unbound* and finding in it, indeed, some of Shelley's quintessential
poetry, find themselves less than enthusiastic about the play as a
whole.

Shelley claimed in the Preface to *Prometheus Unbound* that
didactic poetry was his abhorrence, although he was in some
ways one of the most didactic of poets. He went on to explain that
he wished to influence people's minds in an indirect way:

> My purpose has hitherto been simply to familiarize the
> highly refined imagination of the more select classes of

readers with beautiful idealisms of moral excellence; aware that until the mind can *love, and admire, and trust, and hope, and endure,* reasoned principles of moral conduct are seeds cast upon the highway of life, which the unconscious passenger tramples into dust, although they would bear the harvest of his happiness.[16]

He makes a similar point in *The Defence of Poetry* when he speaks of love as the great secret of morals, and argues that poetry by stimulating the imagination, increases our capacity to love.[17] We may notice that the qualities he enumerates in the Preface (which I have italicized in the passage just quoted) are nearly the same as the 'spells' mentioned in Demogorgon's final speech:

Gentleness, Virtue, Wisdom, and Endurance,
These are the seals of that most firm assurance
　　　Which bars the pit over Destruction's strength;
And if, with infirm hand, Eternity,
Mother of many acts and hours, should free
　　　The serpent that would clasp her with his length;
These are the spells by which to reassume
An empire o'er the disentangled doom. (IV.562–69)

The moral purpose here is sufficiently explicit: when Shelley directed his writing to the reformers and their sympathizers, rather than 'the more select classes of readers', he no longer sought to camouflage his didactic intentions.

In *The Cenci* there is a tension between the avowed moral of the play and the sympathy, admiration, and even approval, aroused by Shelley for Beatrice's killing of her father. In the Preface he claims, as Auden did, that the greatest art 'teaches us to unlearn hatred, and to learn love':

The highest moral purpose aimed at in the highest species of drama, is the teaching the human heart, through its sympathies and antipathies, the knowledge of itself; in proportion to the possession of which knowledge, every human being is wise, just, sincere, tolerant and kind.[18]

Then he goes on to say that a drama is no place for the

enforcement of dogmas, but he declares that Beatrice acted wrongly:

> Undoubtedly, no person can be truly dishonoured by the act of another; and the fit return to make to the most enormous injuries is kindness and forbearance, and a resolution to convert the injurer from his dark passions by peace and love. Revenge, retaliation, atonement, are pernicious mistakes. If Beatrice had thought in this manner she would have been wiser and better; but she would never have been a tragic character . . . It is in the restless and anatomizing casuistry with which men seek the justification of Beatrice, yet feel that she has done what needs justification; it is in the superstitious horror with which they contemplate alike her wrongs and their revenge, that the dramatic character of what she did and suffered, consists.[19]

Shelley seems to be accepting what he condemns in our attitude to Milton's Satan, that is, he excuses Beatrice's faults because of the wrongs she suffers, while recognizing at the same time that she is a more satisfactory dramatic heroine than Prometheus is a dramatic hero. As for his ideal prescription for converting the injurer, he has so depicted Count Cenci that he is clearly not convertible.

One poem which compromises between didacticism and beautiful idealisms is 'Julian and Maddalo', ostensibly the report of a conversation between Shelley and Byron. The Madman, fictionally but not actually visited by the two friends, is to some degree a portrait of Shelley as he imagined himself in the autumn of 1818, following the death of his daughter Clara and the resulting estrangement from Mary, (who held him largely responsible). But one should not exaggerate the autobiographical features of the poem. Byron was not an Italian Count and Shelley was not mad, even though he incorporates in the Madman's portrait some of his own characteristics, as when he describes himself as

> a nerve o'er which do creep
> The else unfelt oppressions of this earth. (ll.449–50)

The Madman can be used both by Julian and Maddalo in support of their points of view—Julian's belief that,

> It is our will
> That thus enchains us to permitted ill.
> We might be otherwise; we might be all
> We dream of happy, high, majestical.
> Where is the love, beauty and truth we seek,
> But in our mind? and if we were not weak,
> Should we be less in deed than in desire? (ll.170–76)

Maddalo scornfully retorts 'You talk Utopia'. He does not believe that mankind will ever be improved.

Wasserman thinks that Shelley was depicting

> the two kinds of paralysis that prevented his generation from pursuing the ideals of the French Revolution—[20]

those who believed that its disastrous failure had demonstrated that its goals were unobtainable, and the Julians, who lacked the will to act. When one considers Shelley's continuous political activity—in prose, in verse, and in deed—it is clear that Julian is not a self-portrait; and presumably Wasserman did not imagine that Shelley lacked will. As we can tell from *The Revolt of Islam*, Shelley's view of the failure of the French Revolution was that its ends were corrupted by the means employed.[21]

There is a fourth character in the poem, Maddalo's enchanting child:[22]

> A serious, subtle, wild, yet gentle being,
> Graceful without design, and unforeseeing;
> With eyes—Oh speak not of her eyes!—which seem
> Two mirrors of Italian Heaven, yet gleam
> With such deep meaning, as we never see
> But in the human countenance. (ll.145–50)

At the end of the poem, when Julian returns to Venice after many years, he meets the child, now grown to womanhood,

> a wonder of this earth
> Where there is little of transcendent worth—
> Like one of Shakespeare's women. (ll.590–92)

The prominence given by Shelley to this character must affect our interpretation of the poem. The Madman is not condemned for the wrongness or impracticability of his views, as Maddalo would seem to imply, but by 'some deadly change in love'. The hope for the future lies in Julian's ideology and in people like Shakespeare's women.

That this is Shelley's meaning can be seen from the last exchange between the two friends before they visit the Madman. Maddalo puts down his lunacy to his optimistic views of human betterment:

> We'll visit him, and his wild talk will shew
> How vain are such aspiring theories. (ll.200–1)

Julian, on the other hand, wants to prove that

> a want of that true theory, still,
> Which seeks a 'soul of goodness' in things ill,
> Or in himself or others, has thus bowed
> His being. (ll.203–6)

He may be one of those who

> demand but this—
> To love and be beloved with gentleness;
> And being scorned, what wonder if they die
> Some living death? This is not destiny,
> But man's own wilful ill. (ll.207–11)

It becomes clear from the Madman's ravings that Julian is in the right, and that Shelley repudiates Maddalo's point of view.

Poetically, the ravings of the madman are not on the same level as the remainder of the poem. Even though only one of Shelley's longer poems, *Adonais*, and the unfinished masterpiece, *The Triumph of Life*, are wholly admirable, perhaps not enough credit has been given the poet for the style of his more relaxed conversational poems, the 'Letter to Maria Gisborne' and 'Julian and Maddalo'. They are written in a diction as simple and unaffected as Wordsworth's—in a style which is able to accommodate actual snatches of conversation as well as an extended and brilliant description of a Venetian sunset:

> we stood
> Looking upon the evening, and the flood
> Which lay between the city and the shore,
> Paved with the image of the sky . . . the hoar
> And aery Alps towards the North appeared

Through mist, an heaven-sustaining bulwark reared
Between the East and West; and half the sky
Was roofed with clouds of rich emblazonry
Dark purple at the zenith, which still grew
Down the steep West into a wondrous hue
Brighter than burning gold, even to the rent
Where the swift sun yet paused in his descent
Among the many-folded hills: they were
Those famous Euganean hills, which bear,
As seen from Lido thro' the harbour piles,
The likeness of a clump of peaked isles—
And then—as if the Earth and Sea had been
Dissolved into one lake of fire, were seen
Those mountains towering as from waves of flame
Around the vaporous sun, from which there came
Their inmost purple spirit of light, and made
Their very peaks transparent. (ll.64–85)

The ease and poise of the conversational poems are found
again in the more argumentative, and more restrained, parts of
*Epipsychidion*, such as the pellucid lines by which T. S. Eliot
professed to be gravelled:[23]

I never was attached to that great sect,
Whose doctrine is, that each one should select
Out of the crowd a mistress or a friend,
And all the rest, though fair and wise, commend
To cold oblivion, though it is in the code
Of modern morals, and the beaten road
Which those poor slaves with weary footsteps tread,
Who travel to their home among the dead
By the broad highway of the world, and so
With one chained friend, perhaps a jealous foe,
The dreariest and the longest journey go.
　　　True Love in this differs from gold and clay,
That to divide is not to take away.
Love is like understanding, that grows bright,
Gazing on many truths; 'tis like thy light,
Imagination! which from earth and sky,
And from the depths of human fantasy,
As from a thousand prisms and mirrors, fills

The Universe with glorious beams, and kills
Error, the worm, with many a sun-like arrow
Of its reverberated lightning. Narrow
The heart that loves, the brain that contemplates,
The life that wears, the spirit that creates
One object, and one form, and builds thereby
A sepulchre for its eternity.[24] (149–73)

All through Shelley's work—half of it literally and necessarily adolescent—we can see how he was tempted to spoil his natural simplicity with inflated diction and imagery. If one compares the 'Ode to Liberty' written in 1820 with the description of what liberty essentially means in *The Mask of Anarchy*, or compares the 'Ode to Naples' (1820) with the 'Stanzas written in Dejection, near Naples', the poems which were not published during Shelley's lifetime were greatly superior to those he thought worthy of publication. The best of Shelley's lines are splendidly simple:

I could lie down like a tired child . . .

The wise want love; and those who love want wisdom . . .

Give yourself no unnecessary pain,
My dear Lord Cardinal. Here, Mother, tie
My girdle for me, and bind up this hair
In any simple knot; ay, that does well.
And yours I see is coming down. How often
Have we done this for one another; now
We shall not do it any more . . .

Some flying from the thing they feared, and some
Seeking the object of another's fear.[25]

Between 1817, when he wrote *Laon and Cythna*, and 1822, when he was composing *The Triumph of Life*, Shelley had gone a long way. The development was not so rapid and spectacular as that of Keats in 1818–19, and there were lapses and relapses. Shelley started and never completed three original plays, some long poems ('The Woodman and the Nightingale', 'Marenghi', 'Fiordispina', 'Ginevra') and scores of lyrics; and the poems he published were as uneven in quality as those he suppressed. Even as late as 1820 he published 'A Vision of the Sea'. But Keats's advice to Shelley to curb his magnanimity and load every rift with ore should not be taken to mean that he indulged, like his skylark, in 'profuse strains of unpremeditated art'. The evidence of his manuscripts suggest that Shelley revised as much as Keats. The word 'magnanimity' may have hinted at Shelley's passion for reforming the world as well as his fecundity. His quality depends on magnanimity in both senses of the word.[26]

## NOTES

1. See Semichorus I, I.567–77.

2. See Prometheus's speech beginning, 'Remit the anguish of that lighted stare . . .', I.597–604.

3. See Maynard Keynes, *The Economic Consequences of the Peace* (1920), 278–9.

4. Published with *Prometheus Unbound* as 'An Ode; Written in October 1819, before the Spaniards had recovered their liberty'. The reference to the Spaniards is a red herring; the toning down of the poem is probably intentionally in keeping with the major new work, but Shelley's fears about possible prosecution may also have played their part.

5. Letter to Leigh Hunt, 1 May 1820, *Letters* ii. 191.

6. *Clark*, 297.

7. Composed at Florence, October 1819, after reading Leigh Hunt on John Hamilton Reynold's skit *Peter Bell, a Lyrical Ballad* and Wordsworth's *Peter Bell, a Tale*, both published April 1819 and reviewed by Hunt in the *Examiner*, 26 April, 3 May 1819. The attack on Wordsworth, as in Shelley's earlier poems about his great contemporary, was largely inspired by his supposed desertion from the popular cause and his celebration of carnage as God's daughter. Cp. ll.636–37 and Shelley's comment on *The Excursion* in his footnote to l.588, 'That poem contains curious evidence of the gradual hardening of a strong but circumscribed sensibility, of the perversions of a penetrating but panic-stricken understanding' (*Poetical Works*, 359).

8. *Clark*, 256, 257.

9. Letter to Leigh Hunt, 14–18 November 1819, *Letters* ii. 153.

10. Preface to *Prometheus Unbound*, *Poetical Works*, 205.

11. English translation by Kenneth Muir and Sean O'Loughlin; see their *The Voyage to Illyria* (1937), 205–6.

12. Preface to *Prometheus Unbound*, *Poetical Works*, 205.

13. Earl Wasserman, *Shelley's Prometheus Unbound* (1965), 86–7, 92.

14. Carl Grabo, *Prometheus Unbound; An Interpretation* (1935), 10.

15. See A. N. Whitehead, *Science and the Modern World* (1932), 105 and cp. Miriam Allott, 'Attitudes to Shelley', p. 1–39 above.

16. *Poetical Works*, 207.

17. *Clark*, 282–3.

18. *Poetical Works*, 276.
19. Ibid., 276–7.
20. Earl Wasserman, op. cit.
21. Preface to *The Revolt of Islam, Collected Poems*, 33.
22. Usually agreed to be inspired by Allegra, Byron's daughter by Claire Clairmont.
23. See *The Use of Poetry and the Use of Criticism* (1933), 92.
24. Another example is in one of the drafts of the poem (*Poetical Works*, 428),

> If any should be curious to discover
> Whether to you I am a friend or lover,
> Let them read Shakespeare's sonnets, taking thence
> A whetstone for their dull intelligence
> That tears and will not cut, or let them guess
> How Diotima, the wise prophetess,
> Instructed the instructor, and why he
> Rebuked the infant spirit of melody
> On Agathon's sweet lips . . .

25. 'Stanzas written in Dejection', 30; *Prometheus Unbound* I.607; *The Cenci* V.iv,158–64; *The Triumph of Life*, 54–5.
26. Shelley had a considerable influence on radical thought throughout the nineteenth century from the chartists to the Fabians. Cf. Kenneth Muir 'Shelley's Heirs' (*Penguin New Writing* 26) and see Miriam Allott, 'Attitudes to Shelley', pp. 1–39 above.

# Shelley's 'Letter to Maria Gisborne': tact and clutter

## ANN THOMPSON

Shelley's 'Letter to Maria Gisborne' is quite literally a letter to an intimate friend; not the kind of verse letter a poet might write for publication but a genuinely informal communication which is dominated and organized throughout by the writer's awareness of a particular correspondent and his deliberate and tactful relation of everything to her. Shelley did not even keep a copy of the letter; his wife Mary wrote to the Gisbornes after his death asking for copies of his 'most interesting letters' to them, including 'that letter in verse'.[1] Reading the poem as a real letter, one is immediately struck by the gracefulness of the exercise as a whole, and by the way in which Shelley unselfconsciously displays his attractive capacity for warm and generous friendships. The tact which pervades the poem is not an awkward politeness or a deliberate glossing over of unfortunate realities but the kind of personal, intimate tactfulness which is a necessity of all close relationships, and indeed of all letters.

But, having said that, one must immediately except most of the verse epistles written in English during the two centuries preceding Shelley's attempt at the genre. Traditionally, such poems were written in rather a formal vein, even when the context was one in which intimacy would have been possible. There is perhaps something paradoxical about using verse couplets (overwhelmingly the most popular format) for a private letter, and of course many verse epistles were in fact directed at a wider audience from the very beginning even though they were ostensibly addressed to individuals.

A typical combination of formality and informality can be seen in an early example of the genre, Donne's epistle 'To Sir Henry Wotton' (c.1597–8), one of the 'Verse Letters to Severall

Personages'. It begins with a characteristically striking image of intimacy

> Sir, more than kisses, letters mingle Soules;
> For, thus friends absent speake . . . ,[2]

but moves rapidly into a more impersonal mode:

> Life is a voyage, and in our lifes wayes
> Countries, Courts, Towns are Rockes, or Remoraes . . .[3]
>
> (ll.7–8)

Donne continues to generalize, and to elaborate his generalizations in a formal, even predictable way: 'Cities are Sepulchers . . . Courts are Theaters . . . The Country is a desert'. When he returns to direct address it is in order to give advice— 'Be thine owne home, and in thy selfe dwell'—though he politely denies his right to do this:

> But, Sir, I advise not you, I rather doe
> Say o'er those lessons, which I learn'd of you. (ll.64–65)

There is in fact no real intimacy in this letter, nor in many other examples of the genre, which was at this time limited by the poet-patron relationship. The epistles are 'full of wise saws and modern instances', given to making moral statements, generalizing, re-stating conventionally approved sentiments. The unfortunate addressee might well feel he is in receipt of a sermon rather than a letter in many cases unless he is being set up as an exemplary figure for others to copy, as in the case of Dryden's 'To my Honour'd Kinsman', John Driden, of Chesterton' (1700), which is as much a panegyric as an epistle. The sententious tone of many verse epistles together with the frequent recurrence of motifs such as the opposition between the country and the city can of course be traced back to classical models, and these influences are explicit and obvious in the work of Pope who was writing epistles of his own (in the form of the *Moral Essays*) at the same time as he was working on his *Imitations of Horace*.

A somewhat lighter and more informal tradition in the writing of epistles can be traced from the Restoration to the mid-eighteenth century in the works of poets such as Cotton, Prior, and Cowper, all of whom, as it happens, avoided iambics for this genre. Cotton's 'Epistle to Sir Clifford Clifton, then sitting in Parliament' (c. 1665) achieves a tone of racy familiarity:

> I receiv'd thy kind letter, good Lord, how it eas'd me
> Of the villainous spleen that for six days had seiz'd me;
> I start from my couch, where I lay dull and muddy,
> Of my servants enquiring the way to my study,
> For, of truth, of late days I so little do mind it,
> Should one turn me twice about I never should find it.
> (ll.5–10)[4]

Cotton combines energetic writing with witty self-deprecation as he describes the chaos of his study and the recalcitrance of his Muse. He manages to maintain the informal tone even when he turns to offering his brother-in-law advice:

> Give his Majesty money, no matter who pays it,
> For we never can want it so long as he has it;
> But wer't wisdom to trust saucy counsel in letters,
> I'd advise thee beware falling out with thy betters;
> I have heard of two dogs once that fought for a bone,
> But the proverb's so greasy, I'll let it alone. (ll.109–14)

Cotton is not exactly parodying the sententious tradition in verse epistles, but his allusions to it are knowing and witty. Prior achieves a similarly light tone in his 'Epistle to Fleetwood Shephard, Esq.' (1689) where he handles his plea for patronage (such a familiar topic in this genre) with a refreshing simplicity and a degree of self-mockery:

> My business, Sir, you'll quickly guess,
> Is to desire some little Place:
> And fair Pretentions I have for't,
> Much Need and very Small Desert.
> When e're I writ to you, I wanted;
> I always begg'd, you always granted. (ll.15–20)[5]

No wonder that Cowper in his 'Epistle to Robert Lloyd' (1754) refers to 'dear Mat Prior's easy jingle' and apparently does his best to emulate this 'sensible' and 'easy' style. Nevertheless, all these epistles have a public rather than a private feel about them; even the raciness of Cotton's is as much the style of its age as a genuinely personal tone.

The same formality and lack of real intimacy is apparent in the epistles Keats wrote to George Felton Mathew, his brother George and Charles Cowden Clarke between 1815 and 1816 and which were published in his first volume of poems in 1817. Reading these poems alongside Shelley's 'Letter to Maria Gisborne' one is immediately struck too by the contrast between the two poets' handling of the couplet form: Keats at this very early stage in his career seems inert and frequently bathetic while Shelley has a vigour reminiscent of Dryden—and a comparable willingness to vary the couplet with the occasional triplet or the single unrhymed line. He knows exactly how to avoid monotony by his manipulation of syntax and *enjambement*; indeed he writes couplets as if they were Shakespearean blank verse. Shelley was clearly aware of the literary tradition of the verse epistle but he avoids its public, didactic dimension. He touches on conventional topics—the problems of writing poetry, the contrast between the country and the city—but he makes them immediate and personal. It is not so much the absolute novelty of his subject-matter (personal letters do not after all need novelty in order to be intimate) but the mode of organization and the overall tone which makes it necessary to read this poem in a different way from other verse epistles and more as if it were what it claims to be, a real letter.

Oddly enough, this approach to the poem has not been employed by its critics who have generally favoured a more piecemeal method, extracting one aspect or another of the poem's varied contents and ignoring Shelley's careful subordination of everything to the tone of the whole. The 'Letter' has not attracted a great deal of critical attention anyway: James M. Hall commented accurately enough in 1969 that 'The "Letter to Maria Gisborne", Shelley's only verse epistle, has been virtually ignored by his students: when it is mentioned it is usually briefly summarized and used, if at all, for biographical evidence or to show that after all Shelley had a sense of humour'.[6] The latter argument bulked curiously large around 1960 when Desmond King-Hele claimed to have found in the poem 'plenty of nails for [the] coffin' of the tradition that Shelley had no humour[7] and Newell F. Ford discussed it in two articles entitled 'Paradox and Irony in Shelley's Poetry' and 'The Wit in Shelley's Poetry'.[8] The anxiety of critics to exonerate Shelley from the charge of humourlessness may seem a little comic itself by now, but of course the argument has to be seen in the context of the criteria of New Criticism (still to some extent dominant) whereby poetry, to be interesting and valuable, must display such qualities as wit, tension, irony and ambiguity. It was important to prove Shelley 'witty' in two senses: he must be capable of being detached from his own work to the point of laughing at himself (i.e. he is not—or at least not always—'self-indulgent'), and his language itself must be 'witty' in the almost Metaphysical sense of being complex and paradoxical. The fact that one has to go to relatively minor poems by Shelley to find these qualities might make one think that the criteria themselves are arbitrary and irrelevant and indeed the whole argument seems dated now, but it is still the case that the 'Letter to Maria Gisborne' has received attention almost exclusively in these terms.

The biographical approach has perhaps worn better though it never led to a particularly full or detailed appraisal of the poem, unless we extend it to cover the method used by James M. Hall himself. After remarking on the general neglect of the 'Letter to Maria Gisborne' he went on to refer to Carlos Baker[9] as 'the poem's best and most thorough critic' and paid him the compliment of following his approach in his own essay. Both men stress the serious side of the poem that they claim underlies the light surface. Baker borrows a phrase from the poem itself to call it a 'visionary rhyme', which he takes to mean an 'intellectual play-poem with serious overtones' in which Shelley deals with 'the predicament of the gentle and acutely sensitive mind in a materialistic environment', and Hall's analysis concentrates on how the 'Letter' makes 'certain basic statements about poetry and its relation to human experience'[10]. Both approaches are based on biographical assumptions, as Baker makes clear in one of his paragraphs on the poem:

> Because Shelley had suffered public neglect, he felt driven to insulate his spirit against public contumely. In order partially to compensate for his having been denied access to the paradise of public popularity, he surrounded himself with the fabric of a vision, a chrysalis of words. A second compensation for public neglect, and one on which the

'Letter to Maria Gisborne' lays great stress, is the consciousness that one has at least a few tried friends who are sympathetic with his visionary aims.[11]

Hall develops the view of the poem as 'a chrysalis of words', as can be seen from his title, 'The Spider and the Silkworm: Shelley's "Letter to Maria Gisborne" '; the insects are images of the poet himself. Hence the 'Letter' becomes self-reflexive, its real subject being seen as poetry itself and the role of the poet: a way of reading poetry which also belongs to a recognizable fashion in literary criticism and one which is perhaps as arbitrary and partial as the determination to read poems as exercises in irony and paradox.

One's suspicions are alerted when one turns back to the poem after reading Baker and Hall and finds that its voice is a much more cheerful one than they would have us believe. Despite the occasional admission that 'the tone of the poem is consistently light' Hall's interpretation makes it seem solemn, as if the lightness is gallantly achieved in the face of despair. He writes, for example,

> The dismal and degenerating human condition in the world of experience is always operating as a force against poetic activity, and Shelley's sense of it breaks through at several points in the poem.[12]

This makes it sound as if Shelley is consciously whistling in the dark, burbling on about trivial matters while 'really' preoccupied with the apparent failure of his own career. But is it in fact the case that Shelley's sense of 'the dismal and degenerating human condition' keeps 'breaking through', and if so, why was it being covered up in the first place? Maria Gisborne was an intimate friend from whom Shelley did not usually attempt to conceal his problems, either domestic ones or those relating to his literary career.[13] The very fact of this intimacy allows Shelley to be brief and even playful when alluding to serious matters and it seems perverse in a critic to seize upon and highlight just those things which Shelley has carefully and successfully subordinated.

I am not arguing that the poem should be read as some kind of 'organic whole' but that it is misleading to extract topics or themes from it and consider them without attending to the purpose and tone of the rest. The tone of the 'Letter' seems crucial to its interpretation and a surprisingly difficult thing to get right. One can easily distort it by putting too much stress either on the witty and whimsical aspects of the language or on the more serious moments. A possible compromise was suggested by Donald Davie as long ago as 1952 when he remarked that in some sense this poem could be called 'urbane':

> It is too exuberant to be called urbane in the usual sense. But it is so, in the sense that the poet is sure of his relationship with the person he addresses, that he knows what is due to her and to himself, that he maintains a consistent tone towards her. She is not a peg to hang a poem on, nor a bosom for him to weep on, but a person who shares with him certain interests and certain friends and a certain sense of humour.[14]

Unfortunately, Davie does not discuss the poem in any detail but his line is worth pursuing. He is surely right to emphasize the sense of confidence and control that comes from Shelley's easy and relaxed intimacy with his correspondent. If anything 'urbane' is slightly too cold a word, with its connotations of a kind of man-of-the-worldliness which could slide into cynicism, and I would prefer to describe the dominant tone as one of tact.

The subject-matter of the 'Letter' is in some ways as difficult to pin down as the tone, and it is perhaps natural that, given such a wide range of material, critics have resorted to the piecemeal approach, implying that there is just no point in pretending that it all hangs together. One's impression is frankly one of clutter: the cluttered setting of Henry Reveley's workshop where Shelley is writing is reproduced in the rich kaleidoscope of thoughts and associations that it inspires. Perhaps we are too accustomed to thinking of Shelley as an abstract, even visionary poet to appreciate the delight he takes in the sheer profusion of material reality, whether in the form of machines, insects or friends. Yet the structure of the poem is carefully and tactfully organized; Shelley moves gracefully from one topic to the next, dividing his attention between his own concerns and those of his addressee with admirable skill. He begins by introducing himself and describing his surroundings (including that mainstay of letters, a description of the weather), then turns to his memories of time spent with Maria and to speculation on her present surroundings and the mutual acquaintances she will be seeing in London. The contrast between their two locations brings him back to speak of Italy and this leads naturally into the enthusiastic invitation to her to visit him next winter with which he closes. In the midst of this he does speak of poetry and the literary life but he accommodates these remarks within his general tone, not belittling or concealing the theme but not dwelling on it or giving it an importance above his other topics.

It is true that he begins with an extended simile, or rather a pair of extended similes describing the activity of the poet. These are the references to the spider and the silkworm which James M. Hall picks out as the starting-point for his interpretation of the poem, but Shelley's tone is light and playful. He refers humorously to his reputation ('So I, a thing whom moralists call worm') and implicitly to his lack of public success, but shrugs it off by declaring he has no intention of spinning 'a net of words in garish colours wrought/To catch the idle buzzers of the day' but prefers to anticipate his fame growing 'in those hearts which must remember me/. . . making love an immortality', thus turning the matter into a statement of his faith in friendship and of course a compliment to this particular friend, Maria.

The vivid and charming description of his immediate surroundings which follows is also in a sense a compliment to her since he is staying in her house at Leghorn and actually writing the 'Letter' in the work-room of Henry Reveley, her son by her first marriage, an engineer with whom Shelley formed a scheme to build a steamboat which would ply between Leghorn, Genoa and Marseilles.[15] Again he starts from a jocular image of the poet:

> Whoever should behold me now, I wist,
> Would think I were a mighty mechanist,
> Bent with sublime Archimedean art . . . (ll.15–17)

but he manages throughout his description of the clutter of strange objects around him to integrate them with his own thoughts and ambitions. He laughs at his ignorance and incompetence in Henry's world as he fails to identify the meaning and function of things, seeing only 'unintelligible brass' (l.47), 'unimaginable wood' (l.50), 'a queer broken glass/With ink in it' (ll.84–5) and so on. He refers to Henry's superior knowledge of the objects he lists—

> A hollow screw with cogs—Henry will know
> The thing I mean and laugh at me,—(ll.76–77)

>            . . . a most inexplicable thing,
> With lead in the middle—I'm conjecturing
> How to make Henry understand; (ll.100–2)

With tongue in cheek, he gives up on this last object:

>                    but no—
> I'll leave, as Spenser says, with many mo,
> This secret in the pregnant womb of time,
> Too vast a matter for so weak a rhyme. (ll.102–5)

This excuse had come up earlier—

>                Upon the table
> More knacks and quips there be than I am able
> To catalogize in this verse of mine:—(ll.54–56)

The effect here is complex but the tone is always under control. Shelley mocks the convention of the epic list by trying to make it accommodate the bizarre clutter of Henry's work-room while at the same time he clearly has a genuine admiration for Henry's skills. He may even be mocking himself directly when he despairs of describing these 'unintelligible' and 'unimaginable' objects, since so often his poetic skills are seriously devoted to describing things on the very edges of perception and comprehension: his poem 'To a Skylark', written, like the 'Letter to Maria Gisborne', at Leghorn in 1820, provides an interesting comparison with its questioning after definition—'What thou art we know not;/What is most like thee?'—and its sense of hidden meanings. In the 'Letter' Shelley laughingly deprecates his own verse and manages to imply tactfully that it is partly *because* he cannot do justice to his surroundings through literal description that he strays into association and fantasy. This is ingeniously done, as for example when the 'dread engines' round the walls of the room make him think first of Vulcan then of the Inquisition—which makes him think of the effect such religious suppression *might have had* on Shakespeare, Sidney, and Spenser, but also reminds him of the happy fact that Spain 'now relumes her fire/On Freedom's hearth.'

The image of Proteus as creator and transformer takes over

from the images of the spider and the silkworm, and it is a more exciting because less predictable image:

> Proteus transformed to metal did not make
> More figures, or more strange; nor did he take
> Such shapes of unintelligible brass,
> Or heap himself in such a horrid mass
> Of tin and iron not to be understood;
> And forms of unimaginable wood, (ll.45–50)

Later Shelley associates his own creativity with this alien technology around him when he sees himself as turning out poetry like some industrial magician:

> And here like some weird Archimage sit I,
> Plotting dark spells, and devilish enginery,
> The self-impelling steam-wheels of the mind
> Which pump up oaths from clergymen, and grind
> The gentle spirit of our meek reviews
> Into a powdery foam of salt abuse,
> Ruffling the ocean of their self-content; (ll.106–12)

The wizard-scientist is a powerful image (was Shelley consciously recalling Mary's *Frankenstein?*) but again the tone is kept light with the tolerant satire of 'the gentle spirit of our meek reviews'. Certainly he was depressed by the way his work was being received, as he hints in various letters written at the time[16] but he does not indulge in bitterness or self-pity. Instead he allows the turbulent images of steam and sea to carry him forward into a dramatic description of the Libeccio, the south-west wind which is blowing outside, and he finishes this section of the Letter thus:

> above
> One chasm of Heaven smiles, like the eye of Love
> On the unquiet world; while such things are,
> How could one worth your friendship heed the war
> Of worms? the shriek of the world's carrion jays,
> Their censure, or their wonder, or their praise?
>                         (ll.126–31)

Clearly it is possible here to extract images like 'the war of worms' and 'the shriek of carrion jays' which could said to illustrate the 'dismal and degenerating human condition' 'breaking through' the surface of the poem, but such an interpretation does not do justice to Shelley's achievement in turning the potentially painful topic into a graceful compliment to his friend.

The next section of the 'Letter' demonstrates that the compliment is not an empty one. His pleasure in his friendship with Maria is conveyed through the detailed reminiscences:

> how on the sea-shore
> We watched the ocean and the sky together,
> Under the roof of blue Italian weather;
> How I ran home through last year's thunder-storm,
> And felt the transverse lightning linger warm
> Upon my cheek—and how we often made
> Feasts for each other, . . . (ll.145–51)

He expresses his specific gratitude for her work in teaching him Spanish ('thou wert then to me/As is a nurse' (ll.184–85), and he struggles to describe what the conversations meant to both of them—

> how we spun
> A shroud of talk to hide us from the sun
> Of this familiar life, which seems to be
> But is not:—or is but quaint mockery
> Of all we would believe, and sadly blame
> The jarring and inexplicable frame
> Of this wrong world:—and then anatomize
> The purposes and thoughts of men whose eyes
> Were closed in distant years;—or widely guess
> The issue of the earth's great business,
> When we shall be as we no longer are—
> Like babbling gossips safe, who hear the war
> Of winds, and sigh, but tremble not; (ll.154–66)

It is almost as difficult to describe as Henry's engines, but the effect of the broken syntax here seems to convey a modest sincerity—an attempt to express the value of what went on without embarrassing Maria. The image Shelley conjures up reminds one of the famous moment in *King Lear* when Lear says to Cordelia

Come, let's away to prison:
We two alone will sing like birds i'th' cage;
When thou dost ask me blessing, I'll kneel down
And ask of thee forgiveness. So we'll live,
And pray, and sing, and tell old tales, and laugh
At gilded butterflies, and hear poor rogues
Talk of court news; and we'll talk with them too—
Who loses and who wins; who's in, who's out—
And take upon's the mystery of things
As if we were God's spies; and we'll wear out,
In a wall'd prison, packs and sects of great ones,
That ebb and flow by th' moon. (V,iii,8–9)[17]

Obviously the relationship is a very different one, but there is the same sense of an intimate retreat from the world ('A shroud of talk to hide us . . .') which is not merely an escape but in some sense an image of superiority and power: Lear and Cordelia will take upon themselves 'the mystery of things' like 'God's spies' while Shelley and Maria can 'anatomize the purposes and thoughts of men' and 'widely guess/The issue of the earth's great business'. At the same time the playfulness and even preciousness of the picture ('like birds i'th' cage', 'Like babbling gossips') would be more appropriate to lovers and conveys in both cases a strong sense of intimacy and affection.

After recounting 'these recollected pleasures', Shelley moves on to imagine Maria's present surroundings in London and the people she will be seeing. The portraits given here have been admired out of context as vignettes of some of the most notable figures of the day, but again the quality which strikes one most forcefully when coming to them as part of the 'Letter' as a whole is the tactful and tolerant generosity that Shelley mingles with the accuracy of his remarks. Most significant in this respect are the lines on Godwin:

You will see
That which was Godwin,—greater none than he
Though fallen—and fallen on evil times—to stand
Among the spirits of our age and land,
Before the dread tribunal of *to come*
The foremost,—while Rebuke cowers pale and dumb.
(ll.196–201)

We know from their correspondence that, since the previous year, Shelley had in fact been troubled by frequent requests for money from Godwin whom he described as 'the only sincere enemy I have in the world' and whose bitter importunities he tried to conceal from Mary.[18] The fact that he can present him here as a tragic figure seems positively magnanimous. Maria clearly had reason to trust in Shelley's assessments of character: from her own letters we can see that she found herself in agreement with his views on some people and was prepared to persevere with others who seemed at first remote and difficult because of Shelley's high opinion of them.[19] With the exception of the often-quoted portrait of Coleridge (whom, alone of this list, Shelley had of course never met), the descriptions are full of warmth and enthusiasm, tempered with affectionate references to what might seem short-comings: Hunt's 'eternal puns' and Hogg's forbidding reserve.

But, apart from these few friends, who are said to be 'all/You and I know in London,' Shelley's vision of the city is bleak. He encourages Maria to look up into the sky to see the same moon that he is looking at and then asks

> But what see you beside?—a shabby stand
> Of Hackney coaches—a brick house or wall
> Fencing some lonely court, white with the scrawl
> Of our unhappy politics;—or worse—
> A wretched woman reeling by, whose curse
> Mixed with the watchman's, partner of her trade,
> You must accept in place of serenade
> Or yellow-haired Pollonia murmuring
> To Henry, some unutterable thing. (ll.265–73)

By contrast, he can look around and see

> . . . a chaos of green leaves and fruit
> Built round dark caverns, even to the root
> Of the living stems that feed them—in whose bowers
> There sleep in their dark dew the folded flowers.
> (ll.274–77)

The rich, complex image of natural life he evokes is far more than the bland pastoral we might expect to be contrasted with the somewhat Juvenalian London. And yet the city is the place

where congenial company can be found, and so Shelley proceeds
naturally into his invitation to Maria to come and see him—
'Next winter you must pass with me'—in an attempt to combine
the pleasures of urban and rural life. Ideally the house in Italy
should contain the friends from London too—'Oh! that Hunt,
Hogg, Peacock, and Smith were there,'—and they will pass their
time happily feasting and talking. Shelley seems to relish the
prospect of busy, free-flowing disorganized conversation even
though it reminds him of the strains that can accompany social
intercourse:

> And then we'll talk;—what shall we talk about?
> Oh! there are themes enough for many a bout
> Of thought-entangled descant; as to nerves—
> With cones and parallelograms and curves
> I've sworn to strangle them if once they dare
> To bother me—when you are with me there. (ll.310–15)

The terms in which he describes both the talk ('thought-
entangled descant') and the 'nerves' ('cones and parallelograms
and curves') take us back to the more literally mechanistic nature
of Henry's puzzling engines with their strange figures and shapes
of 'unintelligible brass' and 'unimaginable wood', their 'Great
screws, and cones, and wheels, and groovèd blocks' (52). These
images seem to dominate the poem as the engines dominate the
room in which Shelley is writing it, giving a sense of tension and
excitement. There are difficulties and dangers involved: the
'nerves' can be as incomprehensible and unpredictable as the
engines, and the sense of jangling strain in the imagery reminds us
that in both cases there is a potential for pain—even torture. Yet
Shelley conveys a kind of exuberance and a sense of hard but
productive complexity: everything seems in a positive confusion
of creation—even nature is seen as 'a *chaos* of green leaves and
fruit'—where the ingredients are cluttered and unknowable but
nevertheless exhilarating. Part of the excitement comes from the
unpredictability of it all: this is again the creativity of Proteus, not
that of the silkworm. Everything in the poem is richly jumbled
and seems on the verge of escaping the poet's grasp to take on a
life of its own: even the list of London friends threatens to get out
of control and Shelley apologizes for teasing Maria's patience
with it.

The linking of the engines and the mathematical figures with the questions of Shelley's social life and his poetry is not merely a formal trick. We get a genuine sense of how important all this clutter is to him and how, literally in this case, it is precisely out of the clutter of people, talk and things that the poetry comes. The 'thought-entangled descant' of conversation and of poetry is no rarified thread spun from ideals and abstractions but, in the end, a tough but flexible machine wrought out of people, places and material objects ranging from 'a most inexplicable thing,/With lead in the middle' to 'an endless host/Of syllabubs and jellies and mince-pies'.[20] It all relates because it can all be referred to and shared with one particular friend and this kind of intimate friendship, though occasionally leading to scandal and tragedy, was crucial to the sustaining of Shelley's poetic talent. The 'Letter to Maria Gisborne' shows us both how good he was at friendship—how tactful and nuanced his attitudes and expressions are—and how well he was aware that the 'visionary rhyme' grows out of the confused detail of the immediate physical world. His joy in the creative potential of this confusion as well as his confidence in Maria's friendship allows him to end, more optimistically than Milton,

'To-morrow to fresh woods and pastures new'.

## NOTES

1. Ed. Frederick L. Jones, *Maria Gisborne and Edward E. Williams, Shelley's Friends, their Journals and Letters* (Norman, Oklahoma, 1951), 92, n.11.

2. Ed. Herbert J. C. Grierson, *The Poems of John Donne* (Oxford, 1912), I, 180–2.

3. Remoraes are sucking fish, once believed capable of staying the course of any ship to which they attached themselves.

4. Ed. John Beresford, *Poems of Sir Charles Cotton 1630–1687* (London, 1923), 265–70.

5. Eds. H. Bunker Wright and Monroe K. Spears *The Literary Works of Matthew Prior* (Oxford, 1971), I, 85–91.

6. James H. Hall, 'The Spider and the Silkworm: Shelley's "Letter to Maria Gisborne" '. *Keats–Shelley Memorial Bulletin* 20, (1969), 1.

7. *Shelley: his Thought and Work* (London, 1960), 253.

8. In, respectively, *Studies in Philology* 57 (1960), 648–62 and *Studies in English Literature* 1,iv (1961), 1–22.

9. See Carlos Baker, *Shelley's Major Poetry* (Princeton, 1948), 202–6.

10. See Carlos Baker, op. cit., 8 and James H. Hall, loc. cit., 1.

11. Carlos Baker, op. cit., 203.

12. James H. Hall, op. cit., 4, 7–8.

13. See, for example, his letters to the Gisbornes, 23 Dec. 1819, 30 June 1820, *Letters* ii. 165–6, 206–7.

14. *Purity of Diction in English Verse* (London, 1952), 141.

15. For details of the steamboat project and references to it, see *Letters* ii. 124, n.2.

16. See his letter to the Gisbornes of 30 June 1820, *Letters* ii. 206, 207.

17. From *The Riverside Shakespeare* (Boston, 1974).

18. See his letter to Amelia Curran, 18 Nov. 1819 and his letters to the Gisbornes, 23 Dec. 1819 and 26 May 1820, *Letters* ii. 156–9, 165–6, 202.

19. See, for example, her comments on Peacock and Hogg in a letter dated 23rd August 1820, and her further comments on Peacock in a long letter dated 28th April–21st May 1822. Both are included in Frederick L. Jones's edition of Maria Gisborne's *Journal and Letters* as cited in footnote 1, 66 and 81–6.

20. This delight in *things* is apparent again in a short passage (ll.73–83, *Poetical Works*, 656) in 'The Boat on the Serchio' (1821) which in the unfinished draft seems quite at odds with the more highly wrought lyrical tone of the rest of the poem.

# Shelley's Narratives and 'The Witch of Atlas'

## BRIAN NELLIST

### I

The bulk of Shelley's poetry is either narrative or makes extensive use of devices most familiar in narrative poetry, yet criticism does not readily think of him as a narrative poet. Leavis flatly states 'Shelley was not gifted for drama or narrative'.[1] His own preferences among English poets, Spenser, Milton, Southey, the Wordsworth of *Lyrical Ballads*, are all devisers of narrative, yet, as G. M. Matthews points out, readers persist in seeing him as preeminently the master of the personal lyric.[2] To search for reasons why Shelley so constantly turns to a form for which he 'was not gifted' might seem to start at the wrong end of the problem: much better to establish first just how he uses it. But the predominance of narrative in Shelley is not peculiar in its period. All the major Romantic poets turned to narrative for their major statements and in that they differ from Augustan poets and are akin to the Renaissance poets. Without involving any theory of the *zeitgeist*, we might accept on empirical grounds the priority of story for the Romantic poet and its comparative unimportance for the Augustan poet. Indeed, the exceptions which immediately come to mind confirm the distinction. *The Rape of the Lock* and *Absalom and Achitophel* certainly involve narrative, but in both poems narrative functions ironically. Achitophel and Belinda become objects of criticism partly because of their willingness to invest the ordinary confusions of life with the grandeur of a tale. This critical use of narrative seems immediately to differ from Wordsworth, say, who can tell the reader of 'Simon Lee' that he should find 'A tale in every thing'.

Speculation as to why certain periods should foster narrative and others be antagonistic or indifferent to it is all too easy. Too many untested and untestable hypotheses spring to mind. A major value of narrative, however, seems to be that it allows a poet to accommodate different viewpoints and yet achieve formal completeness within the composition. Discursive poetry by contrast has to admit the force of different propositions and allow the argument to move back and forth between them. Where a writer faces a problem of intellectual pluralism in a given area of discourse, say the analysis of human love in the late fourteenth century, story allows him to articulate the various possibilities without deciding between them or without submitting the poem to domination by argument.

Strategies manifestly vary. A Renaissance narrative produces separate images for the viewpoints that the narrative is accommodating. In *The Faerie Queene* images evolve out of a continuous dialectic, or in *Paradise Lost* Hell confronts Paradise in massive opposition. Romantic narrative, by contrast, tends to offer the reader a single image, the ascent of Snowdon at the end of the *Prelude*, the Coliseum in *Childe Harold*, which fractures into innumerable perspectives, a play within the image rather than between images. Yet in both cases discovery takes place in, and through, narrative images.

When the Augustan poet tells a story, however, he often seems to use it to discomfort the reader, and that seems to be true even for some eighteenth century novels. Story in these will be used to question the certainties that the reader may be expected to assume, as though it were an argument directed against him, as in *Gulliver's Travels* or *Tristram Shandy*. The Whig tale of progress is painfully inverted in the *Dunciad*. Even the satisfactions of *exemplum* may be qualified. The use of Charles XII 'To point a moral, or adorn a tale' in 'The Vanity of Human Wishes' makes impossible to the reader the moral reassurance that it appears to offer him. The reduction of Charles, for all his energy and abilities, to the status of an *exemplum* represents a deprivation of humanity which punctures complacency and leaves the reader only pity and terror. *Rasselas* does not merely fail to become story: it resists story. It is the hero who wants to submit life to the same control as narrative and direct it to a satisfactory conclusion. *Rasselas* can only end when the hero is brought to the point where he can recognize and smile upon this tendency to elaborate fictions and surrender the conclusions that he fashions out of reverie.

Karl Kroeber's impressive study[3] has helped us to recognize

the primacy of authentic narratives for the Romantic poets. The
difference from Renaissance narrative seems in part an evolution
out of Augustan mistrust. Unlike the use of story by, say, Spenser
or Milton, major Romantic narrative offers not so much a tension
between ideas as a doubt as to whether, or what, ideas or
dominant intellectual assumptions may be possible to the poet.
The poet's mind in a state of crisis itself replaces the field of ideas
as the arena where the narrative is staged. Hence romantic
narrative has to reconstruct story in order to place at the centre of
the tale the poet himself, who seeks knowledge through the story
he contemplates. Among these reconstructions of narrative, the
case of Shelley is especially critical.

Shelley's mind constantly expresses itself in narrative. Even
conceptual terms, which he notoriously uses with an ease that at
times approaches jargon, habitually behave as though they were
participants in an action, as Macaulay recognised.[4] Yet the
narratives remain shadowy in outline. He rarely allows any
distance to come between himself and the object, character, or
event presented. Instead of offering the reader description, he
gives him response. Sentiment, reflection, and action
inextricably entwine in a language which, at its worst, fails to
justify the extreme responses it seems to require of the reader.
Cythna, riding to rejoin Laon at the funeral pyre in the
humiliated city, appears thus:

> They fly—the torches fall—a cry of fear
>   Has startled the triumphant!—they recede!
> For ere the cannon's roar has died, they hear
>   The tramp of hooves like earthquake, and a steed
>   Dark and gigantic, with the tempest's speed,
> Burst through their ranks: a woman sits thereon,
>   Fairer, it seems, than aught that earth can breed,
> Calm, radiant, like the phantom of the dawn,
>   A spirit from the caves of daylight wandering gone.
>                               (*The Revolt of Islam*, XII,viii)

Admittedly, random choice of a stanza from a long narrative
poem can easily falsify the total effect for the reader, and even
here the relevance of the elemental imagery of the horse
answering the cannon of tyranny is immediately apparent. What
bewilders the reader in this case is the presence of a world which

claims some degree of phenomenal reality yet in which space and time are dissolved. It is customary to claim that Shelley is the poet of process and movement yet the sense of time is often what is weakest in Shelley's narratives. He deals more in conversion, in metamorphoses, than with process itself.

The temporal vocabulary of *The Revolt of Islam* is of prime significance here. Where Wordsworth, for example, characteristically conveys the sense of the personal past in verb tenses, 'Was it for this—', Shelley will use a noun formulation, 'In life's young hours' (II,i). Shelley is less the poet of memory than any other major Romantic poet. The ruins among which young Laon wanders do not, as in *Childe Harold*, disturb the present but are a means to dismiss the past and leave Laon stranded in a bitter present—'I wandered through the wreck of days departed' (II,x)—with slight intimations of a better future. Hence when the future breaks into the poem it does so in a moment: 'The chains of earth like mist melted away' (V, xxxvii). Changes, like the response of Reaction to Revolution, become instantaneous: 'and all was done/Swifter than I have spoken' (VI,v); or again, 'Thus sudden, unexpected feast was spread' (VI,viii) and 'When on my foes a sudden terror came' (VI,xix). Time is ejected into qualifiers, 'sudden', 'soon' (which for Shelley tends to mean 'at once') (e.g. IX,iv,v,ix) or becomes a demonstration of the moment, 'Behold', or, typically, when the women of the City gain their liberty, 'They looked around, and lo! they became free' (IX.x). Movement here seems less a matter of transition than of change from one image to another, the dreary 'for ever' engaged in conflict with the hopeful 'on a sudden, lo!'. Or, to put it another way, the poet's mind casts around restlessly seeking escape from story, with its transitions rooted in cause and effect, into the mental liberation of image. Story tends, in fact, to be a pejorative term within Shelley's vocabulary, despite his appeals to it in the preface to *The Revolt of Islam*. He talks in the poem itself of 'the various story/Of human life', 'chroniclers of daily scorn' (II,iii), 'I heard, as all have heard, life's various story' (II,ix); the terms dismiss the past as an unvarying catalogue of illusion and degradation—'I felt the sway/Of the vast stream of ages . . ./It shall be thus no more.' (II,xii,xiii). Indeed, in the *Defence of Poetry* he objects to story precisely because it is subject to 'time, place, circumstance, cause, and effect'.[5]

Before I examine in more detail the causes of this narrative *bloc*, a proviso needs to be made at once. Only a stone-deaf reader would think that he was dealing here with an autonomous 'reality'. The poet's presence throughout is signalled not only by the presentation of the poem as a personal vision in the introductions to most of the major narratives, but by the very extravagances of the narrative method that I have indicated. The narratives are in the lyric mode and the voice is raised in fluency, in a torrent of inventive flow, which floods against and over the despair or doubt which the events of the poems raise. If the narrative in 'Alastor' depicts stasis, the style urges against it a rapid and passionate movement, which constructs for the reader a model of the singer against the world.

It would be rash to accuse the poet of mere ineptitude in his narratives, or the 'immaturity' levelled against him by the New Critics, without at least acknowledging the serious basis of Shelley's difficulties. Underlying the narratives, or quasi-narratives, of most English Romantic poets there lies a fundamental 'tale' which one can roughly distinguish as either the tale of the world, history of Nature's laws, or the tale of the self, confession. Shelley's contemporaries arbitrate between these 'tales' but favour one or the other. Scott and Byron, even Blake in the avatar presented by David Erdmann, are governed by the former, Wordsworth, Coleridge, Byron again, Keats less certainly, by the latter. Shelley's problem is that he cannot trust either of these fundamental 'tales'. History seems a nightmare from which he seeks release in espousals of revolutionary hope, though he can rarely sustain the act of faith needed for release consistently throughout the poem. The self proves an even more critical area and no Romantic poet is less introspective than Shelley. As with the tale of the world, a fundamental scepticism subverts any confidence with which he may claim to map those dark regions. In the notes towards a 'Science of Mind' (1815), after admitting what value would reside in an accurate account of one man's history 'If it were possible', he describes the contradictions and deceptions involved in the act of self-analysis:

> But thought can with difficulty visit the intricate and winding chambers which it inhabits. It is like a river whose rapid and perpetual stream flows outwards—like one in

dread who speeds through the recesses of some haunted pile and dares not look behind. The caverns of the mind are obscure and shadowy; or pervaded with a lustre, beautifully bright indeed, but shining not beyond their portals. If it were possible to be where we have been, vitally and indeed—if, at the moment of our presence there, we could define the results of our experience—if the passage from sensation to reflection—from a state of passive perception to voluntary contemplation were not so dizzying and so tumultuous, this attempt would be less difficult.[6]

What is notable here, and characteristic of Shelley, is that where we might expect denial we find only doubt. He speaks of difficulty not of impossibility. Shelley's predicament, like that of some Augustan poets, is to feel the pull of different intellectual models upon his imagination but to withhold final credence from them. His concern with 'ideas', no adolescent enthusiasm, however it began, becomes an attempt to discover the missing narrative base. His narratives function as tense conflicts between confirming the revolutionary substitute for the fundamental tale, and either its disconfirmation or a detachment from any available viewpoint. His narratives are pulled backwards and forwards between exemplum and irony, between attempted proof and ruefully acknowledged doubt of any secure model which could liberate the mind from its hazards.

If narrative reveals to Shelley the problematic nature of what in the pamphlets[7] he affirms with apparent confidence, this might explain the curious discontinuity of his poetic career. Shelley wrote fast and wrote much, yet until 1819 his works were composed in spasms: 1812 *Queen Mab*, 1815 'Alastor', 1817 *The Revolt of Islam*, 1819 *Prometheus Unbound*. Moreover their direction changes. *Queen Mab* and *The Revolt of Islam* are basically poems about the tale the world tells, 'Alastor' a tale of the self, *Prometheus Unbound* may be an attempt to relate the two. What then makes the readers of Shelley's narrative poems so queasy—the lack of transitions, the distance from a recognizable phenomenal reality, the characterless characters—results from a particular use of narrative. He develops story as a kind of hypothesis to test certain assumptions. Narrative fluidity is another name for the exploration of different attitudes to these assumptions.

The basic narrative hypothesis is displayed in a Romance formula recurrent in his poetry. A liberator comes, often by a journey, often marked out by suffering, to release a transfixed victim and bring to him renewal of life. This Parsifal-like quester either seeks wisdom or brings it with him to heal wounds and restore sight. In 'Alastor,' for example, the hero is at once victim and quester and if the two roles could be united it is the watchful and praying poet of the introductory lines who would be released. In *The Revolt of Islam*, Laon and Cythna undergo torture, separation, and imprisonment, they travel through nightmare tests on faith, like St. Anthony in the Wilderness, to bring release to the City. Cythna is agent for the wisdom of Laon. In 'Julian and Maddalo', Julian wishes by his wisdom to become the healer of his *alter ego*, the maniac. In *Prometheus*, Asia journeys to release her shackled husband, but equally the mind of Prometheus itself painfully travels into the past to release Jupiter from the curse, though the liberation properly belongs to Prometheus himself. In all these cases, however, the narrative hypothesis either cannot be sustained or proves suspect. The problem of how to achieve the transformation proves more intractable than the initial assumptions implied, and the narratives of 'Alastor', *The Revolt of Islam* and 'Julian and Maddalo' end in conclusions that are in part at least ironies. Even in *Prometheus Unbound* the surplus of routes to liberation demonstrates Shelley's customary narrative insecurity and in Demogorgon's last speech the promised end to history becomes only the completing of a cycle.

In the late poems, however, the Romance journey is used rather differently. In the most dubious of these cases, *Epipsychidion*, the final voyage to the island paradise is a provisional flight. The language sets impossible conditions for its fulfilment. Having admitted the claims of the twin lights, sun and moon, to rule his life, the narrator offers his invitation to the single body, the sun. They will follow a path 'No keel has ever ploughed . . . before' (411). Recklessly, he promises that 'The treacherous Ocean has forsworn its wiles' (413) and offers Eden restored. Such images are conceived differently from the mysterious tortures of the past journeys. They are the product of a will to liberation. *Epipsychidion* acknowledges, as *The Revolt of Islam* could not afford to do, that the liberating journey is formulated by reverie. The blighted and halting travels of the earlier part quicken into the projection into Elysium, but the projection is offered not as achievement but as vision. The constructs of the imagination presented by idealizing poetry become the only resource the liberator-poet has finally to offer.

The alteration of the pattern of redemption in *Adonais* is still more radical in its severity, and notably more successful. Spatial references in the poem divide along two axes, the horizontal of the earth-wanderers and the vertical, stretching from the abyss of the grave to the empyrean of immortal poetry. Primary among the earth-wanderers is the 'pard-like spirit'. He has all the lineaments of the victim-redeemers of the earlier narratives (Cain or Christ). The tone here is not so much self-pity as an attempt by the poet to disengage from the older model, to recognize in it the marks of weakness that disfigure the travellers in *The Triumph of Life*.[8] The two images which in Canto I of *The Revolt of Islam* were associated with redeeming vision, the dome and the ship, in *Adonais* belong to the tainted world of horizontals. The dome has to be shattered to let in the light streaming from the vertical axis and the boat voyages without any guide but the star itself:

> my spirit's bark is driven,
> Far from the shore, far from the trembling throng
> Whose sails were never to the tempest given;
> The massy earth and sphered skies are riven!
> I am borne darkly, fearfully, afar . . . (ll.488–92)

Redemption belongs not to the world but to the poet, liberated from the world by death. Some liberation, the reader might mutter. The poem is an elegy, however, and the search for consolation is necessary to it. Death ends the poet's subjection to the world, with hints that the poet has in life carried the world's flaws. Now he is his poetry which is purified in death from the lies that assault it while the poet lives. The claims are close to those Shelley makes in the *Defence of Poetry*. The poet is a vehicle for a truth that neither he nor the world fully comprehends but which attends the future; poets are 'The mirrors of the gigantic shadows which futurity casts upon the present'.[9] In place of the heavenly vision of 'Lycidas', Shelley sets the creative mind itself, raised above the world, serene and aloof.

Hence in the final mysterious fragment, 'The Triumph of Life', the horizontal journey has become the type of the evil courses of the world and the only proper response to it is either the watchful stillness of the narrator or the soaring flight of those who return to the sun, a vertical axis like that in *Adonais*. The saviour figures of the earlier model who claim to bring wisdom to the world are here indisputably subject to its corruption, not least the fallen Rousseau, who with his golden lady of the dawn offers a terrible parody of Laon and Cythna.

The shift that takes place within Shelley's narrative hypothesis, then, to retain that awkward term for the moment, does not lie in a growth from innocence to experience. On the contrary, the earlier poems show a persistent desire that the innocent hero should redeem the realm of experience by a heroic journey. The later poems sacrifice the realm of experience in order to preserve the state of innocence untainted. If a redemptive role remains it lies now in the hero's capacity to reach the sacred spot of the imagination and keep his faith in it. Freedom, creativity, and endurance are now attributed to the poetic imagination itself, defined not by its knowledge but by its attitude of mind. It is that attitude of mind to which he first gives full expression in 'The Witch of Atlas'.

Significantly, around the time of its composition he was concerned largely with satires, all of them written between late 1819 and late 1820. The satires moreover, are negative visions of Experience rather than moral appeals to the reader. Maria Gisborne, in the verse letter addressed to her, which is closely related to the satires, journeys to the fallen world of London from the innocence of her house in Pisa. Her house, from which Shelley writes his poem, is described as though it were a model of the mind in free creative play. Her journey from that innocent spot has no redemptive intention towards London, however, for London is fallen too far to benefit from it. Shelley imagines her rather in the ideal company of the few pure souls that remain there, Godwin, Coleridge, Hunt, and Hogg. Each figure is, moreover, described as in some sort locked away from the world, Godwin as a second Samson 'fallen on evil times' (l.198), Coleridge sitting within the 'intense irradiation' (l.204) of his own mind, Hunt within his room, to parallel the room described at the start of the poem, Peacock, whose 'best friends hear no more of him' (1.237). This is a community only to the imagination. The poet's stance at the end of 'Julian and Maddalo', 'But the cold world shall not know' (1.617), anticipates the benign isolation of these figures.

It is all too easy, of course, to draw diagrams upon the intricate and kaleidoscopic surface of a poet's work, especially a poet whose texture is so complicated as Shelley's, yet if there is any conviction in this argument for a shift in his major metaphor of a redeeming journey, it will help to explain the peculiar form and success of 'The Witch of Atlas'. To argue that the shift happens because of the poem would obviously be excessive. Many factors contribute. Shelley wrote it in one of his mysterious dry periods, though the dryness is here partly attributable to literary experiment, in satire, and above all in translation. He read much, as always, but the reading of late 1819 and 1820 was particularly important.[10] The speed with which he wrote it (in three days after a weekend's solitary expedition to Monte Pellegrino), its uniquely sustained poise and clarity, may be explained as a sudden coming by the poet to himself, an encounter at last with his elusive Muse. Within the organization of his career it is emphatically not to be dismissed as it is in Eliot's footnote,

> He did not, for instance, appear to take his ideas very seriously in *The Witch of Atlas*, which, with all its charm, I think we may dismiss as a trifle.[11]

It is interesting, however, that Eliot picks on the poem and that he should feel slightly hesitant over his dismissal. When Shelley's mind turns in the later poems with such assurance to the sacred spot of the imagination the confidence is of a man who had been there. This poem is a celebration of its *genius loci*. It is all journey, yet unlike the earlier narratives the Witch is not going anywhere. Movement justifies itself by its exhibition of freedom of mind, by a kind of self-contained pleasure. Hence the poem is as much about stillness as about movement. Though tears are attributed to her, the Witch weeps rather for the world than for herself and she is placed beyond suffering. To the Witch and, therefore, to the creative mind she exhibits Shelley awards the attributes of Godhead itself, immortality, impassibility, freedom, transcendant superiority to the world of contingency.

## II

Before I can turn to look at the poem in more detail and attempt to substantiate this claim for its importance in Shelley's career, there is an initial charge to be met, which affects the reading of all his poetry and is intimated in Eliot's essay as a whole; either Shelley takes his ideas seriously, in which case he is a bore and a simpleton, or he does not, in which case he is a trifler. The Witch has not lacked advocates of stature (Yeats, Wilson Knight, and Harold Bloom, for instance), but in general, as the poet predicted in his dedication to Mary, criticism has disapproved of her gossamer quality or patronized her playfulness.[12] Playfulness is the most obvious factor in the poem's style and one, I think, too much ignored by mythopoeic criticism, for all the insight with which Harold Bloom in particular has illuminated the poem. Yet it is the idea of play which gives the work its most interesting relation with Shelley's earlier narratives.

Pontifications about 'play' by academics are liable to make even a tolerant reader wince. As the word is used in phrases like 'Give it more play' or 'The play of mind', the word assumes a condition of freedom. Yet the very notion of 'playing the game' appeals to rules and the logic of the enterprise. For the purposes of this discussion, then, I should like to see 'play' as a means by which the mind seeks to relate the freedom of its imagining to the logic implicit in its assumptions. Such a combination of inventiveness and reason seems at least as important as mimesis, for example, in children's play. It also seems close to the sense of play in say Lewis Carroll, where play offers an equivalent to pastoral in Renaissance literature, an internalized pastoral in which the mind creates for itself its own echoing green.[13] It is play, in this sense, I think, which allows Shelley in 'The Witch of Atlas', to transform the shifting of viewpoint which threatened the integrity of his earlier narratives into a positive virtue.

We read the plots of Shelley's narrative poems, as of most Romantic poets in fact, to resolve an enigma, one which is often propounded in the introductions that preface them. We expect the problem propounded to be resolved positively or negatively. Shelley's conclusions, however, customarily leave us with a sense of increased dubiousness and, at times, even the nature of the problem itself, the thematic matrix of the poem, seems retrospectively to be altered. His desire that the poem should 'come out' along the lines he projects is contradicted by the honesty of his scepticism, as in 'Julian and Maddalo'. This induces in the poet a frustration which finds vent in moments of sudden savagery—the account of the plague in *The Revolt of Islam*, the decay of the garden in 'The Sensitive Plant', and maybe in some instances to moments of self-pity. To exemplify this problem inherent in his narrative I want to look in more detail at 'Alastor' and *The Revolt of Islam*.

Shelley himself recognizes the reader's difficulty with 'Alastor' in the prose Preface he added to it. In its first paragraph he records in apparently neutral but actually excited language the history of the poem's hero, yet in the second paragraph he vacillates between identification of the hero's errors and protective applause. Thus, the gap is already opened between the fiction and its exemplary status. Difficulties with the object of the poet's search, the Lady in the dream, are however to some extent assisted by this preface. Platonic accounts of the poem as the pursuit of an ideal realm, beyond yet within the phenomenal, usually manage only to turn the reader away in bemusement. The language of the Preface belongs rather to religious quest:

> The vision in which he embodies his own imaginations unites all of wonderful, or wise, or beautiful, which the poet, the philosopher, or the lover could depicture . . . He seeks in vain for a prototype of his conception.[14]

The hero in the work pursues the wraith of the *deus absconditus*, the God of natural theology. For Shelley to identify this figure as God would be to resolve precisely what is problematic to the poet, namely, how far the experience of the Divine is possible without benefit of the divine Name and how far the process is an illusion. Hence the narrator who prays only to Nature, 'I have loved/ Thee ever, and thee only' (ll.19–20), watches the Hero by turns with reserve, anxiety and admiration. Is the female figure a projection in his dream of the hero's isolation, a transcendental subliming, even, of a basically sexual impulse? In so far as the vision heralds a moment of psychic crisis, is the search for her no more than an objectified and spoilt process of self-discovery, a narcissism by which the desire for truth within the devotee himself is projected upon the world? If this problem is to remain a problem, the narrative must offer hints yet avoid giving answers. Its viewpoint constantly hesitates between granting validity to the quest and imputing illusion. When the hero asks, 'Does the dark gate of death/Conduct to thy mysterious paradise,/O Sleep?' (ll.211–12) he may be discovering that the world is insufficient to satisfy human longings or confessing that his obsessions disable the religious man from entering life.

It is the sequence of landscapes composing the poem that constitutes the heart of the problem. Their dizzying sequence constantly intimates significance yet they fail to compose themselves into a stable meaning. They are organized in a sequence of oppositions; a journey East to the Vale of Cashmire through the ruins of the past, a journey West to the Caucasus through the evidences of nature. In the Chorasmian (Caspian) marshes the traveller envies the free flight of the swan, then is immediately rapt on a magic boat journey with speed across the sea. Movement towards the abyss on the underground river is followed by ascent of the waterfall to the stream in the forest bower. This behaviour of the landscape against the expectations of nature hovers on the edge of symbol, or even of allegory, but this is not, *pace* Harold Bloom, a confused mixing of 'allegory and mythmaking'.[15] Either mode would decide the issue that the poem holds in question by its scrupulous preservation of an indeterminate mode.

Typical of the poem's style is the description of the cedars; 'The pyramids/Of the tall cedar overarching, frame/Most solemn domes within.' (ll.433–35). That observation of the different shapes presented by the tree—from the outside and from within looking up to its boughs—typifies Shelley's precision at its best. Is the tree essentially dome or spire? How can the two impressions be made to yield the unity which the hero so universally seeks? Only to the mind is the cedar a single entity. At his death, the hero becomes significantly an Endymion presence, yet prematurely wasted and aged as he is, how can he be the beloved of any goddess? The moon above the mountain pass remains numinous but silent.

Yet in the conclusion, where we might expect the enigma to be resolved and the futility of the search to be admitted, the poet turns in scorn upon the world for failing to recognize the worth of the hero who throughout has either ignored or consciously rejected its claims. The narrator himself yearns towards the 'poisoned chalice' of God and the dream of the alchemist, though the whole poem has apparently conceded the emptiness of such attempts. The failed hero becomes poetry's true elegiac subject, the 'surpassing Spirit,/Whose light adorned the world around it' (ll. 714–15). The religious spirit apparently justifies itself, indeed turns into the Godhead hymned by the poet. In the last lines he acknowledges the loss of a being, in the hero, beyond the Nature that was all in all at the start of the poem.[16]

It is this flickering between different intellectual assumptions which makes the poem so difficult to hold steady in the memory, yet the poem seems directed to produce precisely this result. It is all too easy to claim that what a poem does is necessarily the poem's aim, that an apparent flaw is in fact a purpose. Yet it must be granted that these reversals of judgement in the conclusions of Shelley's narratives are recurrent and amount to a narrative style if not demonstrably to a method.

It is when Shelley allows his narratives to hover on the edge of different possibilities and interpretations that he is most successful. Myth, in so far as it supposes a stable viewpoint, all too often tempts him into the inert abstractions in which he strives to render his cherished ideas. The difficulties of *Prometheus Unbound* maybe originate in the poet's mistaken attempt to articulate a myth and its successes lie in its attempt to accommodate contradictions and acknowledge uncertainties. Its desire for stability, however, may have been prompted by the radical instability revealed in the immense narrative spaces of *The Revolt of Islam*. There is not time to indicate more than casually a few of these. The introductory Canto disposes the reader to expect in the narrative a resolution of the enigma propounded there. The narrator is granted a vision of an eagle and a serpent locked in conflict above the sea, which is ended only when the snake drops into the waves. The description has scrupulously avoided giving us any grounds for preference between the combatants or any decision as to which creature has won. With the arrival of a visionary lady, however, no room for doubt apparently remains;

we have witnessed one moment in the unending struggle between the people and the eagle of tyranny. Accompanying the wounded serpent, a magic boat takes the narrator and the lady to a temple, dedicated to humanity, and situated amid the polar ice-field and there the serpent's story, if it is indeed the serpent who speaks, is delivered and the poem follows.

Yet the implications of this long story are anything but as clear as we expect. For example, in her childhood Cythna is instructed in the principles of liberty by her foster-brother, Laon. She dreams prophetically that she is to free the Golden City, a prophecy the narrative later confirms. Yet by the end of the poem the city has returned to slavery and the lovers are defeated. On the other hand, her dream ends with the lovers separated whereas in the narrative's last stanzas they are in fact united with their child, travelling to the polar fane. Cythna's corrective comment on her dream is, 'We meet again/Within the minds of men, whose lips shall bless/Our memory.' (II.xlviii). Is then the temple at the opening and close of the poem no more than an image of the domed head of the free man rearing its hopes into a cold and polar world? How substantial are these images meant to be and what confidence are we to repose in our reading of them? Throughout, the love of Laon and Cythna in their separation appears to be the test by which their value as protagonists of revolution is recognized. Yet when revolution fails, it is their Damon-and-Pythias loyalty to each other which seemingly conquers not tyranny but death itself. Whether the tale sees love as the prerequisite for revolution or the failure of revolution as the supreme test upon love remains in doubt.

I am not trying to raise niggling doubts here, let alone encourage any easy sneer at the expense of the poem's issues, but trying to record the doubts deeply experienced within the poem. Does its sympathy lie with the serpent of the people in fact, or with the eagle individual, that is with the great and sighted souls who affirm their aristocratic status by their superiority to the world and their worthiness of each other? The revolutionary voice is insistent in the poem and commands respect, yet it is not so much the suffering of the masses that we are shown as the courage of Laon and Cythna (and the poet) and the ravaging of their tender and developed sensibilities by the horrors of plague and reaction. As narrative, the poem seems honestly to admit defeat but then wavers in its interpretation of that fact between progressivist history and a celebration of the undaunted individual. Shelley's change of title from *Laon and Cythna; or, The Revolution of the Golden City* in 1817 to *The Revolt of Islam* in the following year may be the consequence not so much of political censorship as a doubt about where the poem's thematic centre really lies.

Much detail is given to Laon's dark dreams of life in his imprisonment, an early prefiguring of 'The Triumph of Life', and on his release he sees his reflection in the water showing burning eyes and a consumed youth, like the hero of 'Alastor', worn out by illusion. Yet, equally, political tyranny is endowed with the status of nightmare. Which dream tells the truth? Is the dark dream a test on faith or is the good dream of revolution an illusion, plunging the dreamer into a yet deeper horror, from which he is saved only by love? Medwin describing Shelley's dreams during 1811 says,

> it had more than once happened to him to have a dream, which the mind was pleasantly and actively developing; in the midst of which, it was broken off by *a dream within a dream*—a dream of the soul, to which the mind was not privy; but that from the effect it produced—the start of horror with which he waked—must have been terrific.[17]

These dreams Shelley distinguished as the Phrenic and the Psychic and *The Revolt of Islam*, flawed poem as it is, is most alive as a testing of the narrative by Phrenic and Psychic interpretations.[18]

These shifts and indecisions maintain in the forefront of the reader's mind the presence of the poet, seeking consistency yet moving back and forth under the pull of different assumptions. No style could be further from Dante's, Eliot's point can be safely granted, where the steadiness of the eye confirms the coherence of the poet's intellectual world. The viewpoint that constituted despair for the position from which he begins the narrative, may by the end have to be embraced as a kind of consolation, as in 'Alastor', or perhaps as a strength, as in 'Julian and Maddalo'. This process might seem at first not very different from the process at work in other Romantic narratives. The serenity maintained at the end of 'Michael' or 'The Ruined Cottage' derives from the story mysteriously. Yet Shelley achieves a more precarious sense of rest at the ends of his narratives and seems much more anxious about their dubiousness. He carried a greater burden of cherished ideas than other Romantic poets, Blake alone excepted, and his poetry is prone to a kind of teleological surfeit. The formal source of the problem for Shelley's temper of mind lies, I would suggest therefore, with narrative itself, with story's need for an ending. The problem, again, is familiar in Romantic poetry and the unfinished narrative, the situation which never finds its conclusion, is practically a Romantic genre, as we can affirm with no more than the instances of Coleridge and Keats before us.

To come by this long route back to the issue of 'play' then: what 'play' offers Shelley is a means of entertaining in a narrative design such different points of view as, for example, *The Revolt of Islam* exhibits, while evading the anxiety of deciding between them. Instead of escaping from the constraints imposed by endings into the composition of a fragmentary piece like 'A Vision of the Sea' (written, incidentally, in 1820) he finds in the kind of 'play' that he achieves in 'The Witch of Atlas' a means, as it were, to deconstruct narrative. Instead of appointing an ending, he multiplies episodes that allow him to remain always in the midst of things, admitting different kinds of viewpoint as integral to his imagining of the Witch's state. The poem originates in a despair of the kind of solution that the narratives seek to yield. Its golden tone is rooted, as we shall see, in dark recognitions. What is only an undertone in that work becomes evident in the late poems, where again he surrenders story for an accommodation of narrative to ritual gesture, the mourning procession in *Adonais*, the negative vision of 'The Triumph of Life'.

As further evidence for this conscious assault on narrative, 'The Sensitive Plant', written in March of 1820, is particularly significant. Of all forms of narrative, fable seems the most completely controlled by its sense of an ending. 'The Sensitive Plant' is classically controlled by the expectations of the form. In Canto I the garden is filled with love and renewal in the spring; in Canto II the Lady becomes the focus of that love, protects and cherishes the garden in summer—and dies; in Canto III, the garden is invaded in the Autumn by loathsome decay and in the

Winter finally withers away. No tale could be simpler in its reproduction of a beginning, a middle, and an end. It is a story of death in which natural process is a trap, fertile only in multiplying the sources of death. The style increases in precision and detail as decay increases.[19] Shelley relishes sadistically this investing of death with the vitality of life, culminating in a parody of resurrection, 'But the mandrakes, and toadstools, and docks and darnels,/Rose like the dead from their ruined charnels.' (III.112–13). Yet the apparent conclusiveness of this narrative, projected by the poet irresistibly and with such satisfaction to its ending, is in the teasing tones of the 'Conclusion' itself thrown into doubt. 'It is a modest creed, and yet/Pleasant if one considers it,/To own that death itself must be,/Like all the rest, a mockery.', (III.126–29). Allusions to Plato here really do not help much and inflate the 'modest creed'.[20] It is a tone rather than an argument that we are asked to respond to. To the imagination, the delight in mutual feeling described in Cantos I and II has been as real as the description of decay in Canto III. The poem is told according to the simplest of narrative progressions—birth, flourishing, death—and then the rules are suddenly changed: 'For love, and beauty, and delight,/There is no death nor change.' (III.134–35). In place of the unchangeable sequence offered by time, Shelley wittily offers us in retrospect an interpretation that disregards time. What reader would want to disagree with a narrator so sophisticated in his appeal to imaginative possibility; 'in this life/Of error, ignorance and strife,/Where nothing is, but all things seem,/And we the shadows of the dream', (III.122–25)?

'The Sensitive Plant' is the first of the late poems in which Shelley does not simply use story but asks what story is and remains throughout in control of the implications it has for his meanings. Where in the earlier poems, the shifting viewpoint to an extent preyed upon story, with consummate intelligence Shelley has now found in the playful style a means of holding tentativeness within the poem's structure. In this discovery of how to liberate narrative images from the claims of narrative progression, Shelley's career has a parallel with Keats's. In these late poems as in Keats's Odes, narrative is decreated to leave the reader facing the moment of transition, without the writer needing to describe the conclusions into which transition leads.

## III

In its sequence of transitions without any posited ending 'The Witch of Atlas' is indebted to *Don Juan*. But then it is the very abundance of its literary models which helps it in its flight past the nets cast for it by any single interpretation. For a reason which will become clear the poem is better described as burlesque hymn than as narrative, a celebration of the birth and acts of a deity who belongs to no Pantheon. Its 672 lines divide into episodes, though different readers would put the boundaries of its sections in different places. We are told of the Witch's birth and recognition as deity by the mythological creatures of the locality (stanzas 1–13). The description of her magic powers (hence 'Witch') clearly makes her at once a being who uses Nature and a being beyond and above it, and it is this section which attributes to her a function in effect parallel to that of the imagination in poetry (stanzas 14–30). This involvement in natural process, yet superiority to it, is displayed in her magic boat and the journeys she takes in it, powered by her creation, the Hermaphrodite (stanzas 31–47). The two centres of her activity are her playground on the Austral Lake (stanzas 48–56) and the Nile, where she brings dreams to guilty and thwarted men (stanzas 57–78).

Clearly, these 'acts' differ from the unique events of a narrative, which reveal themselves by inevitable consequences. The poem has no internal design shaped by argument or action. In one sense the poem is endless, like *Don Juan* itself. But it is difficult to see how it could have been longer without gravitating towards legend. Its mastery lies in avoiding the temporal which had perplexed Shelley's earlier narratives. Activity here furnishes episodes but never composes a sequence. It comprises all the elements of narrative without ever settling into a cause and effect or a before and after.

Appropriate to hymn, the poem is confessedly, then, 'vision' rather than tale. His translations of Goethe and Calderon gave Shelley new confidence in 'visionary rhyme' ('To Mary', l.8). But the model of vision that he specifies in his dedication to Mary, Wordsworth's *Peter Bell*, he mentions in order to attack. In the introduction to his own poem Wordsworth had rejected the magical sky-boat, 'Shaped like the crescent moon', which offered to be his muse.[21] It is this boat that Shelley bestows on his Witch. Wordsworth turns away from the boat to the rooted origins of his poetry, offering to the imagination certificates of naturalization, as it were. But it is precisely Wordsworth's belief that imagination displays itself in event which had produced in Shelley's earlier narratives the restless movement between assent and scepticism. Here Shelley breaks free from event to celebrate imagination in its high noon. The pure logic of the imagination only becomes clear when it is liberated from the phenomenal world. As so often, then, Shelley's poem originates in part from an intimate quarrel with Wordsworth's poetry. The paradoxical claim of the poem is that its playfulness makes it not less serious than *Peter Bell* and, indeed, more truthful. Wordsworth in *Peter Bell* analyses the moment of conversion, as always in his most important poems, but from Shelley's point of view conversion means subjugation, the taint of servitude to the world imposed on the imagination's freedom. Hence Peter, seen nakedly, is 'Scorched by Hell's hyperequatorial climate' (l.42).

Where Wordsworth presents a would-be saint, a figure transitional between worlds, then Shelley presents a god: 'If you unveil my Witch, no priest nor primate/Can shrive you of that sin' ('To Mary') (l.46). The disparaging reference to official religion shows that what Shelley needs here is a tone which will imply reverence without demanding belief. His most immediate model to achieve this was undoubtedly the Pseudo-Homeric 'Hymn to Mercury', translated only three months before into the same *ottava rima*.[22] Unlike Keats in *his* dealings with the happy gods, Shelley preserves that mingling of prankishness with power which he found in his originals. The substantiality of the divine in the Greek hymns rescued Shelley from that habitual ease with which he could refer to abstractions as though they were realized presences. More importantly, it allowed him to use narrative incident as episode rather than as story, to rescue fiction from the certainties of myth. Mercury's theft of Apollo's cattle in the 'Hymn' is justified by the dexterity of mind it displays, the exchange of music it leads to, by Mercury's confidence in his claim to sit among the Olympians. By rendering divinity as assumption rather than as argument, Shelley saves himself in the Witch from the unease about its status which torments 'Alastor'.

Where the 'Hymn' could offer him a procedure, a style was available in the burlesque romance. *Don Juan* had shown how comedy's serious purpose could be recovered in a style capable of moving swiftly between high and low styles. Mary and Shelley had recently been reading a belated and crude essay in the same tradition, the *Ricciardetto* (1738) of Niccolò Forteguerri.[23] Burlesque's urbane mockery of the high style which it nevertheless employs allowed Shelley access to his habitual manner yet helped him to grant its absurdities, consciously. The laughter, despite Eliot's earnest disclaimer, helps the reader to admit the poem's seriousness.

Many sources contributed to the poem's mythology, Virgil and Spenser most notably.[24] The poem is geography as much as a legend and it is significant that its image of Northern Africa derives from Pliny and from Herodotus. That historian's baffled response to Egypt, and his notorious incapacity to distinguish truth from lie in what he was told there, allows Shelley entry to a mode of discourse where invention mingles with authority, rather as it does in Spenser. To Pliny, the Nile forms a kind of Southern parallel to the Danube (Ister), both rivers being boundaries to the known world. Shelley can therefore turn Africa into an inverted world, an answer to the familiar and rational regions of Europe. The proverbial mystery of the Nile's sources allows the poem to intimate, if not directly to state, two separate origins; the fount in Atlas where the Witch is born and the Austral Lake where she plays.[25] Hence the poem is like a journey from the hidden places of the Witch's power to the Lower Nile where she touches upon human life. But by keeping the poem's design simply to the shape of the river itself, Shelley can avoid a sequence based on narrative, which would raise his habitual teleological anxieties. The river does not exist for the cities of the Lower Nile though it makes their life possible.

This extraordinary range of influences, analogues, and models allows the poet to fend off interpretation. In his dedication to Mary he uses her doubts about the poem to answer the charges made by his own earlier creative self. The poem defies narrative; his verses 'tell no story, false or true' ('To Mary', 1.4). Equally it escapes the demands of argument; it describes a time 'Before those cruel twins . . ./Error and Truth, had hunted from the Earth/All those bright natures which adorned its prime.'

(ll.49–52). It is free of time and hence his comparison of the work to the evanescent 'silken-winged fly' ('To Mary', 1.9) is no gratuitous bitterness. The poem, like the fly, carries the flavour of the sun, with its 'eternal smile' ('To Mary', 1.15), while the ambitious 'Winged Vision' ('To Mary', 1.17) that he had offered to Mary (*The Revolt of Islam*) died before the sun set. Ironically the images contradict the apparent argument; the evanescent poem shares in the power of the eternal sun where the poet's attempt to conquer time in the earlier poem was doomed to failure. Hence, Wordsworth's slowness in writing *Peter Bell* is the very cause of its subjection to taint 'Watering his laurels with the killing tears/Of slow, dull care' ('To Mary', 11.27–28).

Already in this dedication Shelley is helping the reader to see the poem in the right way and doing so by addressing an answer to his wife as a critic who is misreading the work. Our rational expectations are systematically assaulted; the poem is neither truth nor falsehood, the instant lasts longer than time itself, holy Peter Bell is a devil in disguise. To ask what the Witch 'means' in the face of such a style is to ask the wrong question.[26] The Witch does not have a meaning; she has a function—to enable the poet to produce this kind of inversion of the reader's viewpoint. The poem is a kind of contest between the world which the reader brings with him and the poet who defeats that world by the process of the poem's strange logic.

Thus the Witch like all good deities is granted a genealogy, daughter to the Sun and one of the Atlantides. *Before* the Witch's birth, her mother is granted the supreme honour of stellification; she becomes a vapour, a sunset-cloud, a meteor and finally 'one of those mysterious stars/Which hide themselves between the Earth and Mars' (ll.71–2), one of the newly discovered asteroids.[27] Apotheosis apparently is a matter of becoming progressively more elusive: the deity in the mind must have an origin yet the originating presence is nugatory. The Witch is born fully grown and it is her birth which warms the womb-cave, not *vice versa*. She is not, as it were, anterior to her conception but what is necessary to her life is there not only when, but because, she comes into existence.

The best analogy for her form of birth is the poem's own process of coming into being. It is not that the Witch represents poetry but that in conceiving her Shelley is forced to write poetry that uses language in the way he describes in *A Defence of Poetry*:

> language is arbitrarily produced by the imagination and has relation to thoughts alone; but all other materials, instruments, and conditions of art have relations among each other which limit and interpose between conception and expression.[28]

The style is maintained throughout. In the Witch's cave, for example, are stored the objects of the senses:

> sounds of air,
> Which had the power all spirits of compelling,
>      Folded in cells of crystal silence there;
> Such as we hear in youth, and think the feeling
>      Will never die—yet ere we are aware,
> The feeling and the sound are fled and gone,
>      And the regret they leave remains alone. (ll.154–60)

The impression is being described without either the antecedent cause or the ears of the actual listener, yet this strange state is rendered with precision by the poetry, the bounds of the experience defined by 'crystal silence'. What is remarkable in the poetry is the combining of unfamiliarity with exactness, apparent extravagance with logic, in analysing the laws governing the mind.

The celebration of the pure mental act is combined here with a sense of its price, however. The end of the stanza might seem at first to have modified towards that demand for gratuitous pity which apparently infects Shelley's poetry at intervals. Adequate cause justifies the modulation here. Experiences which seem enduring in youth, itself transitory, yet which vanish to leave only the sense of loss in human life, remain forever in the Witch's cave both in *potentia* (in cells) yet actual, having the power to compel. In a poem which celebrates the deity within the mind, Shelley persists in recording also the regret that it exists only there or only realizable in just such a poem and on such conditions. Shelley is constructing 'something upon which to rejoice'; he chooses to stay besides the lotus-pool, no less conscious than Eliot of its fictive nature and therefore confessing recurrently 'the waste sad time/Stretching before and after'.

What is remarkable here is the degree of conscious control Shelley exercises over the process of reading. He describes, in stanza XXVI for instance, the Witch working on a tapestry by the light of her sandal-wood fire. Having made us attend to the precious materials of combustion, however, he suddenly castigates us for neglecting the beauty of fire itself; then he compares it to a precious stone, and, having thus aroused our concupiscence, sternly indicates that beauty properly belongs to all who love it. Yet the end of the process is that the Witch does not notice the fire at all, absorbed in her embroidery 'that dimmed the burning brand' (1.264). The whole stanza has been a means of placing the tapestry, itself a pictured tale, in a position superior to the natural world which we are blamed for ignoring. The function of the style is to startle the reader into altering his customary valuations. The freedom of mind over its circumstances, of imagination over fact, become assumptions the reader has to grant in order to read the poem at all.

If it is the method of narration rather than the object of narration which gives the poem its centre, then mythic explanations might seem mistaken, at least in their emphasis. Harold Bloom, for example, makes the Witch's farewell to the Nymphs the central episode of the poem.[29] The shaping of that incident is a more important fact than its imagery, however. The Nymphs, to us the sign of Nature's immortality, come to the Witch to offer their love but the Witch points out that they will die and with tears admits that they are therefore no fit companions for her. The poignancy is exactly rendered, 'over me Your leaves shall glance—the streams in which ye dwell/Shall be my paths henceforth' (ll.238–40), but the Witch weeps for the Nymphs, not for herself; Shelley's debt here is significantly to the defeat of the Nymphs by the Christchild in Milton's 'Nativity Ode': 'A knell/Of sobbing voices came upon her ears/From those departing Forms' (ll.245–47). The reader is invited to mourn for the transitoriness of apparently immortal forms by which he is accustomed to measure his own evanescence. Yet what follows is the stanza about the fire and the tapestry, just discussed. Through the alternation of tones the reader is finally led to rest in the resources offered by the tapestry, 'the pictured poesy/Of some high tale' (ll.252–53). The Nymphs after all are fictions which have meaning only because of the powers offered them 'in poesy'.

But the process by which the reader is led to this conclusion concedes its bleakness as well as its consolations. The imagination is an uncomfortable home.

It is the playfulness of the tone which allows Shelley so deftly to combine dark and bright recognitions in the poem. This is especially true for the episode of the Hermaphrodite and again, I think, Harold Bloom gives too much weight to what the creature *is* and not enough to what it *does* in the poem. Its creation is subordinate to the making of the boat in which the Witch intends to ride. Undoubtedly the mingling of fire and snow in the composition of the Hermaphrodite is founded upon the making of the False Florimell in the *Faerie Queene*. But to infer from that borrowing sinister connotations and to describe what amounts to a fall in creation, 'a robot' which is also 'the best *permanent* being she can create',[30] seems to me to miss the wit of the poem. Shelley certainly borrows from Spenser but that does not imply the presence of the original context. Snow and fire, attraction and reserve, are the usual constituents in the Petrarchan tradition of love, that icy flame.[31] Spenser uses the imagery to describe a courtly simulacrum of the true snow and fire of Amoret and Belphoebe. But Shelley unites cold and heat in the Hermaphrodite to show the completing of what love everywhere aspires towards. His use of the word 'It' for the creature signalizes no fall from true relatedness *à la* Martin Buber, but a sign that relationship is completed within the Hermaphrodite itself, neither he nor she but, in its world-excluding completeness, an 'It' to everything in that world. Shelley is not recording an inadequacy in the Witch but addressing a notional inadequacy in the reader. We shiver before this chilling absolute in love. The logic of what the love-poet everywhere assumes is here completed and all the language of frosty flames and of growth-together derives, as it were, from this serene and mocking image. If the critic dislikes the soporific surrender of the thing to its dreams, he should at least recall that throughout the poem dreams are the model for the valid self-containment of the mind. Love is one of the Witch's fictions, complete only within these apparently impossible yet recognizable terms, which typify the regrets and celebrations of the poem. If Shelley introduces love to power the Witch's boat it is because he is taking as literally true the metaphorical power of love to conquer the world,

Under floods that are deepest,
  Which Neptune obey;
Over rocks that are steepest,
  Love will find out the way.[32]

Dreams, dreams: 'Hesperian fables true,/If true, here only'.

So far I have been selecting moments from the poem to demonstrate its reversed logic, but the last two episodes demand attention together because their connectedness has not been recognized. Indeed, embarrassed silence broods over the first of them. Yet eleven stanzas are devoted to the Witch's interlunar games on the Austral sea 'Beyond the fabulous Thamondocana' (1.424).[33] In 1820 Shelley composed his elemental odes 'The Cloud' and 'To a Skylark', which are obviously baffled attempts to enjoy the ideal freedom attributed to the Witch in her playground. Everything in this episode comes back to front. At the centre of the clouds, which bring storm to the world, the Witch finds a still and serene home. While the world suffers and 'The spirits of the tempest thundered by' (1.432) the Witch plays games, a parody of epic games in that they involve no competition. Insubstantial vapours become crags to be scaled. Space becomes an island within the cloud mass. The spirits that attend her bring news of the earth at which she weeps and laughs, yet if from our point of view that seems to justify her function, Shelley slyly adds, 'These were tame pleasures' (1.481). The Witch finds executing a slalom in the wake of lightning-flashes more to her taste than participating in human existence. 'And sometimes', she joins the chorus of the upper spirits; 'Mortals found/That on those days the sky was calm and fair' (ll.492–3), bringing to them happy thoughts 'too sweet to last' (1.496). No wonder the reader is puzzled by all this. Shelley seems first to invite and then to frustrate a normalizing perspective founded on humanism. Consequences for humanity certainly follow from some of the Witch's actions but they are never the causes of those actions. The temporal transitions are arbitrary, 'And sometimes', 'And then', 'She would often'. No reasons are given or traceable. The Witch's actions remain free and therefore arbitrary.

We might shrug our shoulders and concede that to seek anything of moment in the description would be to break a butterfly on a wheel. Yet the poetry is accurate, substantial, manifestly more successful than, for example, 'The Cloud'. What inspires the poem is precisely this frustration of what the reader wants to find there. Total freedom is feasible only on these terms: the ideal world to which Shelley's earlier poetry aspired is made present in 'The Witch of Atlas' but is present only on these conditions. The poem's glee is rooted in melancholy acknowledgements.

Therefore, when Shelley presents in the final episode a version of the redeeming journey motif, he introduces it not with a new seriousness but with an intensification of the language of play:

> But her choice sport was, in the hours of sleep,
>    To glide adown old Nilus, where he threads
> Egypt and Aethiopia . . .(ll.497–499)

Where the reader seeks a justifying purpose, a culmination of the poem, Shelley offers us transitions so casual as to create stasis. We are offered not 'this, and then that' but alternatives, like the different origins given for the Witch's magic boat, 'this *or* that *or* the other'. When the Witch visits the dreams of tyranny and superstition among the Egyptian sleepers 'Little did the sight disturb her soul' (l.545). Far other is the response Shelley expects in his readers:

> We, the weak mariners of that wide lake
> Where'er its shores extend or billows roll,
>    Our course unpiloted and starless make
> O'er its wild surface to an unknown goal:—
>    But she in the calm depths her way could take,
> Where in bright bowers immortal forms abide
> Beneath the weltering of the restless tide. (ll.546–552)

Her visit has consequences. In her sportiveness she brings correcting dreams to priest, king, soldier, and timid lover. As in his satires Shelley rarely implies any ability in his rhetoric to change the world, so here the dreams do little to affect waking conduct, except maybe in the lover. What in an earlier poem would have been triumph, the soldiers 'Beating their swords to ploughshares' (l.645), is here achieved only within the special laws of the Witch's world. It is not an end for the Witch, only an end to the poem. Yet not everything has to be surrendered. Peter Bell's dream is uttered by his central self, the hidden being behind his behaviour, proper to the confessional mode. Shelley is concerned with the general characteristics of the mind itself. If we were to say that Wordsworth is Freudian, then we should have to say that Shelley, here a Jungian, attempts a model of the collective unconscious, with the Witch as a guiding Anima, the 'Psychic' tutoring the 'Phrenic'. If the dreams of this final section are for each role-playing man the absolutely unforgivable mistake that he must never make (the Priest declaring that Apis is only a bull, the king dressing up a monkey in his own state robes), in the poem they are the 'mistakes' the mind yearns for, the jokes that effect release from the imprisoning role.

Shelley's earlier poetry had hesitated between dark and bright interpretations of experience. More particularly it had started from a dark account and had tried to find a narrative road to lighter places of the mind. C. S. Lewis is surely right in arguing that Shelley's attempt to say goodnight to the Christian religion led him, selectively, to admit its terms without using its terminology.[34] Doubt in Shelley arises not about the value of the bright region but about how to reach it and how to define it. 'The Witch of Atlas' presents a positive vision only because it is static. There is no road here between the two regions, only an occasional abutting of the one on the other which merely confirms the dark nature of habitual experience. If the strange processes of reading that he compels upon the reader are the only means by which he can present the secure imagination, then its position surely seems hazardous. Shelley's reading in 1820 included *Paradise Regained* and the extreme quietism of that work, the rejections necessary for the achieving of the serene state of mind, find a certain equivalent in Shelley's poem. The logic by which the Witch survives is at once impossible to human circumstance and yet a model for the way in which ideally the imagination may be said to act. Even here, however, Shelley has to admit a qualifying doubt.

> 'Tis said in after times her spirit free
>   Knew what love was, and felt itself alone. (ll.585–6).

Whether the purity of the imagination that passes 'with an eye serene and heart unladen' (l.592) is bought in the poem at too great a cost confronts the reader with something of the same problem he meets in his response to the unfallen Adam and Eve in Milton's Paradise.

'The Witch of Atlas' makes necessary 'The Triumph of Life' as the reverse of the same double vision. In 'The Witch of Atlas', like many eminent Victorians, he celebrates a holy and divine region of the mind without benefit of Godhead. With a clearer and more accurate understanding of the issues than Carlyle, maybe, he presents it as intact only within a fictive world, unable to energize Human action directly unless Shelley were to create a spurious theology. In 'The Triumph of Life' he gazes without flinching at the consequences of that recognition for action and thought. If the solution denied Shelley his old topic of the journey between bright and dark worlds, nevertheless, taken together with the claims for the imagination that he made in the *Defence of Poetry*, it points towards a new celebration of poetry as itself the only region where the mind can find its proper liberty. Such a belief in the liberating value of fictions gives a peculiar modernity to Shelley's later work.

## NOTES

1. *Revaluation* (1936), 206.

2. 'Shelley's Lyrics', *The Morality of Art*, ed. D. W. Jefferson, (London, 1969), 196.

3. *Romantic Narrative Art* (Madison, 1960).

4. 'Out of the most indefinite terms of a hard, cold, dark, metaphysical system, he made a gorgeous Pantheon, full of beautiful, majestic, and life-like forms', 'John Bunyan' (December, 1830), *Critical and Historical Essays*, 3 vols. (London, 1848), i. 414.

5. Clark, 281.

6. Ibid. 186.

7. Such as *An Address to the Irish People* and *A Letter to Lord Ellenborough*, both 1812, *A Proposal for Putting Reform to the Vote*, 1817, and 'A Philosophical View of Reform', 1819–20: see Clark, 39–59, 72–80, 158–62, 229–61.

8. G. M. Matthews maintains that the draft shows the 'frail form' originated as a historical figure antedating Napoleon, maybe Rousseau, op. cit., 197.

9. Clark, 297.

10. 'The astonishing scope and magnitude of Shelley's reading' is demonstrated in Appendix VIII 'Shelley's Reading', *Letters* ii. 467.

11. *The Use of Poetry and the Use of Criticism* (1933), 93 n.

12. Shelley himself sounds apologetic in writing to his publisher, Ollier: 'I send you the "Witch of Atlas", a fanciful poem, which, if its merit be measured by the labour which it cost, is worth nothing' (*Letters* ii, 257). I shall argue later in relation to the Dedication, however, that lack of labour was to Shelley a sign of the work's value, hence the comment may be a wry joke addressed specifically to a publisher. Critics have been ready to take Shelley's word for it, however;

Desmond King-Hele accepts it as a 'kittenish frolic' (*Shelley, His Life and Thought* (London, 1962), 260); Carlos Baker, to whom all students of Shelley are indebted, thinks the poem most interesting as 'a literary hybrid' (*Shelley's Major Poetry* (Princeton, 1966), 214), a valuation in which J. R. de L. Jackson concurs, adding 'a fanciful personification of the spirit of love' (*Poetry of the Romantic Period* (London, 1980), 302; even G. M. Matthews dismisses it as 'a long holiday-poem written in three days' (*Shelley, Selected Poems and Prose* (Oxford, 1964), 14). Kenneth Neil Cameron, in a phrase which counters dismissals, describes its underlying mood as 'one of skeptical exasperation' (*Shelley, The Golden Years* (Camb. Mass., 1974), 275).

13. See J. Huizinga, *Homo Ludens* (in German, 1944, English trans., London, 1970) esp. chap. 1. Shelley himself uses the child's expression of its internal creativity in play as an analogy for the poet (Clark, 277).

14. *Poetical Works*, 14–15.

15. *Shelley's Mythmaking* (New Haven, 1959), 8.

16. See Miriam Allott, 'Keats's *Endymion* and Shelley's "Alastor" ', *Literature of the Romantic Period 1750–1850*, ed. R. T. Davies and B. G. Beatty (Liverpool, 1976), 151.

17. Quoted in Richard Holmes, *Shelley, the Pursuit* (London, 1974), 65.

18. *OED* glosses 'phrenic' as 'mental' but offers no reference earlier than 1835 for this meaning (Medwin's *Shelley* is of 1847). Whatever the origin of the terms themselves, the distinction between mind and spirit was of general interest to Shelley's contemporaries.

19. Cp. Donald Davie, *Purity of Diction in English Verse* (London, 1952), 150. The chapter on Shelley also singles out 'The Witch of Atlas' for particular praise.

20. But see James A. Notopoulos on the Conclusion constituting 'one of Shelley's finest expressions of Platonic faith and idealism', *The Platonism of Shelley* (Duke University Press, 1949), 268.

21. *Poetical Works*, ed. E. de Selincourt, 5 vols. (Oxford, 1940–49) ii. 331.

22. For expert discussion of the translation see Timothy Webb, *The Violet in the Crucible* (Oxford, 1976), 70ff.

23. See *Letters* ii. 474.

24. Any account of the sources is indebted to Carlos Baker, op. cit., 206.

25. D. Bush, *Mythology and the Romantic Tradition* (Cambridge, Mass., 1937), 138; the most complete recent account is by Frederic S. Colwell, 'Shelley's "Witch of Atlas" and the Mythic Geography of the Nile', *ELH* (45) 1978, 69–92.

26. The most extended study of 'The Witch of Atlas' as a kind of allegory is Carl H. Grabo, *The Meaning of the Witch of Atlas* (Chapel Hill, N.C., 1935).

27. Desmond King-Hele, op. cit., 258.

28. Clark, 279–80.

29. *Shelley's Mythmaking*, 188.

30. Ibid., 200.

31. For the dissemination of the tradition in the Renaissance see L. W. Forster, *The Icy Fire: Five Studies in European Petrarchism* (Cambridge, 1969).

32. 'Over the mountains' in Percy's *Reliques of Ancient English Poetry*, 2 vols., (Everyman's Library, London, n.d.) ii. 336.

33. 'Thamondocana' is something of a crux in the poem; commentators since Carlos Baker assume the name refers to Timbuctoo (even so scholarly a critic as F. S. Colwell, in the article cited above) without offering authority for this. Yet contemporary travellers like Mungo Park, whose accounts Shelley had read in December 1814, refer to the town by its familiar name, as does Tennyson in his prize poem which appeared only nine years after 'The Witch of Atlas' was written. The trading centre close to the Niger was not founded until the eleventh century and received its first visitor from the outside world in the person of Ibn Battuta in the mid-fourteenth century. Since that time it appears to have been known by its familiar name or some variant of it, 'Tambutu' in Leo Africanus and 'Tombuto' in Hakluyt. The only name at all similar that I have been able to find is Pliny's version of the Greek name for Mt. Kakulima, Theon Ochema (*Hist. Nat.* V.10), in the section immediately preceding the discussion of the Atlas range. Shelley was a good Greek scholar, of course, but he may well have garbled the name from his memory of the translation of Pliny he made as a schoolboy (T. J. Hogg, *Life of Shelley* (London, 1906), 268).

34. 'Shelley, Dryden, and Mr. Eliot', *Rehabilitations* (Oxford, 1939), quoted from *English Romantic Poets*, ed. M. H. Abrams (New York, 1960), 257; Lewis also speaks of 'the muscular, sustaining power' of 'The Witch of Atlas', 259. The 'religious' toning of the poem could maybe be best accounted for in an aphorism of Novalis as translated by Carlyle; 'It depends only on the weakness of our organs and of our self-excitement . . . , that we do not see ourselves in a Fairy-world. All Fabulous Tales . . . are merely dreams of that home-world, which is everywhere and nowhere. The higher powers in us, which one day as Genies, shall fulfil our will, are, for the present, Muses, which refresh us on our toilsome course with sweet remembrances.' (*Critical and Miscellaneous Essays* (7 vols. London, 1872), vol. 2, 217). Shelley often seems closer to the German transcendental tradition than to the other English Romantic poets.

# Transforming Presence: Poetic idealism in *Prometheus Unbound* and *Epipsychidion*

## GEOFFREY WARD

A common factor among poets of the Romantic period is the urge to call into question both the philosophical inheritance of dualism, and the social inheritance of institutionalized hierarchies. These two legacies were viewed by the Romantics as a single evil, a false and debilitating version of reality wherein the self was a discrete entity, forever estranged from, and yet in a prefixed relationship with, the not-self. In consequence, Romantic works search for, celebrate, betray anxiety over—in short, privilege—any moments of experience that challenge this orthodoxy.

Yet behind the united front, there are strong temperamental and conceptual differences between the approaches of each poet. In this regard, we might read Wordsworth's poems, for example, as providing a spectrum of experience, offering, at one end, the dissolution of the perceiver into unity with the perceived, recorded by the poet largely as a morally necessary alteration; but at the dark end of that spectrum of changing selfhood appears a *contre-coup* of anxiety in which the prospect of such dissolution carries the threat of annihilation. Wordsworth also records an analogous and vertiginous discrepancy between buoyant voyages of self and their aftermath in guilt or torpor. The activities of the 'egotistical sublime' may involve impetuous selection from the objects presented to perception, objects that may be human but which are still catalysts merely for an expansion of consciousness so terrifically self-reflexive that it neglects them. This produces a contraposition of deflated remorse over the act of crushing that is often embodied, for Wordsworth, in guilt at local transgressions of a quasi-pantheistic code. By contrast, Coleridge's most crucial poems are interior, their narratives and environments psychological; formed in a half-light where traditional hierarchies can neither be supported nor abandoned, they always generate fear. Hierarchy in 'Kubla Khan' or 'Christabel' is oneiric, an evasive compromise; it may, as in the former poem, release an expanded awareness, but the new order is opaque, threateningly incomplete, or refuses to remain stable and so cannot be trusted or even properly recalled. So, although Wordsworth and Coleridge in their different ways give priority to experiences that subvert standard beliefs, even the most intense or splendid instances are beset by doubt and contradiction.

Of course it is Blake among the Romantics who shows most confidence in dismissing customary taxonomies, social, and moral structures injurious in his eyes to the potential of the self. Rather than recording moments or voyages of released selfhood that might easily be viewed as mechanisms of *escape*, Blake sought to fight the enemy on its own territory, seeing clearly the conceptual foundations of the orthodoxy, and labouring to construct a rival world, also conceptually grounded, and poetic by virtue primarily of its bardic tones. Unfortunately the degree to which this new poetic order becomes applicable to the non-poetic world is coextensive with the increasing privacy of its details and ramifications of myth. In addition, Blake's apparent alternatives to traditional structures may be viewed as *parody*, precisely at those points where Blake strives most to give his world independence; his Bible of Hell would be nothing without the orthodox Bible.

I intend by this cursory summary only to note certain cardinal difficulties attaching to the Romantic preoccupation with received hierarchy—the gradations of dominion and class in any context—and dualism. It might almost be said that hierarchy signifies in 'vertical' terms the oppressions that dualism sustains on a 'horizontal' axis; by 'dualism' is meant, here, a division in principle between subject and object, applicable also to the relations between people. I shall argue that Shelley's writing is vehement in its subversions of dualism and hierarchy within perception, politics, and philosophy, and not merely in epiphanic moments—though his work is rich with those—but habitually, indeed almost as a starting point. It could not be argued that for Shelley these problems are transcended with seraphic immediacy. Few poets exercise their reader's reasoning habits so fiercely while simultaneously pursuing a Utopian trajectory. At the same time I would put forward *Prometheus Unbound* as a paradigm of the Romantic concerns sketched above, which consciously anticipates and deals with certain of the snares of anxiety and contradiction that trouble the other Romantic poets I have mentioned. And I hope to show that *Epipsychidion* does not merely epitomize but lays bare the Romantic attitude, by displaying it *in extremis* together with a possible critique of, or limit to, that attitude.

I

It is hard to view *Prometheus Unbound* as a play. It makes little use in theatrical terms of either character or action, and the poet deals so swiftly with the pivotal dramatic incidents of Jupiter's overthrow by Demogorgon (III.i,63) and Prometheus's liberation by Hercules (III.iii,1) as to seem to want to dispose of them as quickly as possible so that the questing flow of poetry may be reasserted. In fact the drama, to Shelley, is simply one more poetic genre, as he makes clear in *A Defence Of Poetry*:

> The drama being that form under which a greater number of modes of expression of poetry are susceptible of being combined than any other, the connexion of poetry and social good is more observable in the drama than in whatever other form.[1]

And so Shelley's adoption of the dramatic form is in this case equivalent to an announcement of the social orientation of his poem's concerns. In a limited sense Shelley did find a model for his text in the drama of Aeschylus, but showed no loyalty to it and kept or rejected what he wished; as he states in the Preface to the poem:

> . . . in truth, I was averse from a catastrophe so feeble as that of reconciling the Champion with the Oppressor of mankind.[2]

The close of the poem entails no such Aeschylean reconciliation. We may take Shelley's poem to be wholly independent or see it as subversive of its source; either way, the autonomy of the text is emphasized finally. (It could in any case be argued that it is a ploy of Romantic poems to deal ambivalently with 'source' material, which is included but rewritten, referred to but excluded, as it were present and absent, conducive finally to a tendentious multiplication of meanings.)

Shelley had considered Tasso and Job as potential subjects for the poem, but he may in part have been led to settle on Prometheus by the very *pliable* nature of this myth, the classical sources of which differ greatly. Hesiod provides the familiar story wherein Prometheus steals fire from the gods to bring down to earth, but in so doing angers them, and brings to an end the prelapsarian age. But for Shelley, Edens were never lost in the mists of time, but always to be constructed, a preference to which Aeschylus's *Prometheus Bound* is more akin. There, Zeus is angered by the emancipation among men caused by the theft of fire and artistic and scientific skills, and has Prometheus shackled in the mountains where a bird pecks daily at his liver. Prometheus knows but will not reveal that if Zeus marries Thetis, he will produce a son who will topple him, just as he unseated Cronos in his time. This promise of change gives Shelley space in which to introduce his libertarian themes: the avenging son is in Shelley's poem Demogorgon, a figure of multiple function.

The militant departure from feeble catastrophe at the close of *Prometheus Unbound* is of course the unseating of Jupiter 'the tyrant of the world' (III.iv,183), embodiment of institutional and inherited subjection, who has bound Prometheus to an icy precipice in the Indian Caucasus where he is tortured continually for his refusal to acquiesce to the tyrant's rule. Sustained by his love for Asia, Prometheus is liberated finally by forgiveness and the retraction of his curse against Jupiter. The latter is overthrown at the height of his tyranny:

> Rejoice! henceforth I am omnipotent.
> All else had been subdued to me; alone
> The soul of man, like unextinguished fire,
> Yet burns towards heaven with fierce reproach, and doubt,
> And lamentation, and reluctant prayer,
> Hurling up insurrection, which might make
> Our antique empire insecure, though built
> On eldest faith, and hell's coeval fear; (III.i,3–10)

Only tradition ('eldest faith') and fear of penalties for

transgression prevent the progress towards emancipation that Prometheus's commitment to active love and Demogorgon's actions as the embodiment of cyclical change will effect in the poem, and which by analogy Shelley wishes for the non-poetic world. Man becomes in the poem, and in Shelley's eyes ought everywhere to become,

> Sceptreless, free, uncircumscribed, but man
> Equal, unclassed, tribeless, and nationless,
> Exempt from awe, worship, degree, the king
> Over himself; . . . (III.iv,194–97)

This constellation is akin to Godwin's man without hierarchy. By the time of the composition of this poem Shelley had jettisoned the hortatory programme exemplified by the 'Notes On *Queen Mab*,'[3] and in the Preface to *Prometheus Unbound* he eschews didacticism as being a mode natural to prose but not poetry. Nonetheless, *Prometheus Unbound* is unequivocally a poem of opposition, arguing a compassionate socialism which invokes the figure of Christ while repudiating organized religion, and which supersedes but does not betray the poet's adherence to Godwin's *Political Justice*.

And yet Prometheus is not a New Man, nor indeed a discrete entity, and we might subscribe to the reading of the poem offered by Earl R. Wasserman to the extent that the other 'characters' in the work be seen as aspects or projections of the central voice.[4] However most readers would probably not see the need to establish, as Wasserman does, a distinction between the 'One Mind', that Prometheus finally is, and mankind. It may suffice to accept the description of Prometheus volunteered by Shelley in his Preface, whereby

> . . . Prometheus is, as it were, the type of the highest perfection of moral and intellectual nature, impelled by the purest and the truest motives to the best and noblest ends.[5]

Prometheus, then, is humanity at an idealist extreme and outside the bounds of time and discrete identity—or at least this becomes the case after the retraction of the curse against Jupiter. As Wasserman notes:

> But since tyrannic power is only an efficient fiction constituted of the mind's willful abdication of its own will,

> Jupiter has no real and independent existence in the sense
> that Mind or Power does. Tyrannic evil is a lapse of
> the Mind, its negative mode, its reflection in a distorting
> mirror . . .[6]

Jupiter is a fiction, the embodiment of energy relinquished by
mankind, hence reified and institutionalized to the extent that,
although unreal now, it may exercise a tyranny over the human
mind which in fact created it but which, via the progressive
alienation of custom, is unable to overthrow it. So the Phantom of
Jupiter, in repeating Prometheus's original curse against the
'deity' (I.i,262–301) is the shadow of a fiction. In cursing Jupiter,
Prometheus had shown himself enslaved still by the language of
hate—forgiveness dissolves self's connection with the mental
categories of oppression. At this stage in Shelley's idealist
metaphysics, what is real is good: what is evil is finally unreal.
The Phantasm is Jupiter cursing himself, and Jupiter is only an
hallucination prompted by Prometheus's—that is the human
mind's—estrangement from its own truth.

The following lines show how Asia, like the other pseudo-
characters, is also an aspect of central Mind. Panthea speaks:

> And Asia waits in that far Indian vale,
> The scene of her sad exile; rugged once
> And desolate and frozen, like this ravine;
> But now invested with fair flowers and herbs,
> And haunted by sweet airs and sounds, which flow
> Among the woods and waters, from the aether
> Of her transforming presence, which would fade
> If it were mingled not with thine. Farewell! (I.826–33)

The 'vale' is nothing outside of Asia's 'transforming presence'
which has graced it with flowers and herbs and music, but her
person itself would 'fade' to nothing if it were disconnected from
the presence of Prometheus, not simply in a figure of speech of
love, but because she is an aspect of Promethean Mind. (In
addition, line 830 echoes a speech by Caliban in *The Tempest*,
beginning:

> Be not afeard—the isle is full of noises,
> Sounds and sweet airs, that give delight and hurt not:
> (III.ii,133–34)

It may be argued that the isle in Shakespeare's play is contained

and activated by the central Mind of Prospero, just as the actions
and characters of Shelley's poem are contained in the Mind of
Prometheus.)

In one sense the whole poem is an extended articulation of
'transforming presence', since whatever purely narrative or
dramatic material exists in the work is subordinated to a tirelessly
energetic supply of metaphor and simile, the component
elements of which tropes are generally of equal weight, that is to
say not a matter of decoration or rhetorical emphasis, but rather
the substance of the poem's prime moves. Density and difficulty
in the verbal surface are not therefore a temporary impediment
to a proper reading, a block which ought to disappear after
habituation to the text has taken place; the sum of tropes forms
the poem, and language here draws attention to its own
materiality. In Act IV, in particular, it is no longer relevant to
ask what is 'happening' in any usual sense, whereby language
would merely be a transparent medium through which reference
might be made to events supposedly persisting outside the
purview of the work. Act IV is arguably an extended
development of the lyrics interspersed in the first three Acts of the
poem. At the level of design, these lyrics are pendants, clearly, or
provide respite from the main discourse, but they are also a minor
component that will swell at last into a major theme. Comforts to
Prometheus, they are glimpses of the transformed world we will
see in Act IV after the downfall of Jupiter.

> *Ione*:                    Even whilst we speak
>       New notes arise. What is that awful sound?
> *Panthea*: 'Tis the deep noise of the rolling world
>       Kindling within the strings of the waved air
>       Æolian modulations.
> *Ione*:                    Listen too,
>       How every pause is filled with under-notes,
>       Clear, silver, icy, keen, awakening tones,
>       Which pierce the sense, and live within the soul,
>       As the sharp stars pierce the winter's crystal air
>       And gaze upon themselves within the sea.
> *Panthea*: But see where through two openings in the forest
>       Which hanging branches overcanopy, . . .
>                              (IV.i,184–95)

If we were to expect of these lines descriptive reference to

common experiences outside the poem then they would seem
pretty but thin, at best. Panthea's first reply would communicate
little, albeit grandly, and her second reply might seem to follow
too sharply the most climactic burst of images in these lines. They
should be read not as pointers towards an external reality but as
constituting reality itself. Acts of perception in Shelley's texts are
nothing if not phenomena thrown up by this ceaselessly changing
'real', and objects are nothing if not productions of signifying
perception. Panthea's first reply engenders metaphorical music
punctuated by silence ('every pause') which cannot be nothing
since the 'pauses' are distinctly perceptible. They are then
supplanted by phenomena lacking existence outside this poem
('under-notes'), whose connotations engender 'awakening tones'
which find their being 'within the soul', itself, as we know now,
yet another projection of the poem's idealized central Mind.
These 'tones' are compared to, and indeed—the rhetorical bias is
so forceful—effectively *become* those stars, self-reflexive but
humanized in an image-cluster so autonomously powerful that it
rejects its expected status as decoration and takes its place as
primary element in the lines' meaning. In addition, these two
lines,

> As the sharp stars pierce winter's crystal air
> And gaze upon themselves within the sea . . . , (ll.192–93)

although depicting the entry of one phenomenon, the stars, into
two other media, the atmosphere and sea, use words whose
connotations are the same for all three elements. In other words,
'crystal' follows naturally from and might directly be applied to
'sharp stars', in terms of connotation, and the same might be said
for the 'sea', since 'gaze' is such an appropriately hard and sharp-
edged verb. Given this, and the fact that the stars have travelled
from limit to limit of the earth, from beyond the atmosphere to
the depth of the ocean, self-reflexively gazing on themselves as
they go, the whole world is as it were included in these lines. Yet
even this miniature crystal world is immediately supplanted, as
sound creates sense in the move from 'sea' (l.193) to 'see' (l.194).
The writing *enacts*, and does not *describe*, the ceaseless movements
of non-dualistic, non-hierarchical reality, a point emphasized by
the fact that the next 'image' to follow the crystalline world is the
presence of an absence ('two openings'), signifying again that

what is perceptible must in some sense *be*, and with a non-hierarchical equality, whether we're dealing with stars or small spaces. In addition I would suggest that poetic autonomy is stressed here by a deliberate echo of lines from the opening of the poem, where the protagonist says:

> The crawling glaciers pierce me with the spears
> Of their moon-freezing crystals . . . (I.i,31–32)

Here by contrast (IV.i, 188–93), to be 'pierced' by ice is to be entered with pleasure by sound recalling humanized stars. Discrete, local identity, as Prometheus endures before the bursting of his bonds, feels the ceaseless change perfusing the material world as a threat, as I said might be the case for the Wordsworthian 'sublime ego.' To apprehend reality fully is to recognize that we produce it constantly and give it meaning through cognizance, which is nothing if not one more production of reality.

Here is another example:

> Hark! the rushing snow!
> The sun-awakened avalanche! whose mass,
> Thrice sifted by the storm, had gathered there
> Flake after flake, in heaven-defying minds
> As thought by thought is piled, till some great truth
> Is loosened, and the nations echo round,
> Shaken to their roots, as do the mountains now.
> (II.iii,36–42)

We begin with an external landscape which is made suddenly psychological in line 39 by an unexpected reversal of the conventional use of simile; we might expect 'as thought by thought' to come first, stressing the dualistic difference between mind and avalanche, subject and object, but the unusual reversal casts doubt on the external nature of the landscape, shifting the bias of the poetic action to mind rather than mountain. Yet no sooner have we become used to that than line 42 returns us to the 'mountains'. We expect one half of a metaphor or simile, the first as a rule, to be privileged over the other, but those lines will not submit to that procedure. Meaning oscillates constantly between what is 'inner' and what 'outer', implying not only that each gives the other meaning, but that each is to be found within the other. It need not be stressed that such tropes in Shelley's work do not come to rest or fit inside each other with a 'Chinese box' effect, but proceed immediately to dissolution succeeded by new phrases. At times, this is done by association, at times by allowing the second pictorial component in a metaphor to spawn images inherent in its own logic, which then in turn produce what is to be the first element in the next line. And at times sound creates sense. It is probably correct to read instances of this in Shelley's work as the fruits of excitement during composition, though this shouldn't either devalue them, or send the reader back to a romantic image of the Poet, pouring out his lines in a fine frenzy. Even these merely local effects illustrate the Romantic view that perceptual organization, and truth, make use of analogy as well as linear cause-and-effect. This production of sense by sound can be sharply distinguished from onomatopoeia, the echoic linkage of sound with sense. Shelley makes comparatively sparing use of onomatopoeia; it is notable that Tennyson's writing, which uses it habitually, tends often towards the hypnotic and towards a quite un-Shelleyan fixation of interest, productive of realism rather than the enacted real. (Tennyson's poetic realism offers a plausible mimicry of the surface of a perceived phenomenon: it is an aural technique that often has a visual result, which, conjured in the reader's mind may, paradoxically, falsify reality by its vividness, as in photographs and films certain vivid visual effects tend to push the perceiver into an unnatural detachment from the perceived.)

Shelley's politics and poetics argue unqualified rejection of the *status quo* throughout his career. It is axiomatic now that there is no poetic technique or form that does not carry with it a corresponding political belief, even where the author may have been unconscious of the political component in his or her text. Just as Shelley in life did not waver in his opposition to the Jupiters of church, state, and private morals, so his poetic forms habitually offer wastrel action, investments of celebrant attention that are lateral, forgetful of hierarchy and dismissive of the enforced taxonomies of property, sex, and selfhood, as is exemplified by his regeneratively explosive use of metaphor. But it would I think be misleading to impose the codes of contemporary poetry or contemporary politics on his work, or to imply that it merits praise to the degree with which it conforms to our present-day preoccupations. (This topic is awkward, because it is also the case that a text cannot be abstracted from a certain historical context, that context being not the author's, but the reader's. For while the latter includes an obviously subjective component, the former is available only through acts of reconstitution, which must by their nature include a subjective component too.) Even in the early *Address to the Irish People*,[7] a prose tract composed at a stage in Shelley's career when his preferred rhetoric could be fiery and extreme, the poet's advocacy of the overthrow of English imperialism, followed by advance towards socialism, insists on non-violent reformism rather than revolt. In the same way, his purely poetic trajectory, while militantly subversive of fixed meaning, does not aim for the abolition of memory, as the oneirically socialist programme of the Surrealist movement in our own century has done, with a nihilistic squandering of all revered signification. Shelley does choose to maintain a purchase on certain revered signs. The figure of Christ in *Prometheus Unbound* is one example. Towards the end of Act I, during the torture of Prometheus by the Furies, Panthea tells Ione she has seen:

A woful sight: a youth
With patient looks nailed to a crucifix. (I.584–85)

It is (properly) unclear by the lights of Shelley's beliefs whether or not this figure is Christ seen by Prometheus or Prometheus himself under torture, both in Shelley's eyes being man raised to his ideal potential. The sentiment of these lines is humanist, though it is clearly a tendency of Romantic poetry to voyage into areas previously occupied by religion, unable to accept its answers but continuing to pose its questions. Shelley was vehemently against the church but adhered to the militant pacifism and egalitarianism based for centuries, and pre-eminently in the West, in the figure of Christ.

In Shelley's work perception and morality cannot be separated. The mechanisms of liberation in *Prometheus Unbound* hinge always on forgiveness and love, and I would contend that the operations of love and the operations of poetic language are exactly analogous to Shelley. In *A Defence of Poetry* he treats of 'the manner in which poetry acts to produce the moral improvement of man' and proceeds via the formulation that poetry

> . . . awakens and enlarges the mind itself by rendering it the receptacle of a thousand unapprehended combinations of thought.[8]

And so the production of manifold meanings described earlier is related directly to moral good. Shelley continues:

> The great secret of morals is love; or a going out of our own nature . . .[9]

and it would not be simplistic to claim that a fundamental poetic operation in *Prometheus Unbound* is the discharge of words out of their customary and singular nature into areas of proliferating, thence indeterminate, thence inexhaustible meaning.

To support this we might look to the lines spoken by Demogorgon in the poem. It is hard to say what Demogorgon represents in Shelley's metaphysics, and the only sure conclusion is that his, or its, symbolic function is by its very nature veiled. By the standards of the rest of the text, this character's utterances are curtailed, cryptic and marked by a stress on their conditional nature, their merely local or temporary applicability. Jupiter asks:

> Awful shape, what art thou? Speak!
> *Demogorgon*: Eternity. Demand no direr name.
>
> > (III.i,51–52)

and Asia's dialogue with Demogorgon is equally opaque:

> *Demogorgon*: All spirits are enslaved which serve things evil:
> > Thou knowest if Jupiter be such or no.
> *Asia*: Whom calledst thou God?
> *Demogorgon*:                    I spoke but as ye speak,
> > For Jove is the supreme of living things.
> *Asia*: Who is the master of the slave?
> *Demogorgon*:                    If the abysm
> > Could vomit forth its secrets . . . But a voice
> > Is wanting, the deep truth is imageless;
> > For what would it avail to bid thee gaze
> > On the revolving world? What to bid speak
> > Fate, Time, Occasion, Chance, and Change? To these
> > All things are subject but eternal Love.
>
> > (II.iv,110–20)

Line 113 stresses the relativistic and limited nature of linguistic communication: to 'speak but as ye speak' is to say not what is utterly true, but what makes sense within 'your' limited terms of reference. The line is not a repudiation of linguistic multiplicity but a pointer to areas literally unspeakable and beyond identity, no matter how generalized and idealized. Asia, as noted earlier, is ultimately an aspect of the Promethean Mind but beyond 'mind' are processes unassimilable by the poem's attitudes. We might interpret these lines and Demogorgon's function as signifying that, from the poet's coign of vantage, language, no matter how multiform, does not of itself give us the world entire. The list of conditioning factors given by Demogorgon—fate, time, occasion, chance and change—are linked by their limiting nature and propensity to *end* human activity. Only love escapes because whatever its context, linguistic or pre-linguistic, it pre-empts stoppage, stasis or decay.

## II

That *Epipsychidion* exemplifies Shelley's characteristic practice in its ardour and fiery lyricism is commonly agreed. A greater and peculiar importance may be claimed for the poem if we recognize its attempt to push Romantic idealism to the uttermost limit, while at the same time offering a critique of that extremism and providing illustrations of failure attaching to it. While the figure of Prometheus represents an ideal, whose significance nevertheless has a profoundly important bearing on the everyday social world, the speaker and his subject in *Epipsychidion* stem from what is nakedly subjective. Yet the poem struggles away from the initiating confessional mode in order to reach towards commonly shared experience, lyrical though the expression may still remain at the close. Demogorgon stands in relation to the rest of *Prometheus Unbound* as evidence that Prometheus, although he is idealized central Mind representing Man, cannot convey the whole truth of existence. Demogorgon does not provide an impediment to the principal movement of the verse, but his utterances are in a markedly different key, and he embodies the possibility of immense additional 'outside' factors, which though they do not inhibit it, nevertheless imply limits to human capability. *Epipsychidion* is more ardent but less optimistic than

*Prometheus Unbound* and, alongside its poetic successes, the poem offers a series of failures (in some ways structural analogues to Demogorgon), certain of which may be seen as imaginative flaws, while others are tendentious but capturing admissions of defeat for the projects of idealism.

The dangers of attaching poetic effect to biographical cause are axiomatic, but *Epipsychidion* stems pointedly from encounters and relationships in Shelley's life. However, it may be useful to consider Emilia Viviani, the poem's inspiration and dedicatee, not only as a person who has entered literature, but as one who in her own person carried connotations of the literary, even before the composition of the poem.

Emilia was a Contessa, and at the age of nineteen was forced to undergo a traditional Italian custom of being incarcerated in a convent while her parents looked around for a husband of appropriate wealth and standing. She clearly excited Shelley's commiseration and desire, in a manner it would be fruitless to try precisely to define and quantify. It can only be concluded that whatever the nature of the private feeling expended on Emilia, she was extremely useful to the poet as a subject. In a most vivid way, she had been reduced to an object of exchange in the social stakes. A victim of sexist prejudice and familial scheming, she lay at the mercy of many of the social evils Shelley inveighed against at a theoretical level in his writing. In addition, she seems to have taken pains to present herself in a literary light, and in his biography of the poet, Tom Medwin compares her within the space of only a few lines to 'a Greek Muse in the Florence Gallery', busts by Bartolini and portraits of Beatrice Cenci, drawing so many veils of idealized beauty around her that no real contours remain.[10] Her letters to Shelley seem to have been consciously Petrarchan, and so she was in a sense a literary artefact from the outset, a self-conscious prototype of the poetic ideal both in her own and the poet's eyes.

Shelley's reading at the time of this friendship naturally enough included Dante's *Vita Nuova*, and the invocations of *Epipsychidion* repose on that work, as they do on Petrarch's sonnets, Spenser's *Epithalamion* (perhaps partly responsible for Shelley's title), *The Song of Songs*, and the whole genre of erotic yet idealist adoration. But it cannot be concluded that the poet viewed this genre as a settled tradition to which his poem made genuflection and within which it might finally take its place. In *Prometheus Unbound*, clearly neither Shelley's use of Neoplatonic ideas about the relationship between the real and the ideal, nor his echoes of Milton and the Old Testament make him a believer or a copybook Platonist; rather they show him using or subverting what he chose from a common literary store whose contents also furnished fixed platforms along a daring trajectory which required such points of stability both for himself and his reader. And so, with regard to *Epipsychidion* the poet's attitude to the books of love is dissenting, self-consciously problematic and content only in making local use of what it steals. The poem projects a secular idealism of its own, echoing sources to evidence a certain degree of seriousness that does not entail allegiance. At the close, delighting in but finding wanting its own Utopian drive, the poem ceases abruptly, leaving the reader to construct a judgement or solution. Shelley probably anticipated a misreading of his text and a reader unwilling to engage in this labour to construct meaning rather than remain passively in receipt of it. Certainly his Advertisement to *Epipsychidion* refers to a class for whom it

> . . . must ever remain incomprehensible, from a defect of a common organ of perception for the ideas of which it treats.[11]

The 'defect' may not merely be an ignorance of the surface relations of a poem to events and to previous poetries, or a crass reaction to the transiently scandalous, but an unwillingness to let words work at a theoretical level, for conceptual adventure is wedded to, but need not in all instances have sympathy for, the emotional specifics of a poem.

Shelley's references to *Epipsychidion* in letters reinforce a reading of the poem as being simultaneously dissenting and idealistic. In a letter to John Gisborne of 18 June 1822, the poet said of this work:

> It is an idealized history of my life and feelings. I think one is always in love with something or other; the error, and I confess it is not easy for spirits cased in flesh and blood to avoid it, consists in seeking in a mortal image the likeness of what is perhaps eternal.[12]

The movement from cavalier dismissal of Emilia ('something or other') to contemplation of the eternal is startling but accurate, surely, to the dual sense in which this catalyst would be discarded, without cruelty but in favour of whatever stimulus came next, while yet remaining 'a mortal image' of what is beyond mortality.

*Epipsychidion* begins and ends in tendentious failure. I propose a division of the poem into three sections, siting the first between lines 1 and 190. The first seventy lines of the text constitute a failed attempt to find tropes adequately descriptive of the speaker's ideal love, while the remainder of that section draws Pyrrhic victory from the attempt by turning attention away from the single form to be described and toward the variety of metaphors summoned in the describing. Is Emilia a 'bird', 'Heart', 'Seraph', 'Moon', 'Terror', 'Mirror', 'Lamp', 'Smile', 'Lute', or 'grave'? The 'world of fancies' volunteers a gorgeous cascade of comparisons, often contradictory; each trope is discarded as soon as it is voiced. And yet although language has in a sense failed its non-linguistic target, she is far from distant:

I am not thine: I am a part of *thee*. (1.52)

In failing to reach her the poèt fails simultaneously to reach two aspects of selfhood, of one of which he is himself a part, an ideal to which he is raised and whose proliferations power the verse. But *Epipsychidion* is troubled by the original aim which the writing may not quite relinquish—the presentation of Emilia as a single, bounded entity. This conflict between the multiple ideal and the limited actual persists in the poem, but at this stage the dominant idea is that although discrete identity may not be conveyed accurately, the variety of images engendered by the thought of Emilia may finally say more about her true value than a portrait or apt comparison drawn from the 'world of fancies' ever could.

So at last Emilia is:

A Metaphor of Spring and Youth and Morning; (1.120)

This line prompts some slight visualization but its primary action is conceptual, making us read Emilia as an agent of vitality rather than sterility, of what is abundant rather than single. Without at all leaving its originating subject, the writing now takes theoretical wing and range, broadening its compass in its attack

on the notion of the singular, be it in 'modern morals' or
philosophical contemplation. The poet's love is not possessive or
exclusive, and the final worth of Emilia lies not in her own
person, as object, but in the revision of the world she causes in her
relations with the poet as he continues to live in the world. The
consequences of this for conventional marriage ties are made
absolutely clear:

> I never was attached to that great sect,
> Whose doctrine is, that each one should select
> Out of the crowd a mistress or a friend,
> And all the rest, though fair and wise, commend
> To cold oblivion, though it is in the code
> Of modern morals, and the beaten road
> Which those poor slaves with weary footsteps tread
> Who travel to their home among the dead
> By the broad highway of the world, and so
> With one chained friend, perhaps a jealous foe,
> The dreariest and the longest journey go. (ll.149–59)

These lines move at the steadiest tempo of any in the poem. The
production of images is not fast and furious as is the case with the
earlier rhapsodic lines addressed to the girl, and the argument is
straightforward. It may therefore be worth examining the
reasons why the lines might be misread, as they were by Desmond
King-Hele who says of Shelley in connection with this passage:

> Though theoretically he still favoured the free love of
> *Political Justice*, he would probably, like Godwin, have
> admitted that human nature was too imperfect for abolition
> of marriage ties to be a desirable reform. Caught in this
> equivocal attitude, he took refuge in a good-humoured
> protest against convention . . .[13]

I lay stress on this misreading because it is typical of a kind of
foisted rehabilitation of Shelley common particularly perhaps to
British critics who have tended to represent the poet's
libertarianism as something which he had in *Queen Mab* but let go
by degrees, conforming to the familiar liberal stereotype of
radical youth made sadder, wiser, but more presentable by time
and experience.[14] Shelley's abandonment of the hortatory
programme has at least as much to do with rhetoric and poetics as

it has with any sign of a change of heart, and *Epipsychidion* is as heretical a text as 'Song to the Men of England'.

To return to the quotation from King-Hele, the pivotal term here is 'probably'; in other words it is not certain, at all, that Shelley would have balked at the disappearance of 'marriage ties', but this particular reader would rather that he had. And if he *had* balked at such a change in *mores*, taken for granted in our own day, then perhaps he would indeed have been 'caught' in an 'equivocal attitude'. But it may be argued to the contrary that the import of these lines from *Epipsychidion* is as clear as daylight. The term 'good-humoured' is not in any way appropriate to the tone of this passage for it connotes genial relaxation when the writing is in fact poised between severity, in its attack on custom, and saddened commiseration, aroused by the 'poor slaves'. The 'great sect' is clearly the broad mass, coerced by custom into monogamy, life with one who is at best a 'chained friend' and at worst 'a jealous foe'. The passage shows an adept balance in its range of tones, caustic at a theoretical level and yet kept far from being patronizing or dismissive by a lucid sensitivity to the human mistakes it describes. There is a fierce Romanticism in the preference for variety over constriction, but the writing, which employs, curiously, the pentameters and rhyming couplets favoured by Pope, might also convince by the clipped and astringent delivery of its thought.

It is not even monogamy alone that is attacked, but any form of exclusive choice that restricts human potential:

> Narrow
> The heart that loves, the brain that contemplates,
> The life that wears, the spirit that creates
> One object, and one form, and builds thereby
> A sepulchre for its eternity. (ll.169–73)

In a deliberate undercutting of the conventional poem of ideal love, Shelley makes it clear that Emilia is not to be a life-partner, or an object of obsessive or exclusive attention. Rather she is to be a sign, a stimulus or catalyst, an instigator of release of imprisoned meaning, expression of the endless change perfusing the material world and offered in truthful opposition to the restrictions of any dogma.

I take the second section of *Epipsychidion* to run from line 190 to line 387, where the word 'Paradise' announces the final movement, with its ambiguous closing articulation of Utopian flight together with descent to the universe of dualism. This second, middle, section draws on past experiences to support the assertion that being in the world is synonymous with participation in and furtherance of ceaseless change. This truth is not merely unacknowledged in the public world, but is a perception won by the poet only through lived experience: it is not innate. He tells of his unwise efforts to recapture the past after the death of a lover:

> And half bewildered by new forms, I passed,
> Seeking among those untaught foresters
> If I could find one form resembling hers . . . (ll.252–54)

These failures to forget the old and face the new lead only to a sterile encounter (ll.256–66). There follow enactments of more equivocal *liaisons* prior to the return of Emily as ideal. Although this middle section of the poem reinforces dramatically the espousal of multiplicity in experience announced by the opening section, it is the weakest stretch of writing in the text. The explosive idealism of the first section, finding hidden victory in the inadequacies of descriptive language, is symmetrically aligned with the Utopian trajectory of the poem's closing movement which finds Pyrrhic victory again in death (and so perhaps in this case a possible union with the ideal). Similarly, both sections contain a seed of doubt: in the first, that the single stable self *is* the true identity, which cannot be conveyed by language: and in the last, that the world as it is conflicts catastrophically with the world as we would have it.

This central section sags: forward motion is impeded as Shelley elects to return to narratives of the past, and the writing swerves indecisively between veiled autobiography and symbolic utterance. The first woman described seems based on the suicide Harriet, Shelley's first wife. The vampire figure 'whose voice was venomed melody' (1.256) may by the account of the poet's latest biographer be a prostitute, as prematurely grey hair, mentioned here, was thought at that time to be indicative of venereal infection.[15] The next lover mentioned is based on Mary Shelley; Claire Clairmont, who drifted for a while between Shelley and Byron, and bore a child by the latter, also makes a brief appearance. But these figures are not sufficiently detailed as portraits to be referred ultimately to the women in Shelley's circle. Yet neither are they sufficiently potent to be responded to as archetypes, whether void of autobiographical components or not. The writing is overloaded and perhaps spoiled by the attempt to describe experiences as being at one and the same time unique and psychologically typical. It is at this point that the failure of the projects of idealism to consort with the knowledge of the actual is different in kind from the tendentious 'failures' of the first and third sections—valuable risks of self as they are—and becomes a flaw. Shelley cannot decide the degree to which he wants to offer archetypally active signs, whose tendency would naturally be towards common experience, or autobiographical data, whose drift is always backwards to a single source.

The final section commences with the line:

The day is come, and thou wilt fly with me. (1.388)

The poet describes a Utopia, a 'favoured place' (1.461) owing something to the landscape of 'Kubla Khan', to which he and Emilia might fly to live out the poem's libertarian and aesthetic ideals. This 'wreck of paradise' (1.423) is externalized, made a habitable place, but it is primarily a psychological landscape of unfettered selfhood. It is a projection into the future but also a present-tense articulation of prelapsarian yearning. Utopias occur frequently in Shelley's work—towards the end of *Prometheus Unbound*, for example—but failure is built into the experience of this isle, making it untypical.

The persistence historically of urges towards such versions of Paradise lends support to the view that Romanticism was not a bounded movement ending with the death of Sir Walter Scott, but actually the dominant artistic mode of the last two hundred years, taking as its central, abiding project the investigation of selfhood. Just as this investigation can be carried out against a religious background even while producing anti- or post-religious conclusions, so behind the freest, most open non-metrical verse-form (in Europe at least), fixed form can still be discerned, not necessarily as a residue, but with a new offended status. Romanticism holds the poetries of our own time within its compass. Just as the poetics of expanded awareness have had to deal with residual dualism as a Caliban within the new settlement, so the idea of Paradise has divided what might for the sake of brevity be termed a 'light' from a 'dark' Romanticism. The poets of light, for example Blake, Shelley, or Whitman, tend often to approach the idea of paradise as a projection into the future, present to us only as a possibility, but to be constructed. For the dark Romantics—Poe, or Baudelaire—paradise is not to be discovered, but is rather a garden from which we are cast out, embodied here by childhood, there by rhapsodic episode only temporarily a warrant against detachment or despair. On the dark side, death may prove ironically to be a saving grace, providing the unity of being that life promised but then withdrew. In *Epipsychidion*, Shelley tries for the light, aims to make of bliss a communicable possibility. But at the close of the poem, the aspiring urge towards the breaking up of the final bonds, those of the singular self, hits, and cannot negotiate, the facts of death.

> Woe is me!
> The wingèd words on which my soul would pierce
> Into the heart of Love's rare Universe,
> Are chains of lead around its flight of fire—
> I pant, I sink, I tremble, I expire! (ll.587–91)

There is climax here, on a level that has been thought to connote orgasm, but on a theoretical level *Epipsychidion* has no conclusion, as such; it simply ceases to proceed. It is a text of such extremity that it lets the voyaging self beat against the final bars of death in an admission of possible failure, incarceration at the point of most nearly boundless bliss, mirroring, with 'wingèd' and 'flight', the imagery of Emilia's incarceration in the convent of St. Anna that occurred at the beginning of the poem:

> Poor captive bird! who, from thy narrow cage,
> Pourest such music . . . (ll.5–6)

The possibility of failure is thrown open to us, together with the postmortem projection of the isle, not in weakness, but rather as an invitation to complete, to act, ourselves. The poem lays bare the ultimate tendency of Romanticism, and our own poetries are still quite within its concerns. Shelley's pre-eminence in this connection should not be seen from the vantage point of a retrospective avant-gardeism, which given the extremities of

Romanticism in our time would be pleased by a precedent extremism, but should be accorded him in connection with his treatment of problems of dualism. These are not, in his work, stumbling blocks on the way to a non-dualistic end, but are included in his poetry from the far side of achieved non-dualistic and veridical writing. Although the texts are autonomous, their successes in this sphere draw attention to Shelley's politics; though it is the business of poetry to interpret the world and the business of politics to transform it, a hope implicit in these poems is for the inauguration of a mutually-defining dialogue between the two.

## NOTES

1. Clark, 285.

2. *Poetical Works*, 205.

3. *Poetical Works*, 300–35.

4. 'Prometheus has no antagonist but himself . . . The only real and autonomously existing actors in Shelley's cosmic design are the One Mind', Earl R. Wasserman, *Shelley's Prometheus Unbound: A Critical Reading* (1971), 112.

5. *Poetical Works*, 205.

6. Wasserman, op. cit., 258.

7. Written Jan.–Feb. 1812; see Clark, 39–40.

8. Clark, 282.

9. Clark, ibid.

10. Thomas Medwin, *The Life of Percy Bysshe Shelley*, ed. H. Buxton Forman (1913), 279.

11. *Poetical Works*, 411.

12. *Letters* ii. 434.

13. Desmond King-Hele, *Shelley: His Thought and Works* (1971 edn.), 273.

14. On modern critical responses to Shelley's ideas see further Miriam Allott, 'Attitudes to Shelley', pp. 1–39 above.

15. Richard Holmes, *Shelley: The Pursuit* (1974), 638.

# The Transformation of Discourse:
## *Epipsychidion, Adonais,*
## and some lyrics

### BERNARD BEATTY

I

We have become accustomed, in England especially, to two
Shelleys. One is the supreme lyricist of Palgrave's *Golden Treasury*,
dethroned by Scrutineers and New Critics. The other is the
'urbane' Shelley of Donald Davie's splendid essay in *Purity of
Diction in English Verse*.[1] This second Shelley seems to have been
accepted as a respectable figure and has thus effaced the New
Criticism sterotype much more extensively and rapidly than
F. A. Pottle had thought possible in 1952 when he wrote that,

> The disesteem of Shelley is going to become general and it
> may continue for a century or more.[2]

One result of this improved reputation is that we are much less
likely to patronize Shelley than, say, the Scrutineers were. Even
Davie felt obliged to preface his demonstration of urbanity in
Shelley's familiar style by a few orthodox gestures of demolition.
Shelley has his faults of course but we are much less likely to
assume that we know all there is to know about them. May it not
be, for example, that there is a closer and much more conscious
relation between Shelley's urbanity and his lyrical extravagance
than Davie assumed?

Byron wrote in *Don Juan* (a poem much admired by Shelley),

> The night—(I sing by night—sometimes an owl,
> And now and then a nightingale) (XV.xcvii)

and thus acknowledged neatly the relation between discourse
and lyricism in his poem. Clearly *Don Juan* is a poem which juxtaposes the two for complicated purposes, one of which certainly

is to defend the possibility of a discursive base for poetry at a time when, as Byron divined correctly, that base was under attack. Shelley never saw it like this and his lyrics were used later in the century as vindications of the opposite opinion. Yet Shelley could and did write excellent verse based on discourse and never saw the necessity to cut himself off wholly from habits of diction, genre, and general procedure that had been established in Augustan poetry. The contrast with Keats is striking and wholly to Shelley's advantage.

To establish however the continuation of Augustan harmonies in Shelley's verse alongside his experiments in lyrical dissonance is insufficient. What is the relation between the two and how conscious is Shelley of that relation? Consider for instance these lines from a securely 'urbane' poem:

> and when we die
> We'll toss up who died first of drinking tea,
> And cry out,—'Heads or tails?' where'er we be.
> Near that a dusty paint-box, some odd hooks,
> A half-burnt match, an ivory block, three books,
> Where conic sections, spherics, logarithms,
> To great Laplace, from Saunderson and Sims,
> Lie heaped in their harmonious disarray
> Of figures . . . ('Letter to Maria Gisborne', ll.89–97)

The habit of mind behind these lines appears to be not so very different from that of Pope's noting the harmonious disarray of Belinda's dressing table. Shelley, like Pope, assumes too that snatches of conversation can be accommodated naturally in verse. Nor is there any suggestion that human artifacts, scientific equipment, non-literary proper names, arranged in what Keats called disenchantedly,

> the dull catalogue of common things ('Lamia' II 233)

need disperse the charms of poetry. A few lines further on, Shelley gives us another list:

> the thunder-smoke
> Is gathering on the mountains, like a cloak
> Folded athwart their shoulders broad and bare;
> The ripe corn under the undulating air

Undulates like an ocean;—and the vines
Are trembling wide in all their trellised lines—
The murmur of the awakening sea doth fill
The empty pauses of the blast . . .
              ('Letter to Maria Gisborne', ll.116–23)

We could hail this passage as more distinctively Romantic in its
earnest, almost portentous, concentration upon and elevation of
natural phenomena. Yet it is, in rhetorical outline, clearly
derived from the carefully composed pictorialism of Augustan
taste[3] and emphatically generalized. Moreover the sense of
wonder that informs these lines has its urbane roots in a precisely
late Augustan sense of how a pastoral and picturesque scene can
be elevated to sublimity by a thunderstorm. Second thoughts, as
usual, are the best. The first list (lines 89–97), that Apollonian
catalogue of artifacts, is less urbane than we might think. For
when Shelley wants to suggest a transformation of ordinary
consciousness into some more direct participation in the
everlasting flow of universal life he frequently uses the device of a
list, shifting from one reference to another with bewildering
rapidity and consciously confusing mental and physical
phenomena. The word 'consciously' may be justified by Shelley's
Preface to *Prometheus Unbound*:

> The imagery which I have employed will be found, in many
> instances, to have been drawn from the operations of the
> human mind, or from those external actions by which they
> are expressed. This is unusual in modern poetry, although
> Dante and Shakespeare are full of instances of the same
> kind: Dante indeed more than any other poet, and with
> greater success.[4]

This reference to Dante is very much to our purpose for Dante is,
supremely, the poet of urbanity and lyricism. *The Divine Comedy*
composes its lyrical intensities in an evidently rational and
categorizing structure yet that structure itself proceeds from and
terminates in lyrical impulse. Shelley's admiration for the kinship
with the great Florentine, which C. S. Lewis defends so ably,[5] is
thus far a matter of poetic temperament and procedure. But for
Shelley, the interrelation of urbanity and lyricism was necessarily
a problem, one might say *the* problem, in a sense that it was not
for Dante.

Behind Dante lies Scholasticism and the Fathers. The ultimate coincidence of History and Providence, Roman Empire and Roman Church, Reason and Faith, Discourse and Logos, City and Song, was not the fruit of Dante's own anguished speculation nor kept in being simply by his verse. Behind Shelley lies an Enlightenment that his friend Peacock had presented as finally scotching the anti-urbane myths upon which poetry depends. Shelley, of course, wrote *A Defence of Poetry* to disprove this thesis. But he would not have done so had he not felt the damaging force of Peacock's argument.[6] Moreover though we read Shelley's tract rather than Peacock's, we do not do so for its argument but for its fervour and its fine phrases. This is indicative as we shall see. Only in the French Revolution and its surrogate eruptions is there, from Shelley's point of view, an apparent coincidence of reason and song which exists outside the poetry called into being by it. At the very least, the possibility must have been maddeningly present to Shelley's mind that Peacock's views, reinforced as they are by such celebrated contemporaries as Walter Scott and Chateaubriand, were right and that Dante's Europe depended upon a creative fusion which modern Reason had knowingly repudiated.

The picture is not as clear as I am making it. In different ways, many of Shelley's poems rely on some state of affairs which pre-exist the poem. We hear, from Shelley as well as from his commentators, of Shelley's Platonism, Godwinism, belief in 'the one Spirit's plastic stress' (*Adonais*, l.381) and much else besides; moreover the scientific accuracy of many of Shelley's apparently impressionistic lines is well-established and an important factor in his rehabilitation. Nevertheless if we have erred in the past by not crediting Shelley with this kind of hard-headed fidelity to fact, we need not fall into the opposite error of supposing that scientific accuracy necessarily guarantees the objectivity of what is asserted. Why is it necessary for some extra kind of excitement to be generated, in the verse as in the *Defence of Poetry*, in order to make us accept Shelley's intention? Take for instance these lines from one of the fine passages in *Epipsychidion*:

> The glory of her being, issuing thence,
> Stains the dead, blank, cold air with a warm shade
> Of unentangled intermixture, made

By Love, of light and motion: one intense
Diffusion, one serene Omnipresence,
Whose flowing outlines mingle in their flowing,
Around her cheeks and utmost fingers glowing
With the unintermitted blood, which there
Quivers, (as in a fleece of snow-like air
The crimson pulse of living morning quiver,)
Continuously prolonged, and ending never,
Till they are lost, and in that Beauty furled
Which penetrates and clasps and fills the world;
Scarce visible from extreme loveliness. (ll.91–104)

Timothy Webb, in his recent selection from Shelley's poems,
comments:

This passage seems to combine the language of science with
that of religious devotion.[7]

He goes on to explain the science but does not specify the religious
devotion. That is understandable. The devotional language is
clearly Dantesque. What is unclear, both obscured and brought
into prominence by the scientific imprecision, is the status of this
'language of religious devotion'. Is 'Love' (l.94) as substantial as
light? Dante devotes a whole section of *The New Life*[8] to clarifying
his use of the word 'Love', establishing very carefully the sense in
which 'Love' is a conceit and an entity. In Shelley's lines, we
encounter a conceit posed as an entity. Shelley's conception here
to that of Dante is as Fonthill Abbey to Chartres. The distinction
I have in mind is evidenced most clearly by the engaging self-
consciousness that informs 'The Witch of Atlas'.

Clearly this poem is both urbane and lyrical. Nor does this
fusion depend upon excitement but upon calculated
whimsicality and open acknowledgement of the lack of
corroborating beliefs necessary to substantiate its fictions. This
acknowledgement frames the poem. The first stanza admits that
in the present time, all too conscious of the distinction between
Error and Truth, we are left with

nothing to believe in, worth
The pains of putting into learnèd rhyme . . . (ll.53–54)

The last lines of 'The Witch of Atlas' complete the frame around
it. The poem will be continued at another time,

for it is
A tale more fit for the weird winter nights
Than for these garish summer days, when we
Scarcely believe much more than we can see. (ll.669–72)

Needless to say this 'frame' does not call attention to some solemn
crisis of faith but is a deliberate enabling device analogous to an
extended conceit yet delicately in touch with Shelley's real sense
of human limitation and his unsuppressed need for some
validating vision of human life. However, if Shelley knows that
this is in fact the firmest—certainly the coolest—base available to
him for that fusion of discursive enquiry and visionary certainty
which he recognized in Dante then what did he intend us to do
with *Epipsychidion* and *Adonais?*

## II

*Epipsychidion* certainly is intended to excite us. Shelley can
elongate sentences, piling up clauses and couplets so as to render
his reader breathless, agitated, and susceptible. This is, in the first
instance, a physical effect. We know that Shelley took a peculiar
pleasure in frightening young ladies of his acquaintance by
nightmare stories.[9] He manipulates his readers in a disturbingly
similar fashion. 'The Witch of Atlas' is disarmingly free from such
intensifiers. It is written in stanzas not across them. In almost
every case the concluding couplet of each octave terminates in a
full stop. There is consequently a cool regularity in its movement
quite distinct from the extract from *Epipsychidion* (ll.91–104)
quoted above. This has fourteen lines and almost as many clauses
yet it is one sentence. We scarcely perceive it as such. The effect
and intention of lines like these is to dissolve the logic of sentence
construction and imply another model for human consciousness
than that provided by discourse. It would be wrong however to
assume that discourse is discarded altogether or that here we have
some pure lyrical voice. On the contrary, Shelley establishes the
language of discourse in order to transform it. Let me be more
specific about this.

An obvious starting point is Shelley's disquisition on free love
(ll.147–89) which follows immediately upon the excited passage

which I have quoted in part. Couplet and sentence now coincide in manifestly urbane equipoise:

> True Love in this differs from gold and clay,
> That to divide is not to take away. (ll.160–61)

This passage raises its own difficulties if we try to relate it thematically to some containing argument within the poem as a whole. Let us consider a different question. What is the relation of the reader to the speaker at this point? Do we ask in effect—why is there a sudden intrusion of urbane colloquy in a declaredly lyrical conception? Or do we note some effort here by the speaker to recover his self-control after giving way to unwarranted excitement? That we do neither of these suggests that we must have attributed some governing sense of procedure to the speaker. We trust him sufficiently to grant that this excitement may have been calculated or, at least, tolerated, and that his present urbanity is, potentially, lyrical.

Potentiality is an important concern of Shelley.[10] *Epipsychidion*, like so many of Shelley's poems, is a tribute to a potentiality. What is more remarkable is that *Epipsychidion* is itself an instance or working model of the potentiality which it celebrates. This extended section on free love establishes, we might say, the poet's credentials. He is not simply a prisoner of the lyrical moment. He can look before and after. He can present cool arguments, cite precedents, satirize opposed opinion. Since the poem, if given in bald outline, celebrates an escapist extravaganza and, specifically contrasted with Dante's *The New Life* who seeks only Beatrice's freely bestowed greeting, appears to sanction some kind of transcendental rape of Emily, this gaining of the reader's trust is undoubtedly necessary. If we stand back from the poem we can see more clearly how it works.

*Epipsychidion* begins rather flatly with a strong sense of Emily's imprisonment and of the poet's separated existence. Almost at once (l.21) an ecstatic list of vocatives (ll.21–32) presents a transformed version of the same situation in which Emily becomes a figure of transcendent power ('Veiled Glory of this lampless Universe!' l.26) and the poet is caught up in her transfiguration. This sudden flight is as dramatically ended by an acknowledgement of the impossibility of sustaining it in ordinary language ('dim words', l.33). The poem then assumes a kind of middle register (l.41) as though this were its base. This in turn yields abruptly to another flight (ll.53–69) terminated by another acknowledgement (ll.69–71). The next lines appear to reassume the base register (ll.72–75) but are set aside by a more elaborate flight terminated by yet another acknowledgement ('Ah, woe is me!/What have I dared?' ll.123–24). This in turn gives way, in the extended account of free love, to what we earlier and mistakenly took to be the base register of the poem. Nevertheless this 'base register' as it re-emerges from line 130 onwards, though discursive, is tinged with excitement. The argument for free love, for example, is presented as inspired by Emily:

Thy wisdom speaks in me, (l.147).

Nor are we likely to expect this base register to be sustained, for the first section of the poem has already been interrupted three times by a flight of lyricism, each flight longer than its predecessor. What we anticipate therefore thematically and conceptually in the second part of the poem—that the account of Shelley's life and loves will terminate in a recovery of love's force in the figure of Emily—we also anticipate with our senses, provided that we are acknowledging the poem with more than our eyes alone. We have experienced a sudden access of force in the three lyrical passages which, by making great physical demands on the reader's lungs, ensure that he is in a state analogous to excitement. We anticipate some even greater demand that is going to be made upon us, some flight of verse so daringly extended that it will replace the base register altogether and thus allow us to experience what it is like to have discursive language transformed into some unimaginably continuous present tense. It is in this sense that the poem exhibits the potentiality which it celebrates. The device is one which is familiar in horror stories and pornography. We read *Epipsychidion*, one might say, with a sense of 'mounting expectation'. This finds release in the two hundred line section (ll.388–587) which is the poem's dazzling culmination. This section, as we would expect, is terminated by the most elaborate of the series of acknowledgements in which the poet bemoans his inability to sustain flight indefinitely:

Woe is me!
The wingèd words on which my soul would pierce
Into the heights of Love's rare Universe,
Are chains of lead around its flight of fire—
I pant, I sink, I tremble, I expire! (ll.587–591)

It is not ironical that these lines are perhaps the most readily remembered from *Epipsychidion*. The rapture sections of the poem are not meant to be quoted outside it. They will make no sense in the world of ordinary discourse which they exist to transform.

It might be felt that our discourse is a trifle puzzling at this point. Reference to Dante and to the audacious transformation of ordinary consciousness may suggest the highest praise whereas the poem's stated proximity to the procedures of horror-stories and pornography may suggest disparagement even in our earnestly indecorous society. Both perspectives are puzzlingly appropriate. *Epipsychidion* is an urbane fantasy which dramatizes a real problem that cannot otherwise be resolved. Certainly Shelley could not let his 'beliefs' emerge without some corroborating excitement. To an extent this can be justified by reference to the inadequacies of ordinary language and the necessarily impassioned character of poetic communication. Nevertheless it is not poetry alone that we encounter when we read poetry. Shelley's beliefs won't do for Shelley what Dante's beliefs did for Dante. There is, as it were, some leeway that has to be made up. *Epipsychidion* is, in part, gesture[11] and suffers in consequence. But the terms with which we disparage its full achievement are, as is typically the case with the best Romantic poems, provided by the poem itself. We must take this into account as part of the achievement of the poem. We are not directed finally to pathos in the lines quoted above (ll.587–591) but rather to a dramatization of opposed extremes which, indeed, the poet feels and the poem expresses, but not without urbanity and from a certain distance. Hence the Advertisement, introduction and envoy play a real role in *Epipsychidion* and the poem is closer in conception to a more evidently dramatized production like 'Julian and Maddalo' than we might at first think.

*Adonais* confirms this reading of *Epipsychidion* by proceeding in the opposite direction with uncanny precision. Pastoral elegies customarily entail transformations of death-bound consciousness by religious lyricism. The genre itself therefore instructs the reader to anticipate a glowing conclusion. It is likely too that we will encounter the same problem of belief in a new situation. Does Shelley have a sufficiently stable and discursively lucid basis to resurrect Keats in some form or another? If he does not, will he have to make up the difference by lyrical excitement and then dramatize the unstable result? He does the exact opposite.

Since I will have to talk about 'breathless excitement' again here, it will perhaps be as well to dispel some possibly misleading associations of the phrase. From Shelley's point of view, it is curious that a trance-like condition in which,

> the breath of this corporeal frame
> And even the motion of our human blood
> Almost suspended, we are laid asleep
> In body, and become a living soul,
>
> ('Tintern Abbey', ll.43–46)

should be associated, despite its blatantly corpse-like appearance, with 'the life of things'. For Shelley, both the life of things, which is in everlasting flow, and the closely associated world of spiritual life, exist in rapidity. Hence the conversation between Julian and Maddalo flows like the rapturous conclusion to *Episychidion*:

> So, as we rode, we talked; and the swift thought,
> Winging itself with laughter, lingered not,
> But flew from brain to brain,—such glee was ours,
> Charged with light memories of remembered hours,
> None slow enough for sadness:
>
> ('Julian and Maddalo', ll.28–32)

Similarly, quick breathing is the sign of inspirational life. The more breath a poet has the better even if it means asking the Wild West Wind, that 'breath of Autumn's being' to,

> Be thou, Spirit fierce,
> My spirit! Be thou me, impetuous one!
>
> ('Ode to the West Wind', ll.61–62)

Thus Shelley's problem in *Adonais* is bizarrely simple. How can Keats, poet, pre-eminently an example of spiritual life, hence of rapid, excitable, breath-filled conceptions, now lie permanently inert and breathless? The dead Keats, like Prometheus in chains, presents a bewildering inertia which the elegy can first establish in its laboriously restrained Spenserian stanzas and then excite into life. In part, these expectations are fulfilled. We can identify very precisely two places where the revivification takes place.

The first of these is worked by the Italian Spring that assailed Shelley as he wrote the poem. Surely Keats, who died at the very end of winter, cannot resist this magical rebirth of Nature?

> Through wood and stream and field and hill and Ocean
> A quickening life from the Earth's heart has burst
> As it has ever done, with change and motion,
> > (*Adonais*, ll.163–65)

It is characteristic of Shelley's poetry that the verse itself should speed up at this point so that the reader, here as in *Epipsychidion*, experiences an increase of breath and of 'quickening life' in himself. This quickening then extends to Keats's body:

> The leprous corpse, touched by this spirit tender,
> Exhales itself in flowers of gentle breath. (ll.172–73)

Such eerie participation by the dead in breathing life is closely related to the wonderful section in 'The Witch of Atlas' where the Witch, having thrown the coffin 'with contempt into a ditch' (stanza LXX), summons up a science-fiction image of an alternative eternity:

> And there the body lay, age after age,
> > Mute, breathing, beating, warm, and undecaying,
> Like one asleep in a green hermitage,
> > With gentle smiles about its eyelids playing.
> > > ('The Witch of Atlas', ll.609–12)

In *Adonais* however this quickening should be supported by ontology rather than whimsicality. Clearly, whatever Nature's force, it does not actually reanimate corpses and so,

> the intense atom glows
> A moment, then is quenched in a most cold repose.
> > (*Adonais*, ll.179–80)

The poem itself is restored by these long vowels to its slow, sad presumption of mortality.

The second attempt to excite Keats into life is presided over by the Muse. Poetry, like Nature, is ceaselessly animating Forms. Keats, as part of Nature, cannot resist Nature's Spring re-birth. Similarly Keats as a poet cannot resist the breath of inspiration merely because he is dead. Once again therefore, as in some Gothic and ghastly tale by Edgar Allan Poe, the corpse is briefly restored to blood and breath:

> In the death-chamber for a moment Death,
> Shamed by the presence of that living Might,
> Blushed to annihilation, and the breath
> Revisited those lips, and Life's pale light
> Flashed through those limbs. (ll.217–21)

In both these instances, Shelley is giving force to ancient conceits by picturing them literally. *Adonais*, in this and other respects, is baroque in character. There is an evident affinity between Shelley's methods here and those of Donne in, say, 'The Dampe' or 'A Nocturnal upon S. Lucies day', or Dryden's in 'To Mrs Anne Killigrew'. Harold Love has argued[12] for example, that Dryden wrote in an age when there was general uncertainty as to whether the analogies between mental and natural phenomena upon which classical and mediaeval poetry had relied were literally true. Dryden, he suggests, theatrically over-states these analogies in order to dramatize a moral truth but also to share with his readers this radical uncertainty. These terms fit the first part of *Adonais* surprisingly well and support my contention that urbanity and lyricism are not necessarily more separate in Shelley's art than they are in Dryden's.

Unlike *Epipsychidion*, these two eruptions of quickening life in *Adonais* fail to infect the established speed or mood of the poem which is again re-asserted (stanza XXX onwards). We neither anticipate nor encounter some further transformation on the model of the earlier ones. If Nature and Art cannot permanently revivify Keats, what can?

Yet *Adonais* concludes with seventeen convincing stanzas of final affirmation. It is difficult at first to see how this trick is managed given the carefully manifested failure of Shelley's lyric resources to quicken Keats and the inadequacy of any urbanely pondered belief that Shelley could actually recommend to his readers. The solution to this conundrum may appear a little disappointing. It is rhetoric.

Two elements are always crucial to rhetoric's success. Shelley uses both consummately well. The first is the right ordering of material, which we might now call 'strategy'. The rhetorician must always do things in the right order so that his audience passes through an apparently comprehensive and emotionally extensive sequence. The second is sheer force of assertion. It is easy to underestimate this. If an audience has come to trust a speaker and been through a difficult emotional sequence with him, they will finally accept unqualified and unsupported assertions from him, provided that he appears to be convinced himself and can produce impressive and memorable formulations in which to express these assertions. If this is Satan's formula in *Paradise Lost* as well as Hitler's at Nuremberg, it is also Shakespeare's in Sonnet 116, 'Let me not to the marriage of true minds admit impediments' and, in any event, it works.

Shelley's strategy in *Adonais* reverses that of *Epipsychidion*. In the latter, his demonstrated urbanity sanctioned his lyrical trustworthiness. In *Adonais*, the emotional excitement of the two lyrical 'resuscitations' of Keats and their manifest failure to be more than conceits, suggests authenticity and thus authorizes the trustworthiness of the final quasi-dogmatic peroration. The sequence too, deftly concocted from precedents, is a perfectly natural one. We begin with the fact of death, pictorially vivid and indignantly resisted. Emotion is allowed its fantasies of revival but cannot alter the case. The funeral procession begins to distance us from the corpse as we recognize and observe the appearances of the mourners one by one. This realization of the present world of mourners naturally recalls those who stand apart or who threatened Keats, actually or symbolically, in life. From here, it is a small, natural, though not logical, step, to attribute a kind of continuing existence to Keats, whose corpse we have begun to forget, in the familiar formula, 'He is better off where he is' or, more memorably:

He has outsoared the shadow of our night. (1.352)

Shelley is thus able to suppress memories of the inert, non-conscious Keats, so vividly given their due earlier in the elegy, and accommodate him casually to the continuing processes of Nature:

> He is made one with Nature, (l.370)

> He is a portion of the loveliness
> Which once he made more lovely. (ll.379–80)

This is not because Shelley has found a new sustaining belief or recovered an old one. Nor is it in contradiction with that earlier vignette (stanza XX) where Keats, though touched by Nature's force, remains outside its capacity to transform. There we had a fantasy of possible experience like the conclusion to *Epipsychidion*, here we have pure rhetorical assertion:

> The splendours of the firmament of time
> May be eclipsed, but are extinguished not. (ll.388–89)

> The One remains, the many change and pass. (l.460)

It is not surprising that everyone recalls these celebrated quotations from the conclusion of *Adonais*. It is not simply that they are better written than the end of *Epipsychidion* but that they are intended to be self-validating. They need to sound convincing because there is no other external basis for the conviction which they carry though, of course, they exploit a mixture of Stoical, Platonic, Pantheist, Deist, and popular sentiments. The distance we have travelled from the early part of the poem is shown most clearly by stanzas XLV and XLVI.

> The inheritors of unfulfilled renown
> Rose from their thrones, built beyond mortal thought,
> Far in the Unapparent. Chatterton
> Rose pale,—his solemn agony had not
> Yet faded from him; Sidney, as he fought
> And as he fell and as he lived and loved
> Sublimely mild, a Spirit without spot,
> Arose; and Lucan, by his death approved:
> Oblivion as they rose shrank like a thing reproved.

> And many more, whose names on Earth are dark,
> But whose transmitted effluence cannot die
> So long as fire outlives the parent spark,
> Rose, robed in dazzling immortality.
> 'Thou art become as one of us,' they cry,

It was for thee yon kingless sphere has long
Swung blind in unascended majesty,
Silent alone amid an Heaven of Song.
Assume thy wingèd throne, thou Vesper of our throng!,
(ll.397–414)

Against the commendably vague 'Unapparent' (l.399), the
profiles of Keats's predecessors emerge in sharp definition. No
attempt is made to transform them, rather their death image is
recalled and associated skilfully with their enduring fame. In the
next stanza however, we do attribute some sort of transformed
existence to the nameless 'many more' (l.406) who welcome
Keats with as much gusto and credibility as the dead Napoleon
was welcomed by the heroes of Ossian. Our tendency to scoff
should be firmly resisted for the vapidly notional realization of
these worthies ('robed in dazzling immortality', l.409) is
intentional. It would be impossible for Shelley, committed as he
was to potentiality, to produce a particularized image of
resurrected life, though we see from *The Triumph of Life* that he
could produce an entirely convincing image of Hell. I merely
want to point out that no reader raises objections to stanza XLVI
though, quoted out of context, it is unimpressive and, when
juxtaposed with the vivid earlier evocation of Keats's corpse, it
should seem too ridiculously insubstantial to form part of an
acceptable affirmation. Yet it does. The reason for this is
instructive.

The energy which fuels this final section of *Adonais* proceeds
not from any conviction of Keats's apotheosis but from contrary
resources of indignation. It is only by continually adverting to the
horrors of present existence in this 'dull dense world' (l.382)
which, naturally, would oppose or even murder young poets such
as Chatterton, Sidney, and Lucan, that Shelley can generate,
rhetorically, conviction in himself and his readers about some
other order of exemplary existence. Such other order of existence
must necessarily appear notional in this world as it is. All the
more necessary therefore to assert it with complete confidence in
the teeth of all available evidence. How skilfully, for example,
Shelley places his most convincing stanza ('The One remains
. . .' stanza LII) immediately after his account of Keats's grave
which is dramatically orchestrated, in the manner of characteristic sections of Byron's *Childe Harold's Pilgrimage*, into a great

outcry against Time and Sorrow amidst the Ruins of Rome. The one validates the other and, as with all great rhetoric, it is scarcely recognized as such.

There is one further factor in the conclusion's success. Shelley must himself appear convinced of the validity of his assertions. Indignation will initiate them; the tributary force of ancient philosophies and commonplaces will support them; but something more is needed to tip the balance. Here we come tantalizingly close to the situation and idiom of *Epipsychidion* which, up to now, the poem has studiously avoided. The last section of Adonais is fired by indignation at human life as it is which in turn generates a sense of the superiority of Death's world. However Shelley, though he relies on the language both of the One and the Many and of Pantheist inclusiveness, does not formally believe in either. At the same time, the compulsion to celebrate some other order of existence beyond the grave is forced on him by the logic of emotion. So the longer his affirmation is sustained (it should be a matter of exalted but urbane assertion), the more he will have to admit to a celebration of Death's potentialities come what may. But such a celebration of a Death-wish unsupported by an ontology provokes excitement and fear:

> Why linger, why turn back, why shrink, my Heart?
> (1.469)

The last three stanzas of *Adonais*, though we may detect the gathering excitement in earlier undertones, could not be described as urbane or rhetorical. The contrast with *Epipsychidion* is thus complete to the last detail. That poem falls from its lyrical height to bounded time and ends with dramatic distancing devices. *Adonais* concludes with dogmatic assertions that are suddenly transformed by a final lyrical flutter of fearful excitement as the rhetoric of the poem rebounds on the poet and fills him with a sense of terrified potentiality:

> The breath whose might I have invoked in song
> Descends on me; my spirit's bark is driven,
> Far from the shore, far from the trembling throng
> Whose sails were never to the tempest given;
> The massy earth and spherèd skies are riven!
> I am borne darkly, fearfully, afar (ll.487–92)

All these factors contribute to and, I would claim, largely explain the triumphant plausibility of the poem's final affirmation, if not indeed the success of the poem as a whole.

I have been concerned with *Epipsychidion* and *Adonais* but certain recurring features of our enquiry are more widely relevant. Shelley manipulates the tempo of his poems for serious and original purposes more consistently, perhaps, than any other poet. This habit is particularly important in his short lyrics which notoriously resist the analysis of practical critics, though we have been much helped recently by Judith Chernaik's excellent book on the subject.[13]

### III

In the lyrics the matter is not usually that of establishing a discursive base, which can be dramatically quickened or suspended, but rather of establishing a definite speed at the outset to which the life and meaning of each poem can be held throughout. Since medium pace is obviously related to discourse and Shelley's lyrics are, in the first instance, vehicles of mood, this means that his lyrics can be divided quite straightforwardly into slow ones and quick ones. Like jazz, the manipulations of rhythm here are subtle and elaborate but the simple, more or less erotic, division into 'blues' poems and 'hot' poems, if a little bizarre, can also be helpful and calls attention to the importance of 'performing' these poems rather than glancing through them. Simplicity of mood held to a single pace but artfully elaborated by metre is manifest in 'A Lament', a particularly good example of a poem which depends upon performance:

> O World! O life! O time!
> On whose last steps I climb,
> Trembling at that where I had stood before;
> When will return the glory of your prime?
> 5 No more—Oh, never more!
>
> Out of the day and night
> A joy has taken flight;
> Fresh spring, and summer, and winter hoar,
> Move my faint heart with grief, but with delight
> 10 No more—Oh, never more!

It is readily apparent that the first line, thought short, must be said very slowly because of its six long vowels and three necessary pauses. It is less obvious but unavoidable in spoken performance that maintaining this snail's-pace in the long lines 3 and 4 and, more especially, the enjambed lines 8 and 9, will use up more breath than the reader anticipated at the outset. Hence he will draw a large and noticeable breath immediately before lines 5 and 10. He will thus find himself with too much breath for the final line of each stanza. This will precipitate a sigh-like expenditure throughout these lines, with the effect accentuated by the internal pause. These effects are built into the poem and may appear comical in this kind of descriptive analysis, but are wonderfully expressive. They could not be achieved without skill and discrimination by the poet. Shelley is a master of them.

'Ode to the West Wind' manifestly inverts the procedures of 'A Lament'. The reader is in considerable doubt as to whether he is going to be allowed to snatch a breath at all:

> O Wild West Wind, thou breath of Autumn's being,
> Thou, from whose unseen presence the leaves dead
> 3 Are driven, like ghosts from an enchanter fleeing,
>
> Yellow, and black, and pale, and hectic-red,
> 5 Pestilence-stricken multitudes: O thou . . .

From the beginning of line two until the colon in line five, there is no opportunity for taking breath. Already uncomfortable by line three, we anticipate some sort of closure both because of the sense and the encouraging prospect of a printed space between this and the next tercet. Instead we encounter a dependent line of adjectives which cruelly push the sense in front of them onto the next line. The reader of the poem, provided that he is using more than his eyes, is forced to read the verse at a tremendous speed in order to cope at all and finds himself poised between panic and exhilaration. Nor is this, any more than in 'A Lament', simply a supernumerary thrill which ought to be rebuked for obstructing some more pertinent meaning. The Ode is about breath, breathing, 'inspiration'. Poet and poem are finite, enraptured, yet unstable embodiments of an irresistible force of breath. Like *Epipsychidion*, the poem exhibits directly in its lyrical process what it can only point to indirectly in its discursive ransacking of potential metaphors. There is more to it than this of course. The onrush of each stanza is regulated by a categorizing rhetoric which distinguishes each of the poem's five sections. Moreover, unlike 'The Cloud', which is also built round unresisted motion, the Ode does not depend upon the identity of poet and West Wind but upon their willed and unstable convergence. This convergence is as precariously maintained as the necessary energy to speak the poem. Instead of finally collapsing, as we might expect, this risky animation, though it wavers in the penultimate section, is restored by the rhetoric of potentiality (i.e. prophecy) to an entirely workable conclusion. We can associate the pattern of this poem then with the more complex shifts of *Adonais* and *Epipsychidion*. Nevertheless, 'Ode to the West Wind' is a single lyrical conception tethered by syntax and enforced pace to a single mood. Indeed most of Shelley's lyrics can be pigeon-holed without distortion as *adagio* or *vivace* on much the same lines. For example the device of setting a single pace for lines of markedly different lengths is used in:

> The flower that smiles today
> > Tomorrow dies;

and, most effectively of all, in 'To a Skylark'. One might imagine that the skylark, like the west wind, would be realized from the outset in quivering motion. Instead the first stanza insists upon a flat, dead pace:

> Hail to thee, blithe Spirit!
> > Bird thou never wert,
> 3   That from·Heaven, or near it,
> > Pourest thy full heart
> 5 In profuse strains of unpremeditated art.

Both 'blithe' (line 1) and 'wert' (line 2) doggedly resist rapid enunciation. Hence the final alexandrine, carried at the same pace but twice the length of its predecessors, 'like a wounded snake, drags its slow length along',[14] but does so for a dramatic purpose of which Pope would have thoroughly approved. This purpose is to make it immediately clear to the reader that, whatever happens, the base experience of the poem is not that of the skylark. Thus although the poem quickens slightly to accommodate the customary list of metaphoric alternatives which suggest the rapt intensity of skylark life, we know the poem will neither terminate in nor fully endorse this intensity. The poem will culminate ostensibly in wisdom rather than in joy and this wisdom, when it arrives, fits the prepared rhythm absolutely:

> We look before and after,
>    And pine for what is not:
> Our sincerest laughter
>    With some pain is fraught;
> Our sweetest songs are those that tell
>    of saddest thought. (ll.86–90)

This is very much Maddalo's sentiment in 'Julian and Maddalo':

> 'Most wretched men
> Are cradled into poetry by wrong,
> They learn in suffering what they teach in song.'
>                            (ll.544–46)

The purpose of 'To a Skylark' cannot be to dramatize this alien Byronic insight but rather to accommodate its force in an apparently open context which will discreetly allow, indeed excite, aspirations quite contrary to the restraints of wisdom. The poem enables the reader to inhabit the space between skylark and earth which results from this tension. Even here, therefore, in these prime examples of *Golden Treasury* 'sublimity' which utilize purely lyrical devices such as the management of tempo and breath, we encounter, if not quite urbanity, then at least something of that continuous adjustment of procedure which characterizes intelligent discourse. My point is best made perhaps, finally, in an example where this does not come off quite as it should.

'When the lamp is shattered' has received more than its fair share of commentary. Partly this is fortuitous. Comment breeds counter-comment. Partly too the poem, which is both brilliant and seriously flawed, has come to represent Shelley's flawed brilliance as a whole. This is unfortunate for whatever the poem is, it is not at all typical of Shelley's procedures.

Dr. Leavis's and Allen Tate's celebrated attacks on the poem were inept in this respect.[15] Leavis all too clearly did not understand the poem at all, presumed that there was nothing to be understood and assumed the unlovely stance of licensed corrector of romantic excess. I am far from suggesting that his 'revaluation' should be rehabilitated but his mistake is not incomprehensible and Shelley is partly responsible for it. What is there in the poem itself which might provoke such a misreading?

I

When the lamp is shattered
The light in the dust lies dead—
When the cloud is scattered
The rainbow's glory is shed.
When the lute is broken,                                    5
Sweet tones are remembered not;
When the lips have spoken,
Loved accents are soon forgot.

II

As music and splendour
Survive not the lamp and the lute,                         10
The heart's echoes render
No song when the spirit is mute:
No song but sad dirges,
Like the wind through a ruined cell,
Or the mournful surges                                     15
That ring the dead seaman's knell.

III

When hearts have once mingled
Love first leaves the well-built nest;
The weak one is singled
To endure what it once possessed.                          20
O Love! who bewailest
The frailty of all things here,
Why choose you the frailest
For your cradle, your home, and your bier?

IV

Its passions will rock thee                                25
As the storms rock the ravens on high;
Bright reason will mock thee,
Like the sun from a wintry sky.
From thy nest every rafter
Will rot, and thine eagle home                             30
Leave thee naked to laughter,
When leaves fall and cold winds come.[16]

The immediate impression is of mood and rhythm, though pace as such, significantly, is less important than usual. It is as though each of the three foot lines answers its two foot predecessor antiphonally and appears to close something off.[17] This effect is achieved by alternating suspended feminine and flat masculine endings. This in turn is picked up in the rhythm of the lines which superimpose falling effects ('músĭc ǎnd spléndŏur', 'móurnfŭl súrgĕs', 'pássiŏns', 'réasŏn', 'nákĕd tŏ láughtĕr'), upon a rising metre ('liĕs déad', 'thĕ lámp ǎnd thĕ lúte', 'lĭke thĕ sún', 'wĭll rót'). I know of no other example where Shelley uses these effects so systematically.[18] They culminate in the brilliant last line with its doubling of dead final stresses set against the suspended phrase 'naked to laughter' immediately preceding it.

On the other hand we are aware throughout the poem that some sort of argument is being conducted. When this is examined more closely, it becomes apparent that there is a sense in which the poem is nothing but argument. It is worth setting this out stanza by stanza:

I

When $a$ then $b$, when $c$ then $d$,
When $e$ then $f$, when $g$ then $h$.

II

As $f$ and $b$ depend on $a$ and $e$,
So $i$ depends on $j$, thus without $j$
There is no $i$ but there is $k$ which is like $l$ or $m$.

III

When $n$ then $o$ and, consequently $p$,
Why, $q$, do you cause $p$?

IV

Since $r$ will happen (like $s$),
$t$ will happen (like $u$), $v$ and $w$ will happen,
When $x$ happens.

We have apparently both an advanced musical score and an advanced logical argument. The result should be something like a Restoration lyric such as Rochester's 'All my past life is mine no more', or one of those rare poems in which Donne privileges musical effects like 'Sweetest love, I do not goe'. In the event we encounter something rather more surrealistic than baroque.

The argument of the poem is not as continuous as it appears. It splits into two halves not unlike a sonnet. But each of the parts has so many terms—I have had to use almost the entire alphabet to catalogue them—that it is virtually impossible to hold them in the mind at once. Moreover the argument of the first two stanzas is comparatively loose and depends upon dispensable exempla, whereas the argument of stanzas three and four is concentrated and, however elaborated, depends upon a single figure (Love leaving one nest and remaining in another). Hence the critic, who naturally reads the second half of the poem in the manner of the first, soon loses his way and dismisses the poem as music masquerading as sense. He is absurdly wrong but yet, after all, he is very nearly right for the subject-matter of the two stanzas is not directly connected to that of the first half. The 'When' opening the third stanza looks identical to that of the first but it is not, since it introduces a chain of particular consequences rather than, as we now expect, a mournful epigram. The last four lines of stanza two (ll.13–16), which are particularly unconcentrated ('but there is $k$ which is like $l$ or $m$'), scarcely prepare the reader for this sharper argument or the equally unexpected address to Love (l.21) which persists, to Leavis's and Tate's confusion, into stanza four. This vocative is made possible and was probably provoked by the vivid realization of Love as a quasi-Petrarchan figure at the beginning of stanza three.

All this is disguised by the unusual controlling rhythm, uniformity of mood, and the clever rhetorical stitching which renews the poem in stanza three with an echo of the opening line and repeats it again, in another cadence, in the last line of all. It would be possible, since modern criticism thrives on tolerance of the plausible, to construct an ingenious argument that would praise the conjunction of dispensable formulas in part one with the grotesquely sustained figure of part two, but I do not propose to make it. I would rather point to two factors of another kind. The first is G. M. Matthews's suggestion that 'When the lamp is shattered' was intended to be part of the unfinished drama published as such in the *Poetical Works* (pp. 482–8). It is clear from the plot of this drama and from the opening lyric (as printed), 'He came like a dream in the dawn of life', that the imagery and concerns of both parts of 'When the lamp is shattered' would, in such a context, appear more evidently

connected. Moreover, Matthews notes that in one of the
manuscripts of the poem Shelley has written *second part* above
stanza three. He therefore suggests that:

> The notation *second part* could have been intended in a semi-
> musical sense, of a dialogue in which a second voice takes up
> and answers the first. The imagery changes abruptly in the
> *second part* . . .

Professor Matthews's characteristically persuasive essay[19] argues
that Shelley's lyrics are much more frequently intended for
dramatic situations than we assume. This suggestion provides
supporting evidence for my emphasis on 'performance' and
calculated effects in these lyrics.

The second factor which we should not overlook in any
analysis is the almost crippling exuberance of talent, both
intellectual and aesthetic, exhibited in 'When the lamp is
shattered'. Whatever we do with the poem, we should not
patronize it. Nevertheless, in the end, we should pass a negative
judgement on these verses as they appear in their present form of
context-free lyric. Shelley does not have sufficient room here to
share with the reader his own sense of the precarious
inventiveness of his poem's procedures as he does in *Adonais* or
*Epipsychidion* or, even, 'To a Skylark' and 'Ode to the West
Wind'. That is why Shelley's best short lyrics are much slighter
than this one. 'When the lamp is shattered' is untypical of
Shelley's procedures because it can be approximated to neither
the elaborated nor the spare lyrics of his customary practice. The
latter use less of his powers and are content to be dramatized
simplifications, like 'Rarely, rarely comest thou', or rhetorical
set-pieces like 'Ozymandias' or 'England in 1819'. These should
always find readers and praise but their distinctive existence
should not persuade us, despite Shelley's ability to produce
markedly differentiated forms of verse, that we can readily
separate lyrical and discursive procedures in his major poetry.
Discourse exists in order to be transformed into something else.
Lyricism, on the other hand, retains links with the discourse
which it has temporarily transformed. Poetry is neither one nor
both but is some *tertium quid* dependent upon yet dramatically
distanced from both its constituent resources.

# NOTES

1. Donald Davie, 'Shelley's Urbanity' in *Purity of Diction in English Verse* (London, 1952).

2. F. A. Pottle, 'The Case of Shelley', originally printed in *Publications of the Modern Language Association of America*, lxvii (1952), 589–608 but I quote from the revised version in *English Romantic Poets*, ed. M. H. Abrams (Oxford, 1960), 297.

3. Compare for instance this passage from *The Seasons:*

> Muttering, the winds at eve with blunted point
> Blow hollow-blustering from the south. Subdued,
> The frost resolves into a trickling thaw.
> Spotted the mountains shine: loose sleet descends,
> And floods the country round. The rivers swell,
> Of bonds impatient. Sudden from the hills,
> O'er rocks and woods, in broad brown cataracts,
> A thousand snow-red torrents shoot at once;
> And, where they rush, the wide-resounding plain
> Is left one slimy waste. Those sullen seas,
> That wash'd the ungenial pole, will rest no more
> Beneath the shackles of the mighty north,
>
> (ll.988–99 'Winter') ed. J. Logie Robertson
> *James Thomson: Poetical Works* (O. S. A. edition, Oxford, 1908)

4. *Poetical Works*, 205.

5. C. S. Lewis, 'Shelley, Dryden, and Mr. Eliot' in *Rehabilitations and other Essays* (Oxford, 1939), 3–34.

6. See T. L. Peacock, *The Four Ages of Poetry* (1820). Shelley told Peacock (in a letter of 15 Feb. 1821) that the latter's essay had produced in him 'a sacred rage' (*Letters* ii 261).

7. Ed. T. Webb, *Percy Bysshe Shelley: Selected Poems* (London, 1977), 217.

8. See Dante, *The New Life*, trans. W. Anderson (London, 1964), 82–4. Shelley quotes part of this section in his Preface to *Epipsychidion* (*Poetical Works*, 411).

9. R. Holmes, *Shelley: The Pursuit* (London, 1976), 257–62.

10. See for example D. H. Hughes, 'Potentiality in *Prometheus Unbound*' in *Woodings*, 142–61.

11. Shelley did not share Dante's orthodox view that belief is founded in the will. In a note to *Queen Mab* he argues,

> Belief, then, is a passion, the strength of which, like every other passion, is in precise proportion to the degrees of excitement. (*Poetical Works*, 813)

This does not affect my argument, but clearly it would not command Shelley's conscious acceptance.

12. Harold Love, 'Dryden's Unideal Vacancy' in *Eighteenth-Century Studies*, xii, no. 1 (Fall, 1978), 74–89.

13. Judith Chernaik, *The Lyrics of Shelley* (Cleveland, 1972).

238 *The Transformation of Discourse:* Epipsychidion Adonais

14. See Pope's 'An Essay on Criticism' (1711), l.377.

15. F. R. Leavis, *Revaluation: Tradition and Development in English Poetry* (London, 1949), 203–32. Allen Tate, 'Understanding Modern Poetry', in *On the Limits of Poetry* (New York, 1948), 126.

16. *Poetical Works*, 667–668.

17. The scansion of the poem is not easy though it is clear that there are alternately two and three feet and that the underlying rhythm is anapaestic. Difficulties occur first because it may not be clear that 'When' (lines 1, 3, 5, 7) is unstressed though it is evident from subsequent stanzas and the dominant beat that this is so. Secondly, we may be tempted to run on the last syllable of the shorter lines with the next (shátt/eřed//Thĕ líght) in order to reinforce and tidy up the metre. This is unnecessary and (in lines 13–14, 17–18, 23–24, 25–26, 27–28) often impossible. This suggests however that the poem uses amphibrachs aˊs significant metrical units (e.g. Aš músič/aňd spléndoǔr/), even though metrists from Saintsbury onwards customarily deny that this is possible in English verse.

18. Shelley often balances masculine and feminine endings; a good example is 'The keen stars were twinkling', but not as consistently as here. The closest parallel is perhaps in the brief fragment 'The rude wind is singing' (*Poetical Works*, 661). There are many parallels to the imagery of the poem. Particularly suggestive ones are in *Prometheus Unbound*, I, 801–6 and *The Cenci*, IV, iii, 39–41.

19. G. M. Matthews, 'Shelley's Lyrics' in *The Morality of Art*, ed. D. W. Jefferson (London, 1969), 195–209.

# The Reworking of a Literary Genre: Shelley's *'The Triumph of Life'*.

## MIRIAM ALLOTT

### I

'The Triumph of Life', described by T. S. Eliot in 1933 as Shelley's 'last, and to my mind greatest though unfinished poem',[1] was left incomplete at its author's death in July 1822 and little direct information has come down to us about the circumstances of its composition. It is as tantalizing as *The Ivory Tower* or *The Mystery of Edwin Drood*, with the additional fascination—since Shelley, unlike James and Dickens, died young—that it seems to signal a new stage in its creator's maturing creative sensibility. After many years of incomprehension and neglect it has at last come into its own through the devoted attention of modern scholars, outstandingly Geoffrey Matthews and Donald Reiman, on whom we have come to depend for guidance through the tortuous difficulties of the original manuscript and the maze of literary sources and influences variously at work in the processes of its composition.[2] With their help, and with the help of information pieced together by modern biographers from Shelley's letters, Mary Shelley's correspondence and notes, and various records left by friends and associates, we can now trace in considerable detail the imaginative evolution of this work and arrive at some degree of informed judgment about the nature and quality of Shelley's achievement in it.

Perhaps the most arresting aspect of Shelley's work rests on the delighted rapidity with which his creative sensibility fastens on the multifarious and antithetical in experience at the same time that it struggles to realize the vision of abiding harmony which passionately engages his moral imagination. These dual impulses remain to the end, but while the movement and excitement of the earlier poetry seems to spring from the sustained effort to reconcile contraries in the interests of an ardent and individual holism, the mood of the poems after *Hellas* (1821) suggests that a more urgent personal involvement with the painful realities of existence is shifting Shelley's poetic attention towards unflinching scrutiny of the 'something that infects the world'. Complicating and adding poignancy to the process is the unaltered keenness of his response to the brilliancy, colour and variety of the 'infected' world.[3] His association of 'white radiance' with an ultimate truth lying beyond the 'painted veil' of life is still central. What strikes us in the later work is the intensity with which the emblematic figures which he sets against the 'white radiance' generate images of prismatic light and colour. His use of the word 'stain' to convey their despoiling effect gathers in consequence something of the ambiguous emotional charge which is felt with peculiar sombreness in his broken-off last poem. 'The Triumph of Life' does not end dramatically, as once was thought, with the narrator's unanswered question, 'Then what is Life . . .?' but with Rousseau's unfinished answer,

> . . . Happy is he
> Whom the fold of . . .

From everything that goes before it is hard not to see in these words the first movement towards a restatement of the stoical Greek pronouncement which captured Yeats (in youth one of Shelley's most fervent modern admirers), who renders it at the close of his 'From Oedipus at Colonnus':

> Never to have lived is best, ancient writers say;
> Never to have drawn the breath of life, never
> To have looked into the eye of day . . .

Yeats's version goes on,

> The second best's a gay goodnight and quickly turn away . . .

but there is no hint of this mood in 'The Triumph of Life', which emerges as an honest and powerful attempt to understand what in the nature of things might encourage the wish 'never to have lived' and the desire, which we know Shelley experienced when writing the poem, for the key to an everlasting repose.

## II

From the evidence of the manuscript, which includes dates written on the paper used (in one instance the back of a letter) and drafts of other late poems interspersed amid the main composition, it is plain that Shelley was working intermittently on 'The Triumph of Life' during May and June 1822.[4] We do not know exactly when he began the poem, but there is little doubt that the 547 lines in *terza rima* which we have (the poem breaks off at the first word of the 548th line) were abandoned in their present state on 1 July. This was the day that Shelley set out on the fated journey by sea which first took him, in seven and a half hours, from his home at Lerici to Leghorn and his reunion with Leigh Hunt, and ended a week later on 8 July when, shortly after setting course for home, the *Don Juan* sank in a storm and he was drowned.

The poems other than 'The Triumph of Life' found in the manuscript include besides one or two lyrical fragments the important 'Lines written in the Bay of Lerici' and 'To Jane: The keen stars were twinkling . . .', both of which are now familiar to us as contributions to the fine series of late poems, at once radiant and sad, inspired by Shelley's deepening emotional attachment to Jane Williams during the period from February to July 1822. Jane and Edward Williams—Edward was Shelley's companion on his last journey and was drowned with him—had joined the Shelley circle in Italy during the previous year, arriving at Pisa in January 1821. The friendship grew, for Shelley at first more warmly towards Edward than Jane, and in November 1821 the Williamses took rooms on the ground floor of the Shelley's lodgings at the Tre Palazzi di Chiesa, thus becoming still more intimate with the Pisan coterie of literary exiles which had its social epicentre—to Shelley's growing moral distaste—at the Lanfranchi Palace, the commodious temporary resting-place where Lord Byron with his customary prodigality had installed himself and his entourage. When the Shelleys and the Williamses planned a summer exodus to the Gulf of Spezzia, circumstances again led them to set up house together, this time at the Casa Magni on the bay of Lerici, where they moved on 29 April, now accompanied by the unlucky and embittered Claire Clairmont, whose child by Byron, Allegra, had died on 19 April

in the convent to which her father had consigned her. In a letter
to John Gisborne written in January, when they were all still at
Pisa, Shelley glances ruefully at his tepid early response to Jane.
He now finds her 'more amiable than ever, and a sort of
embodied peace in the midst of our circle of tempests. So much
for first impressions!'[5] His feeling for this conjunction of storm
and calm is important for 'The Triumph of Life'. Walking with
Jane in the countryside, or listening as she played on the guitar
which he had given her, became an enchantment of the heart, an
ur-Dedalian 'epiphany', seemingly situated outside time and the
more intensely felt because of the certainty that it was not so. 'She
left me', he writes in 'Lines Written in the Bay of Lerici',

>             . . . and I stayed alone
> Thinking over every tone
> Which, though silent to the ear,
> The enchanted heart could hear,
> Like notes which die when born, but still
> Haunt the echoes of the hill . . .
> Her presence had made weak and tame
> All passions and I lived alone
> In the time which is our own;
> The past and future were forgot,
> As they had been, and would be, not . . . (ll.9–26)

But with her departure repose is lost, passion revives and with it
guilt:

>               . . . the guardian angel one,
> The demon resumed his throne
> In my faint heart. I dare not speak
> My thoughts . . . (ll.27–30)

The poem, which evokes the surrounding scene of night sky and
sea, closes with the contrast between his restless plight—plainly
now that of the frustrated lover—and the fish which rise to the
lure of the fisherman's lamp and are speared to death (the
penultimate line was left unfinished):

> Too happy they, whose pleasure sought
> Extinguishes all sense and thought
> Of the regret that pleasure [      ]
> Destroying life alone, not peace! (ll.49–52)

The final line, whichever way we read the text,[6] arrests us because the final stress on 'peace' suggests a stance more readily associated with a stoical Arnoldian longing for calm than with the speed and energy, the hylozoic view of the universe, commonly associated with Shelley's major poetry. The same note is struck at the close of 'To Jane: The Recollection', one of the most accomplished of the 'Jane' poems (this time written out in a separate manuscript):

> Though thou art ever fair and kind,
>     The forests ever green,
> Less oft is peace in Shelley's mind,
>     Than calm in waters, seen. (ll.85–8)

The time 'not our own' during these months was dense with the distresses of others. Shelley may have felt with Arnold that 'Calm's not life's crown but calm is well' when faced with Claire Clairmont's venomous battles with Byron over the child whose death set its seal on their unlovely relationship; Mary's increasing ill-health and dislike of the Lerici house where domestic squabbles with Jane and the ceaseless sound of the sea and wind got on her nerves; and the miscarriage in June which left her still weaker and more despondent, consumed with intensified jealousy of Jane and filled with forebodings of impending disaster. Additionally there were worries about Leigh Hunt's delayed journey from England, his safety at sea, and the financial difficulties likely to greet him on arrival (Byron was now blowing hot and cold about the projected new periodical, *The Liberal*, for which he had urged Hunt to travel out in the first place). There were other matters deeply troubling to the creative self. Shelley's own writing seemed to go unnoticed in England (he was especially disheartened about the cool response to *Adonais*)[7] and his disappointment both weakened his incentive to write and added to his already ambivalent attitude to Byron, whose recent work on *Cain* and *Manfred* filled him with admiration but whose personal principles prompted quite different feelings and exacerbated his troubled sense of professional jealousy.

As it happened the 'beautiful and ineffectual angel'[8] acted with the practical intelligence and address denied him in earlier traditions. He kept Byron and Claire apart, shouldered arrangements for Allegra's burial, saved Mary's life by expeditious treatment in the long hours before the doctor came, and brought Byron round with shrewdness and diplomacy. He threw himself with energetic delight into the project to build his little boat and once the 'swift and beautiful' *Don Juan* had arrived on Monday 12 May spent hours on the water with Edward Williams, accompanied by one or both of their young women. 'My boat . . . serves me at once for a study and a carriage', he wrote, 'I read and enjoy for the first time these ten years something like health—I find however that I must neither think nor feel, or the pain returns to its old nest . . .'[9]

The pain in his side had recurred over the years; today we would probably call it psychosomatic. The reference sets up reverberations often felt in the letters of these last months. There are telling passages in his mid-June letter to Gisborne bringing him up to date with the news and one in particular includes lines which serve as an epigraph for his 1822 temper (the italics are mine):

> The Williamses are . . . very pleasing . . . She has a taste for music, and an elegance of form and motions that compensate in some degree for lack of literary refinement . . . I have a boat . . . we drive along this delightful bay in the evening wind under the summer moon until earth appears another world. Jane brings her guitar, and if the past and future could be obliterated, the present would content me so well that I could say with Faust to the passing moment, 'Remain, thou, thou art so beautiful' . . . I write little now. It is impossible to compose except under the strong excitement of assurance of finding sympathy with what you write . . . Byron is in this respect fortunate. He touched a chord to which a million hearts responded, and the coarse music which he produced to please them disciplined him to the perfection to which he now approaches . . . I feel too little certainty of the future, and too little satisfaction with regard to the past to undertake any subject seriously and deeply. *I stand, as it were, upon a precipice, which I have ascended with great, and cannot descend with greater, peril, and I am content if the heaven above me is calm for the passing moment* . . .[10]

## III

Shelley's reference to Goethe's *Faust* in this letter sends a shaft of light into the hidden recesses of a mind occupied—sporadically and against the grain—with expressing in songs for Jane emotions released by this relationship, whose saving repose and harmony were constantly under threat from the destructiveness of time and passion, and more ambitiously with the problem of imaging mythopaeically in 'The Triumph of Life' the larger scheme of things to which this relationship only too plainly and familiarly belonged. The disenchantments of time and change had attended to his youthful relationship with Harriet Westbrook as they had to his more recent affair with the muse of *Epipsychidion*, Emilia Viviani. They were now undermining his marriage, his confidence in his own work, and his belief in any immediately foreseeable attainment of general good. 'I see little public virtue, and I foresee that the contest will be one of blood and gold', he wrote a few days before his death.[11] The terms 'blood and gold' appear in 'The Triumph of Life',

The Anarchs old whose force and murderous snares

Had founded many a sceptre-bearing line
And spread the plague of blood and gold abroad . . .
(ll.285–87),

and are invariably associated with his bitterest attacks on tyranny and injustice.[12] The mood of the letter is akin to the despondency which takes over at the close of *Hellas*, his ostensibly exuberant celebration of the Greek war of liberation written the previous autumn. The final chorus opens with the line,

The World's great age begins anew,
The golden years return . . . ,

but finishes on a note of fatigue:

The world is weary of the past,
Oh, might it die or rest at last!

The celebrated plea to the passing moment uttered by the doomed and impassioned Faust occurs towards the close of the play which Shelley had recently read with renewed enthusiasm when Friedrich Rielzoni's etchings illustrating its first part reached him in Pisa in January. He was still exclaiming enthusiastically over these in April, the month when he was 'reading over and over again Faust':

> What etchings those are! I am never satiated with looking at them. . . . I fear it is the only sort of translation of which Faust is susceptible—I never perfectly understood the Hartz Mountain scene, until I saw the etching.—And then, Margaret in the summer house with Faust!—The artist makes one envy his happiness that he can sketch such things with calmness, which I dared only to look upon once, and which made my brain swim round only to touch the leaf on the opposite side . . . Do you remember the 54th letter of the 1st part of the 'Nouvelle Heloise'? Goethe, in a subsequent scene evidently had that letter in mind, and this etching is an idealism of it . . .[13]

This letter in Rousseau's *Julie, ou la Nouvelle Héloïse* (1761) is written by her lover during ecstatic moments when he finds himself alone at last in her room awaiting her arrival and would have carried a special charge for the man whose room was troublingly close to Jane's in the Lerici house:

> Lieu charmant, lieu fortuné, que jadis vis tant réprimer de regards tendres, tant étouffer de soupirs brillants . . . O Julie! . . . la flamme de mes désirs s'y répand sur tous tes vestiges . . . Je ne sais quel parfum, presque insensible, plus doux que la rose et plus léger que l'iris, s'exhale ici de toutes parts . . . O désirs! . . . o crainte! o palpitations cruelles! . . . On ouvre! . . . on entre! . . . c'est elle! . . . je l'ai vue . . . Mon coeur, mon faible coeur . . . ah! cherche des forces pour supporter la félicité qui t'accable.[14]

In 'The Triumph of Life' the *idée fixe* of this order of romantic passion is transformed into *Walpurgisnacht* images of ugliness and lust. Rousseau himself emerges as a tragic figure haunted by the disastrous outcome of his own life: his narrative is in effect an allegory based on the historical Rousseau's record of the catastrophic movements of his own sensibility, inspired in youth by belief in man's natural goodness and his coming release from tyranny and wrong ('Man is born free, and everywhere he is in chains') but yielding to the seductions of the world and ending in the darkness of a mind clouded by disappointment, resentment, and suspicion. The first signs of this moral decline appeared in the 1740s when Rousseau was in his late twenties, close to Shelley's age in this year of 1822. The implications are obvious for a similarly ardent temperament now facing disenchantment and fatigue and they help to explain the harsh severity of Rousseau's warning role in the poem. Of the two central figures, the narrator and the 'leader' (Shelley takes the term from Dante), the former is like Shelley youthful and with a 'thirst for knowledge'; the latter—who uses the phrase—is old and ruined and when asked his identity replies,

> . . . Before thy memory
>
> I feared, loved, hated, suffered, did, and died,
>     And if the spark with which Heaven lit my spirit
> Earth had with purer nutriment supplied,
>
> Corruption would not now thus much inherit
>     Of what was once Rousseau . . . (ll. 199–204)

Corruption of the best is the worst it seems, but the poem resists such summary statements. Rousseau may be 'extinguished',

> . . . yet there rise
> A thousand beacons from the spark I bore . . .
>                         (ll.206–7),

and his opening address to the narrator makes it clear that men are not brought low by thirst for knowledge, nor yet by knowledge itself, but by its incompleteness, especially in relation to themselves. Those most tragically fettered—'Chained to the car' (l.208)—are,

> . . . The wise
> The great, the unforgotten, they who wore
>     Mitres and helms and crowns, or wreaths of light,
> Signs of thought's empire over thought . . . (ll.208–211),

but their downfall is not strictly a Faustian nemesis:

> . . . their lore
>     taught them not this—to know themselves; their might
> Could not suppress the mutiny within,
>     And for the mourn of faith they feigned, deep night
>
> Caught them ere evening . . . (ll.211–15)

The 'sacred few' absent from the procession are those who have total wisdom. The narrator's phrase, 'they of Athens and Jerusalem', salutes as their highest representatives Socrates and Christ (ll.128, 134–7).

'You unveil and present in its true deformity what is worst in human nature', Shelley had told Byron in October 1821, in the 'wonder and delight' of his first introduction to *Don Juan*, 'This is what the writings of the age murmur at, conscious of their want of power to endure the society of such a light. We are doomed to the knowledge of good and evil, and it is well for us to know what we should avoid no less than what we should seek.'[15] But Byron's 'lore' did not—or so it seemed—teach him to 'know himself'. Mary, in a joint letter with Shelley written in March 1822, speaks of his 'hypocrisy and cruelty', while even in the previous August, when more kindly disposed, Shelley had still declared that he needed his 'canker of aristocracy' cutting out. But he adds, 'something, God knows, wants to be cut out of us all'.[16] Reflections of this order are common in the letters of late 1821 and 1822 and reveal the outlines of an increasingly examined life. Yet obedience to the Greek command, 'Know thyself', was not rewarded by the equilibrium which makes for seeing life steadily and whole; the 'mutiny within' remained unsubdued. Three weeks before his death the author of the poems to Jane could not 'look at' *Epipsychidion*. It is 'a production of me already dead':

> the person whom it celebrates was a cloud instead of a Juno . . . I think one is always in love with something or other; the error, and I confess it is not easy for spirits clad in flesh and blood to avoid it, consists in seeking in a mortal image the likeness of what is perhaps eternal.[17]

This conception is one of the cluster of major impulses behind 'The Triumph of Life' and had been at work in Shelley's mind with other seminal influences since at least the previous autumn. In October, when completing *Hellas*, he had spoken of *Epipsychidion* as a 'mystery', having 'little to do with real flesh and blood'. He also referred to his unsuccessful attempt 'to be what I might have been', his reading of the Greek dramatists and Plato 'for ever', and his admiration for the figure of Antigone:

> Some of us have, in a prior existence, been in love with an Antigone, and that makes us find no full content in any mortal tie . . .[18]

'Close thy Byron, open thy Goethe', Carlyle commanded a decade later in *Sartor Resartus*: 'It is only with Renunciation (*Entsagen*) that Life, properly speaking, can be said to begin.' But his 'full content' depends on 'lessening your Denominator', a procedure foreign to Shelley's temper even in 1822.[19] 'Give up this idle pursuit after shadows and temper yourself to the season', he told Claire Clairmont in March, but the physician could not heal himself. The man whose Rousseau explains that he was overcome,

> By my own heart alone, which neither age,
>
>     Nor tears, nor infamy, nor now the tomb
>    Could temper to its object . . . , (ll.240–3)

is himself too restless to settle to an 'object'. 'I am not well . . . My side torments me. My mind agitates the prison which it inhabits, and things go ill with me . . .' This is the undersong of the final months of his life. 'My faculties are shaken to atoms . . . I can write nothing'; 'My spirits completely overcome me'; '. . . nothing will cure the cunsumption of my purse, yet it drags on a sort of life in death, very like its master . . .'[20] He had about a month to live when he asked Trelawny for '*the Prussic acid, the essential oil of bitter almonds* . . . a great kindness if you could procure me a small quantity . . . I have no intention of suicide at present, but I confess it would be a comfort to me to hold in my possession that golden key to the chamber of perpetual rest . . .'[21]

## IV

Expectedly, Shelley's current reading plays upon these emotions and helps to set in motion the complex responses at work in his last poem. Goethe's *Faust*, Calderon's *Magico Prodigioso*, Plato, Coleridge, and Wordsworth, are brought together in his April letter to Gisborne, but *Faust* most troubles him (the italics are mine):

> I have been reading over and over again Faust, and always with sensations which no other composition excites. *It deepens the gloom and augments the rapidity of ideas, and would therefore seem to me an unfit study for any one person who is a prey to the reproaches of memory, and the delusions of an imagination not to be restrained* . . .

Compensatory feelings turn out to be equally complicated.

> . . . the pleasure of sympathising with emotions known only to a few, although they derive their sole charm *from despair, and the scorn of the narrow good we can attain in our present state*, seems more than to ease the pain which belongs to them. Perhaps all discontent with the *less* (to use a Platonic sophism) supposes a just claim to a *greater* [Shelley's italics], and that we admirers of *Faust* are on the right road to Paradise.

'Paradise', a conception as remote for him as ever it was from the celestial region of traditional belief, gives his thinking a savage turn. His own 'supposition'

> is not more absurd, and is certainly less demoniacal, than that of Wordsworth, where he says,
>
> > This earth,
> > Which is the world of all of us, and where
> > *We find our happiness or not at all* [Shelley's italics]
>
> As if, after sixty years' suffering here, we were to be roasted alive for sixty million more in hell, or charitably annihilated by a *coup de grâce* of the bungler who brought us into existence at first![22]

Ivan Karamazov, whose creator admired *Cain* and *Manfred* and made his own vast contribution to the literature of the Promethean rebel, would have felt at home with this pronouncement and could have translated it verbatim for use in his Legend of the Grand Inquisitor. From these reflections Shelley is led to think of Calderon, scenes from whose *Magico Prodigioso* he had been translating the previous month. These include dialogues between Cyprian and the Demon which foreshadow Goethe's treatment of Faust and Mephistopheles and gave him 'little trouble' in comparison with his 'very imperfect representation' of Goethe. The lines hint at his insight into the nature of literary 'influences' and parallels 'I find', he says,

> a striking similarity between Faust and this drama . . . *Cyprian* evidently furnished the germ of *Faust*, as *Faust* may furnish the germ of other poems; although it is as different from it in structure and plan as the acorn from the oak . . .[23]

Whatever the 'germ' of 'The Triumph of Life', its 'structure and plan' certainly owe nothing to either of the plays but are strongly affected, together with its versification, by Dante and Petrarch, whose use of *terza rima* Shelley emulates with an accomplishment rare in English.[24] Above all, his long familiarity with their work encouraged the projection of his material through exchanges between a narrator and a more experienced figure who acts as interpreter and guide. But Shelley's Rousseau combines with this function that of certain other spirits encountered in the *Commedia*, in particular Arnaut Daniel, Brunetto Latini, and Statius, ravaged creative figures who elicit sympathetic respect as well as pity and pain. Further, Shelley's Rousseau looks to the narrator for help in understanding his own dark story: 'What thou wouldst be taught, I then may learn/ From thee . . .' he says (ll.307–8). The relationship between these figures and the poet in *propria persona* is thus much more closely akin to the nineteenth century exploratory 'dialogue of the mind with itself' than it is to its fourteenth century antecedents. This difference is probably our single most important guide to the nature of the poem and Shelley's concerns in it.

Nevertheless the formal allegiance exists, as we are reminded by the specific reference to Dante,

> . . . whom from the lowest depths of Hell
> Through every Paradise and through all glory
> Love led serene, and who returned to tell
>
> In words of hate and awe the wondrous story
> How all things are transfigured, except Love . . .
>
> (ll.472–76)

The allegiance is strengthened by Petrarch's Dantesque use of a narrator and a 'leader' in the *Trionfi*, the immensely influential series of six poems written in the period from 1338 to Petrarch's death in 1374, whose 'basic metaphor Petrarch had probably drawn from descriptions of triumphal pageants in the works of classical writers such as Ovid and Lactantius and from the Roman triumph itself'. The six 'Triumphs' are those of Love, Chastity, Death, Fame, Time, and Eternity and even if not initially intended as a series have a continuity with each other corresponding formally, in some degree, to the links within each poem between their constituent '*capitoli*' or chapters. The first

three, on Love, Chastity and Death, were written during
1338–49, and in celebrating the power of each in turn also
celebrate the power of the poet's transfiguring love for Laura.
The Triumph of Death, read by Shelley in September 1819,
belongs to 1348—the year of the Black Death and Laura's
demise—and probably suggested the fourth, where Fame
triumphs over Death, a figure which has some affinity with
Shelley's sombre figure of Life. The fifth and sixth shorter pieces
arrived more than twenty years later and show Time's triumph
over Fame and finally Eternity's triumph over Time. All these,
especially the substantial pieces on Love, Death, and Fame,
develop the 'basic metaphor' of the triumphal procession with
the proliferation of allegorical detail which captivated medieval
and Renaissance painters, and was still arresting attention in
1816 when Keats drew on Poussin's 'L'Empire de Flore' and 'La
Vie Humaine' for his own procession of human life in 'Sleep and
Poetry', the most ambitious poem in his first volume, *Poems*
(1817). The opening Triumph, of Love, establishes the pattern.
Cupid appears in his triumphal chariot drawn by four horses and
surrounded by a multitude of captives known in history and
legend. Their identity and destiny are explained by one of their
number who introduces himself to the narrator and is at first
unrecognized, as with Rousseau and the narrator in 'The
Triumph of Life'.

> Toward me there came a spirit somewhat less
> Distressed than the others, calling me by name,
> And saying, 'These are the gains of those who love!'
>     Wond'ring I said to him: 'How knowest thou
> My face? for theee I cannot recognise.'
> And he: 'The heavy bonds that weigh me down
>     Prevent thee, and the dimness of the air . . .'[25]

In the passage singled out by T. S. Eliot for its 'precision of image
and . . . economy new to Shelley' and for its 'greater wisdom',[26]
the narrator in 'The Triumph of Life' tells us,

>                 . . . I turned and knew
> (O Heaven have mercy on such wretchedness!)
>
> That what I thought was an old root which grew
> To strange distortion out of the hill side
>     Was indeed one of that deluded crew,

And that the grass which methought hung so wide
    And white, was but his thin discoloured hair,
And that the holes he vainly sought to hide

    Were or had been eyes.—'If thou canst forbear
To join the dance, which I had well forborne,'
    Said the grim Feature, of my thought aware,

'I will unfold that which to this deep scorn
    Led me and my companions . . . (ll. 180–92)

Shelley's figure is more fearfully reduced by retributive suffering than Petrarch's and the Miltonic echo in 'the grim Feature' suggests a closer emotional affinity with the figure of Death in *Paradise Lost*. Petrarch's victims of love from history, literature, and legend are followed at last by Laura, whose appearance prepares for the final 'chapter' on poets from classical times to the present who have been thralls of love. This pattern is sustained throughout the series, the captives sometimes appearing as individual figures, sometimes as a Dantean unnumbered multitude. Shelley, who in 1819 had already drawn on one tradition of the genre for 'The Mask of Anarchy', uses both the catalogue of particular exemplars and the suggestion of unnumbered multitudes. But the fact remains that his use of them is governed by the highly individual imaginative purposes which he centres in his two speakers.

    The prevailing temper of this Shelleyan 'Triumph' is in effect no closer to Petrarch than it is to works by other writers mentioned earlier in this paper, or indeed to the temper of passages from Milton and Shakespeare from which inspiration is drawn for some of its telling pictorial details. Shelley's response to the most influential of his 'presiders'—Dante, Petrarch, Milton, Rousseau, and the Goethe of *Faust*—is finally one of oblique, largely dissenting, debate. He works with remarkable individuality within his chosen genre, forcing its disciplines to command a vision which is totally at variance with the basic assumptions of his major antecedents. The thought is seductive that he might have planned a sequel, or even a series of 'Trionfi', in order to celebrate Life's defeat by the values which preserved his 'sacred few' from destruction and which kept awake even in so damaged a spirit as his Rousseau some degree of redeeming self-knowledge. But the 'basic metaphor' of the 'Triumph' gets its strength from the accepted conventions of power and authority, the agents of 'blood and gold' who are Shelley's targets here as always, though now joined by remarkably different instances of corruption. The metaphor is entirely appropriate for the subject proposed but might present peculiar difficulties if designed to serve the interests of an antithetical theme.

## V

As we know it, 'The Triumph of Life' falls into roughly five parts, faintly recalling Petrarch's use of '*capitoli*': (I) the induction in which according to the custom of the genre the narrator sets the time and season—here early summer—when first the 'Vision on my brain was rolled' (ll.1–40); (II) the narrator's account of the 'waking dream', which brings him 'the true similitude of a triumphal pageant'· but offers no explanation of the chariot arriving in its mysterious cold bright glare, the fearful 'Shape' within it and the 'mighty captives' fettered to the car (ll.41–170); (III) Rousseau's emergence, his identification of the 'Shape' as 'Life', and the first of his commentaries on the 'captives', many of whom he identifies for the narrator (ll.176–292); (IV) Rousseau's autobiographical history, undertaken to satisfy the narrator's 'thirst for knowledge', which relates 'how and by what paths' he came to be one of the captives and, as the climax of what we have of the poem, vivifies the ambiguous and seductive 'Shape all light' which precipitates the disaster and takes us to the heart of the mystery (ll.292–468); and (V) Rousseau's descriptive account of the procession (ll.469–543)—the *third* in the poem— which this time summons to attention the tragic delusions of mankind in the form of Lucretian phantoms or simulacra, emanating in their thousands from the individuals in the multitudinous procession until,

> The earth was grey with phantoms, and the air
> Was peopled with dim forms, as when there hovers
>
> A flock of vampire-bats before the glare
> Of the tropic sun, bringing ere evening
> Strange night upon some Indian isle . . . (ll.482–86)

The remaining four lines of the poem consist of the narrator's question, 'Then what is Life . . .', his description of Rousseau gazing after the chariot as it rolls away, 'as if that look must be the last', and Rousseau's unfinished reply, 'Happy those for whom the fold/Of . . .' (ll.544–48).

The structure, then, accommodates two autobiographical narratives which correspond to while at the same time commenting and expanding upon each other. What they record occurs in a continuous present. The procession seems to pass three times but the 'triumph of life' in fact perpetuates itself continuously—through human delusion, the last part of the poem seems to say—and is more or less understood, and more or less damaging, according to the stage reached in an individual consciousness. (Rousseau's gazing after its third passage 'as if that look must be the last' refers to his own withdrawal, not to the end of the process.) Both accounts are incomplete through bewilderment and ignorance. The narrator records the first stages of painful awakening from innocence to experience. Rousseau's longer narrative is more bitterly knowledgeable but still expresses bewilderment at the mystery of his fate. Neither figure, of course, is historical. The narrator, in some ways recalling the youthful poet of 'Alastor', is and is not Shelley. With some lapses, the figure functions dramatically as part of the poem's total imaginative statement. This use of his chosen genre's procedures helps to reduce that ambiguity surrounding the nature of the 'I' in certain of Shelley's other poems which makes him vulnerable to the charge of unbalancing subjectivity. 'Rousseau' is a more complex imaginative conception still, since he is compounded of materials drawn from both the historical Rousseau's autobiographical *Confessions* (which incorporate their own fictional distortions) and the ideal portraits in his novels, particularly Saint-Preux and Julie, the lovers in *Julie, ou La Nouvelle Héloïse*.

Distancing devices are needed in 'The Triumph of Life' because of the pressingly personal nature of the themes it explores. In what I have called Parts II and III of the poem, that is the narrator's and Rousseau's first accounts of the procession, much of the emphasis lies on familiar objects of Shelley's angry attention. Even so the discourse soon accommodates new autobiographical themes, modulating in the narrator's case into distressed concern with the darker aspects of sexual passion and, once Rousseau speaks, into the peculiar perils threatening the creative sensibility. This important theme reaches its climax in the fourth part, where the duplicities surrounding the 'Shape all light' are associated with Rousseau's fated imaginative sensibility.

In Part II, even before Rousseau's intervention, the narrator has no trouble in recognizing the representatives of tyranny and self-interest. The blind charioteer, the 'Janus-faced Shadow' whose 'four faces ... Had their eyes banded', prompts the scornful quasi-Augustan aphorism,

> . . . little profit brings
>
> Speed in the van and blindness in the rear . . .
> (ll. 100–1),

and the 'sacred few' are absent because they

> . . . could not tame
>
> Their spirits to the Conqueror, but as soon
>     As they had touched the world with living flame
>
> Fled back like eagles to their native noon . . . (ll. 128–31)

The image, which suggests that they did not survive long enough to court corruption, already hints at the identity of the 'Conqueror'. Whether Shelley intended to display the narrator's quickening insight or had not yet resolved an anomaly, it is clear where many of his own interests still lie. The first vividly delineated figure, with bowed head 'and hands crossed on his chain', is Napoleon:

> The child of a fierce hour; he sought to win
>
> The world, and lost all it did contain
> Of greatness, in its hope destroyed; and more
>     Of fame and peace than Virtue's self can gain
>
> Without the opportunity which bore
>     Him on its eagle's pinion to the peak
> From which a thousand climbers have before
>
> Fall'n as Napoleon fell. . . . (ll. 217–24)

The narrator responds in lines expressing the weary sense of the irreducible 'non-Euclidean' nature of existence which informs the whole poem:

And much I grieved to think how power and will
In opposition rule our mortal day—

And why God made irreconcilable
Good and the means of good; and for despair
    I half disdained mine eye's desire to fill

With the spent vision of the times that were
    And scarce have ceased to be . . . (ll.228–34)

Rousseau's catalogue includes 'the heirs/Of Caesar's crime, from
him to Constantine', the 'Anarchs' who helped to 'spread the
plague of blood and gold', and 'Gregory and John and men
divine' who interpose 'like shadows between Man and God . . .'
(ll.284–91). But Shelley does not allow him to comment on the
narrator's vision of the 'fierce and obscene . . . wild dance' of
sexual passion. This long passage of some thirteen tercets
(ll.137–75) depicts with vivid and precise imagery the young,
'tortured by the agonising pleasure' who go to 'their bright
destruction', and the old, 'foully disarrayed', with their 'grey hair
shaken in the insulting wind', who still strain after the chariot
only to sink at last to the ground where

            . . . corruption veils them as they lie,
    And frost performs in these what fire in those.
                                            (ll.174–75)

    If this appears to be the most pressing of the younger speaker's
anxieties, the main burden of the 'leader's' first discourse is the
confession of his own corruption and his insistence
notwithstanding that its cause and effect make him less culpable
than the other 'spoilers' in the procession:

            . . . those spoilers spoiled, Voltaire,

    Frederick, and Kant, Catherine, and Leopold,
Each hoary anarch, demagogue and sage
    Whose name the fresh world thinks already old,

For in the battle Life and they did wage
    She remained conqueror—I was overcome
By my own heart alone, which neither age

    Nor tears nor infamy nor now the tomb
Could temper to its object . . . (ll.235–43)

Unlike those whose

> power was given
>   But to destroy . . . (ll.292–93),

he is

> one of those who have created, even
> If it be but a world of agony. (ll.294–95),

and he intersperses this part of his narrative with similar reflections, beginning with the assertion,

> . . . there rise
> A thousand beacons from the spark I bore. (ll.206–7)

Allusions to other of the world's famed but flawed creative spirits signal the unease prompting this 'dialogue of the [poetic] mind with itself'. To Voltaire and Kant are added Plato and Aristotle, the former unsubdued by 'gold or pain/Or age of aloth' but corrupted by passion, the latter infected by association with 'Dominion' through his pupil Alexander (ll.245–62). Even his allusion to the major poets of the past has its ambiguities. His 'See the great bards of old' can be read either as an indication that they too are in the procession or merely as an exhortation to the narrator to turn his thoughts to them as creators of 'living melody', a celebratory phrase seemingly supported by the context. They

> . . . inly quelled
>
>   The passions which they sung, as by their strain
>     May be well known: their living melody
>   Tempers its own contagion to the vein
>
> Of those who are infected with it . . . (ll.274–8)

But 'Contagion' and 'infected' carry an emotional charge which recalls Shelley's ambivalent use of the word 'stain' when thinking about the brilliancy and colour of the physical world. The anomalies, telling in themselves, lead on to Rousseau's contrasting himself unfavourably with his predecessors because unlike them he did not 'quell' but indulged the feelings which he portrayed, a danger which his creator almost certainly felt to be at work in himself (and which he may have recognized in the early Byron). Rousseau explains,

>      ... I
> Have suffered what I wrote or viler pain ...

and so his words

>           ... were seeds of misery
> Even as the deeds of others ... (ll.278–81)

This anxiety about a damaging subjectivity is not resolved within the poem either by the narrator or by Rousseau, but their creator's formal procedures suggest a wary effort to balance the inner and the outer. Certainly the juxtaposition of the poem's 'Rousseau' and the 'bards of old' seems to bring us close to Keats's distinction between the 'dreamer' and the true poet in 'The Fall of Hyperion', where the 'dreamer venoms all his days' because he is haunted by the 'miseries of life' in the abstract:

> The poet and the dreamer are distinct,
> Diverse, sheet opposite, antipodes,
> The one pours out a balm upon the world,
> The other vexes it ... (I 199–202)

For both poets intense obsessive feeling, especially where the obsession is with ideal love, imperils the perfecting of the life and the work. Keats had struggled to wrestle into harmony human passion and ideal love in his youthful recipe for life in 'Endymion', but 'La Belle Dame Sans Merci' and 'Lamia', written in 1819 when he was deeply troubled about his feelings for Fanny, his destiny as a writer, and the relationship between these, show the enchantress as at once the source of delight and the agent of destruction. For Shelley to have dreamed of an Antigone 'makes us find no full content in any mortal tie.'

In Part IV of 'The Triumph of Life' he finally confronts this *idée fixe*. What is described in *Epipsychidion* as 'the lodestar of my one desire' now emerges as the compelling 'Shape all light' which quickens the youthful Rousseau's passionate delight but fades and is lost for ever when the rival 'Shape', dark in the midst of its 'bright glare', rides by in triumph and gathers him into its procession of despairing captives. Rousseau's account of this tragic sequence occupies over one hundred lines (thirty-four tercets, ll.337–438), the longest passage in the poem: longer than the narrator's description of the sensualists in Part II and both longer and poetically more impressively achieved than the passages describing the counterpointing shape of Life (or perhaps more accurately Death-in-Life), which occur in the narrator's record in Part II and again in Rousseau's record in Parts III and IV. The characteristically Shelleyan imagery recurs of iridescence and prismatic colour, but with heightened feeling now that these are no longer seen in contrast to 'the white radiance of eternity' but emerge as components in that 'medal of strange alloy' (Henry James's phrase for human life), one side of which is brilliant and beautiful, the other dark and baleful.[27] The figure stands

> Amid the Sun, as he amid the blaze
>     Of his own glory, on the vibrating
> Floor of the fountain, paved with flashing rays,
>
>     A Shape all light, which with one hand did fling
> Dew on the earth, as if she were the Dawn,
>     Whose invisible rain forever seemed to sing
>
> A silver music on the mossy lawn . . . (ll.349–55)

This description expresses a totally captivating charm and grace. But in the figure's other hand—it is a simple enough allegorical device to suggest her duality—is the crystal goblet with its mysterious liquid Nepenthe. Initially, then, this presence arouses a response which might suit Dante's Beatrice, the magnificent emblem of redemption created by the poet who returned, as Rousseau reminds his listener,

>                 to tell
>
> In words of hate and awe the wondrous story
>     How all things are transfigured, except Love . . .[28]
>                         (ll.474–77)

But as it turns out these lines preface Rousseau's rendering of the nightmare vision in Part V, which follows upon his touching with his lips the goblet which the 'Shape' reaches out to him. Similarly in 'The Fall of Hyperion' the poet experiences his tragic vision after drinking from the 'cool vessel of transparent juice', which he finds waiting in the grass beside the emblematic remnants of a pre-lapsarian existence of unalloyed happiness. It is with the disturbing supervening vision that each poet breaks off his unfinished last work. Shelley's bright figure, then, once approached, has nothing of Beatrice's achromatic purity but conjures to the imagination ambivalences which suggest a certain kinship with the complex feelings producing the fated figure of Keats's troubled reveries.

Part V of 'The Triumph of Life' begins with the third description of the chariot (ten tercets, ll.439–78) but introduces a new motif, designed to emphasize the indissociable relationship between the 'Shape all light' of Rousseau's youthful vision and the dark shape in the car. The device linking them is the image of the rainbow, prismatic emblem of the brilliance and variety of life. The lines in Part IV comparing the bright Shape to the Dawn scattering 'silver music on the mossy lawns' are followed immediately by,

> And still before her on the dusky grass
> Iris her many-coloured scarf had drawn. (ll.356–7)

In Part V, as the rival 'new vision, and its cold bright car' advance, Iris is still in attendance as a celebrant encouraging the 'loud million' who now,

> Fiercely extolled the fortune of her star.
>
> A moving arch of victory the vermillion
> And green and azure plumes of Iris had
> Built high over her wind-winged pavilion,
>
> And underneath, aetherial glory clad
> The wilderness, and far before her flew
> The tempest of the splendour which forbade
>
> Shadow to fall from leaf or stone;—the crew
> Seemed in that light like atomies that dance
> Within a sunbeam . . . (ll.439–47)

Shelley had already used this image to suggest the illusoriness of human notions about the beautiful and the good in his Petrarchan story, 'Una Favola', the little tale in Italian which he had written in 1820 and where the false Duessa is Life, 'who had the form of a potent enchantress.' She is Death's sister and comes 'with a gay visage, crowned with a rainbow and clad in the various mantle of a chameleon skin'. She and her equally seductive sister in turn come between the youth and the attainment of his desire, the lady 'in whose quest Love had led the

youth through that gloomy labyrinth of error and suffering . . .'
Both Life and Love are attended by captivating figures who are
at first veiled but once unmasked are seen to be 'each more
hideous and terrible than the other. Their horrible aspect and
loathsome figure so overcame his heart with sadness that the fair
heaven, covered with that shadow, clothed itself in clouds before
his eyes; and he wept so much that the herbs upon his path, fed
with tears instead of dew, became pale and bowed like himself'.
It is now that he is drawn towards Death for solace. He is visited
at long last by the lady of his dream vision, but finally is yet again
threatened by Life, the jealous, rainbow-coloured female
presence. The story breaks off with the conflict unresolved
between the possessive figure of Life and the now almost equally
possessive lady of his quest.

The closeness of this thinking and feeling to 'The Triumph of
Life' hardly needs stressing, the resemblances reaching to the
connection between the hideousness of the unmasked figures and
the fearful images representing human delusion at the close of
Part V. That the themes had been gestating for at least two years
helps to explain how it is that 'The Triumph of Life', incomplete
and unrevised as it is, displays in its complex poetic structure
remarkable firmness and command. It is hard to believe that
Shelley would have added much more to it. It expresses a
particular mood in which there is no resolution for troubling
contraries. It closes with a harsh statement about human
delusion and its last lines leave everything unanswered, but in
defining the mood it arrives at its own order of free-standing
affirmation.


# VI

The poetic qualities determining this underlying strength cannot
be attended to as closely as one would like in the remaining space,
but something should perhaps be said in this concluding section
about the interplay between sameness and difference in the
narrator's story and Rousseau's and the variations in poetic
procedure which accompany them. The outstanding dissimilarity
is of course the absence from the narrator's experience of the
'Shape all light', which is inspired by Shelley's reading of the
historical Rousseau's confessional writings but is of course at once

a product of, and a warning to, his own imaginative sensibility. Both stories describe a movement from delight in the brilliancy irradiating the physical world to a darker state of being where harsh realities press forward and the earlier vision fades. The sequence is informed by a quasi-Keatsian feeling for human inability 'to unperplex bliss from its neighbour pain', a skill[29] reserved by Keats for his Lamia (who derives her power from it). Certainly Shelley had given 'the miseries of the world' a local habitation and a name long before Keats's attempt in 'The Fall of Hyperion' to distinguish between the dreamer, the poet, and the humanitarian man of action. But Keats's precocious intuitiveness (as distinct from Shelley's more systematically informed analytical intellect) had led him to look the 'Medusa face of life' in the eye as early as 'Sleep and Poetry' and, again in his May 1818 letter to John Reynolds, in both of which he reworks from 'Tintern Abbey' Wordsworth's outline of the stages of personal development. In the poem he envisages an initial period of unreflecting delight in 'the realm . . . Of Flora and old Pan . . .', followed by the stage where he must 'bid these joys farewell' for

> a nobler life,
> Where I may find the agonies, the strife
> Of human hearts . . . (ll.101–25)

Thereupon he introduces his symbol for the progress of the creative imagination: a chariot is drawn across the sky by racing steeds, it descends to earth and the charioteer, after contemplating and delighting in the natural world, turns to human life, pictured as a procession of multifarious figures:

> Shapes of delight, of mystery, and fear,
> Passing along before a dusky space
> Made by some mighty oaks; as they would chase
> Some ever-fleeting music on they sweep.
> Lo! how they murmur, laugh, and smile, and weep—
> Some with upholden hand and mouth severe;
> Some with their faces muffled to the ear
> Between their arms; some, clear in youthful bloom,
> Go glad and smilingly athwart the gloom;
> Some looking back, and some with upward gaze.
> Yes, thousands in a thousand different ways
> Flit onward . . . (ll.138–49)

This is like and unlike Shelley's procession, where 'shapes of mystery and fear' eventually obscure the single 'Shape of delight' and the theme turns on the tragic interdependence of these opposites. But both suggest an over-riding desire to comprehend the mysterious relationship between delight, pain, and creativity. As Shelley's Rousseau touches the goblet and the 'new Vision' bursts glaringly on his sight, he still knows

> in that light's severe excess
> The presence of that shape which on the stream
> Moved, as I moved along the wilderness,
>
> More dimly than a day-appearing dream,
> The ghost of a forgotten form of sleep,
> A light from Heaven whose half-extinguished beam
>
> Through the sick day in which we wake to weep
> Glimmers, forever sought, forever lost . . . (ll.424–31)

In 'Sleep and Poetry' the poet's 'awakening' is characteristically Keatsian in feeling, but the emotional sequence is similar to Shelley's.

> The visions are all fled—the car is fled
> Into the light of heaven, and in their stead
> A sense of real things comes doubly strong,
> And, like a muddy stream, would bear along
> My soul to nothingness . . . (ll.155–59)

Keats wrote this when he and Shelley were both frequenting Leigh Hunt's circle at Hampstead, and it is just possible that Shelley had some inkling of the ideas which led Keats to formulate his image for human life as 'a mansion of many apartments'. In his celebrated May 1818 letter the first apartment is described as 'The infant or thoughtless Chamber, in which we remain so long as we do not think.' The second is 'the Chamber of Maiden-Thought', where 'we become intoxicated with the light and atmosphere, we see nothing but pleasant wonders, and think of delaying there for ever in delight'. Then follows,

> that tremendous one of sharpening one's vision into the heart and nature of Man—of convincing one's nerves that the World is full of Misery and Heartbreak, Pain, Sickness

and oppression ... This Chamber of Maiden-Thought becomes gradually darken'd and at the same time on all sides of it many doors are set open—but all dark—all leading to dark passages—We see not the ballance of good and evil. We are in a Mist ... We feel the 'burden of the Mystery'. To this point was Wordsworth come, as far as I can conceive when he wrote 'Tintern Abbey' ...[30]

To this point, we might say, the narrator of 'The Triumph of Life' had also come, and with him his creator, while 'Rousseau' has travelled far down the 'dark passages' and utters his grim warning from experience of their furthest recesses.

Shelley's narrator seems at first to be 'delaying' in the 'thoughtless Chamber'. The induction (Part I) celebrates the sun as the source of vitality and harmony.

> Swift as a spirit hastening to his task
>    Of glory and good, the Sun sprang forth
> Rejoicing in his splendour, and the mask
>
>    Of darkness fell from the awakened Earth ...
>                                     (ll. 1–5)

Snow-covered peaks 'flaming' above the crimson clouds are the sun's 'smokeless altars', the sound of the sea is an 'orison',

> To which the birds tempered their matin lay ... , (1.8)

and the use of 'tempered', as elsewhere in Shelley, points to an ordered activity ensuring harmony. So too with the flowers synaesthetically sending 'their odorous sighs up to the smiling air' and with the unison described in,

> Continent,
>
>   Isle, Ocean, and all things that in them wear
> The form and character of mortal mould
>    Rise as the Sun their father rose, to bear
>
> Their portion of the toil which he of old
>   Took as his own and then imposed on them ...
>                                  (ll. 15–20)

But in fact the narrator is already alienated from this vital creativity:

> thoughts which must remain untold
>
> Had kept me wakeful as the stars that gem
> The cone of night . . . , (ll.21–23)

and as the world quickens to life he sinks to the ground though not to sleep. Instead,

> a strange trance over my fancy grew
> Which was not slumber . . . (ll.29–30)

Rousseau, at the corresponding stage of his story, as recorded in the climactic fourth part of the poem, finds himself 'asleep' in a 'sweet and deep oblivious spell,' lulled by the sound of the rivulet in the grove. The imagery tells us that his history, unlike the narrator's, must be understood to begin at the beginning, with the process of birth into the world. He speaks (echoing *Hamlet*) of 'this harsh world in which I wake to weep' (l.334) and, at the opening of the second stage of his personal record in what I have described as the fifth part of the poem, refers again to 'the sick day in which we wake to weep' (l.430). The birth imagery carries with it some hint of 'a prior existence', the phrase used by Shelley in his letter about the haunting image of an ideal figure, an 'Antigone'. The grove, we learn, is situated,

> Under a mountain, which from unknown time,
>
> Had yawned into a cavern high and deep,

and the life-giving rivulet flowing from it,

> Bent the soft grass, and kept for ever wet
> The stems of the sweet flowers, and filled the grove
> With sound which whoso hear must needs forget
>
> All pleasure and all pain; all hate and love,
> Which they had known before that hour of rest . . .
> (ll.312–20)

The idea is glanced at again,

> Whether my life had been before that sleep
> The Heaven which I imagine, or a Hell
>
> Like this harsh world in which I wake to weep,
> I know not . . . (ll.332–35)

These unWordsworthian intimations of immortality seem to echo Shelley's bitter dismissal of Wordsworth's lines on 'this world in which we find happiness or not at all'[31] and, we may notice, anticipates Yeats's quasi-Platonic lines in 'Among Schoolchildren' where the 'shape' upon its mother's lap,

> must sleep, shriek, struggle to escape
> As recollection or the drug decide . . . (st.v)

In Shelley, the opiate of 'sweet and deep . . . oblivion' ensures that

> A sleeping mother then would dream not of
>> The only child who died upon her breast
> At eventide, a king would mourn no more
>> The crown of which his brow was dispossessed . . .
>>> (ll.321–4)

The narrator, too, Rousseau assures him, will

> forget thus vainly to deplore
>> Ills, which if ills, can find no cure from thee,
> The thought of which no other sleep will quell,
>> Nor other music blot from memory . . . (ll.327–30)

The lines hint at the nature of the narrator's 'troubling thoughts', their connection with Shelley's 1822 anxieties, and his consequent desire for the 'golden key to the chamber of perpetual rest'.

Life in this poem is certainly not 'a sleep and a forgetting' but there is a hovering, perhaps wishful, notion that it is somehow bounded by these and is perhaps obedient to a Karma-like law of continuity making for ultimate perfection. The narrator's sense of *déjà vu* at the start is in keeping, since it directs attention to the similarity between his own and Rousseau's early experience, while still leaving open the question of the ultimate identity of their respective destinies. 'I knew', he says,

> That I had felt the freshness of that dawn,
> Bathed in the same cold dew my brow and hair,
>> And sate as thus upon that slope of lawn
>
> Under the self same bough, and heard as there
>> The birds, the fountain and the Ocean hold
> Sweet talk in music through the enamoured air . . .
>>> (ll.33–9)

Shelley probably remembered from his recent reading
Rousseau's paraphrase (in a footnote to one of the Letters in *La
Nouvelle Héloïse*) of Plato's views about the soul's journey through
successive existences. Rousseau notes briefly that '*les âmes de justes*'
do not return for purification and dwells on those who were in life
'*asservis à leurs passions*' and so carry with them continuously '*des
parties terrestres qui les tiennent comme enchaînées autour des débris de leur
corps*',[32] an idea which clings round Shelley's portrayal of both
Rousseau and Plato:

> All that is mortal of great Plato there
> Expiates the joy and woe his master knew not . . .
>
> (ll.254–55)

'Expiates' perhaps again hints at the direction of Shelley's
current thinking. But the idea of life as a constantly renewed and
perhaps ultimately renovating process is not anywhere explicit.
Nor is there any assertion of revitalizing processes of the kind
informing *Prometheus Unbound* or of the 'progressive state of more
or less exalted existence' celebrated in the choruses from *Hellas*.

On the other hand, a considerable degree of personal
engagement is suggested by the rise in poetic temperature
accompanying the account of the sensualists in Part II and
Rousseau's account of his personal disaster in Part IV. It seems
right to say that when the pageant first unfolds in Part I, bringing
to attention the agents of 'blood and gold', the prevailing
emotional stance is that of a fascinated and moved but not yet
completely involved spectator, and this in spite of the resonance
noticeable in the poet's quickening use of his Miltonic and
Dantean metaphors for the multitudinousness of the 'undone'.
The quality is felt in the description of the hurrying throng,
'numerous as gnats upon the evening gleam', which precedes the
chariot and grows 'wilder' as it approaches (ll.44–79), and of the
advent of the car itself, which contains the 'Shape' and is drawn
by the blind charioteer (ll.79–106). It is after this that the
watcher's 'wonder' quickens into more painful feeling until he is
indeed 'Struck to the heart by this sad pageantry' (l.176) and asks
the questions which provide the cue for Rousseau's appearance.

> 'And what is this?
> Whose Shape is that within the car? And why?'—
> I would have added—'is all here amiss' . . . (ll.177–79)

But it is still excited attention rather than anguish which characterizes the initial tercets in Part II. The sequence as a whole suggests the author's concentration on his inventive 'making', beginning with the gesture towards the opening convention of the *Comedia*,

> Methought I sate beside a public way
>
> Thick strewn with summer dust . . . , (ll.43–44)

his disciplined reworking of traditional similes,

> a great stream
> Of people there was hurrying to and fro
> Numerous as gnats upon the evening gleam,
>
> All hastening onward none seemed to know
> Whither he went, or whence he came, or why
> He made one of the multitude, yet so
>
> Was borne amid the crowds as through the sky
> One of the million leaves of summer's bier . . . ,
>
> (ll.47–51)

and his slowing of tempo in keeping with what is observed rather than at the command of pressing personal emotion:

> Old age and youth, manhood and infancy,
>
> Mixed in one mighty torrent did appear,
> Some flying from the thing they feared and some
> Seeking the object of another's fear . . .
>
> And others mournfully within the gloom
> Of their own shadow walked, and called it death . . .
>
> (ll.52–59)

The picturing of the flowers and trees, the 'melodious dew' of the fountains in their 'mossy cells' which lie on either side of the dusty 'public way' convey an authorial pleasure in sustaining this appropriate natural imagery. Attention to 'the object as in itself it is', conducts his style from the fresh Miltonic-Shakespearian lyricism of his

> over arching elms and caverns cold
> And violet banks . . . , (ll.71–72)

which are neglected by the hurrying crowd, to the crisply dismissive

> little profit brings
> Sped in the van and blindness in the rear . . . , (ll.100–1)

which is prompted by the 'serious folly' of the crowd and the purposeless onward rush of the blind charioteer (and may perhaps derive added sharpness from Shelley despondently now thinking of his career as a sprinter's rather than a long distance runner's). At the same time, his necessary engagement with the preternatural makes him strike off a studied series of impressively strange and sinister conjunctions: the

> cold glare, intenser than the moon
> But icy cold . . . (ll.77–8)

and the arresting macabre variations on the familiar image of the new moon in coming storm ('The old moon with the young moon in her arms' of the ballad),[33]

> Her white shell trembles amid crimson air
> And whilst the sleeping tempest gathers might
>
> Doth, as a herald of its coming, bear
> The ghost of her dead mother, whose dim form
> Bends in dark aether from her infant's chair,
>
> So came a chariot on the silent storm . . . , (ll.81–86)

The faltering syntax in the next verse is a symptom of interruption in the creative momentum. The 'Shape' in the chariot is bent with age and the tercet's first line—'Beneath a dusty hood and double cape'—continues the literal description, while the second—'Crouching within the shadow of a tomb'— risks an absurdity by seeming to do so too (is there a tomb *in* the chariot?), although it is probably intended as a metaphor for mortality. The search for appropriate figurative language through which to realize this grim figure suggests a difficulty seemingly not encountered in the counterpointing passages inspired later in the poem by the 'Shape all light'. Certainly it leads to a more overt kind of borrowing. Milton's Death is the model:

> The other Shape,
> If shape it might be called that shape had none
> Distinguishable in member, joint or limb . . .
> > *(Paradise Lost*, II.666–68)

It is true that Shelley's life is female like Petrarch's Death,

> I beheld a banner dark and sad,
> And a woman shrouded in a dress of black . . . ,

while Milton's is masculine. But the latter has,

> what seem'd his head
> The likeness of a kingly crown had on . . .
> > *(Paradise Lost*, II.672–73)

and Shelley follows,

> And o'er what seemed the head, a cloud like crape
> Was bent . . . ,

The syntax, once again imperfectly under control, leaves us uncertain whether the subject is 'cloud' or 'crape'. The borrowing is not of course in itself damaging, but the use of Milton's Death, whose companion 'shape' is Sin, signals a preoccupation with 'new' themes for whose expression the poet depends on the imaginative reworking of passages which have spoken powerfully home to his current creative mood. Shelley's 'Life', it has been said, 'represents, then, not merely the everyday stultifying mundane existence [of the wandering masses in the public way] . . . It is a positive evil, a destructive force into whose power men are delivered by Sin . . .'[34] But the nature of the 'Sin' is still essentially unMiltonic in that it still bears no more direct reference to orthodox Good and Evil than anywhere else in Shelley's poetry. The same applies to Shelley's reworking for his 'majestic chariot' of the chariot of God found in, among others, Milton, Dante and Ezekiel.

But the main direction of his individual thinking and the force of his emotional and imaginative drive make themselves sufficiently plain once the narrator rises 'aghast' (l.107), the discourse comes again under command of Shelley's peculiar poetic voice and we hear the familiar tones of the castigator who had mocked himself in 'Peter Bell the Third',

> some few, like we know who,
> Doomed—but God alone knows why—
> To believe their minds are given
> To make their ugly Hell a Heaven,
> In which faith they live and die . . .
> (III.xx,242–46)

The poet of 'The Mask of Anarchy' who recorded the

> Destructions played
> In this ghastly masquerade . . . , (ll.26–27)

lines up once more again,

> all those who had grown old in power
> Or misery . . . (ll.120–21)

The quickened feeling now takes its rise from the dismaying sense that whatever is done, even if it is done for good, is vulnerable to corruption and the only escape is to follow the example of those who retired early from life and

> Fled back like eagles to their native noon . . .
> (l.131)

The strength of this Shelleyan form of 'Renunciation (*Entslagen*)'[35] is more noticeable still in the sequences dealing with sexual passion (ll.137–60), where the pressure of feeling produces the sharply observed image of the lovers,

> like two clouds into one vale impelled
> That shake the mountains when their lightnings mingle,
> And die in rain,—the fiery band which held
> Their natures, snaps . . . (ll.155–58)

(Geoffrey Matthews's gloss reads, 'the tension holding each as an individual apart, like an electric potential between two charged clouds, is broken down in sexual union'.)[36] The control ensures the poise of the closing euphemism which juxtaposes impotence and lust as equipollent agents of destruction,

> And frost in these performs what fire in those . . . (l.175)

This imaginative force is felt again in Rousseau's narrative in Part IV, which begins with the passage admired by T. S. Eliot, that is the identification of the ruined figure with the distorted root growing out of the hillside. The poet's eye is 'on the object', as a more recent critic has it, because Shelley is mindful of the historical Rousseau's neglect of the natural world 'in favour of the artificial one'.[37] As the Rousseau of the poem now seems to portray matters, his earlier happier state precipitates rather than merely precedes the crisis. *Post hoc, propter hoc* is what gives its intensity to the connection between his catastrophe and the 'Shape all light' which attends his awakening 'in the April prime' and gathers unto itself the brilliant and enrapturing qualities which quicken his imagination only to leave it almost at once dark and despondent.

The magnificent Appenine landscape, it was long ago shown in a fine early interpretation of the poem,[38] is similar at the opening of both the narrator's and Rousseau's stories, but different aspects of it are thrown into relief in accordance with the imaginative purpose of the two records. Geoffrey Matthews has reminded us that the setting—or, one would prefer to say here, the *use* of the setting, especially in Rousseau's account—is affected by the historical Rousseau's 'situation' at Les Charmettes in 1737–8, described in Books V–VI of the *Confessions* as the only idyllic episode in a career that immediately afterwards (Book VII) plunged into the living storm of social and political life'.[39] Mr. Matthews cites the passage, '*Entre deux côteaux assez élevés est un petit vallon nord et sud au fond duquel coule un rigole entre des cailloux et des arbres*', and continues by quoting the letters describing the ecstatic delight of walking in the countryside with Madame de Warens on that April day in the 1730's—the 'April prime' of the poem—on recapturing '*l'espèce de rêve*' he had experienced seven or eight years before:

> . . . le chant des oiseaux, la beauté du jour, la douceur du paysage. . . tout cela me frappait tellement d'une impression, vive tendre, triste, et touchante, que je vis comme un extase . . . ce qui m'a frappe le plus dans le souvenir de cette rêverie quand elle s'est réalisé, c'est d'avoir retrouver des objects tels exactement que je les imaginés . . . Hélas! mon plus constant bonheur fut un songe: son accomplissement fut presque à l'instant suivi du réveil . . .[40]

The untroubled charm of the pre-natal passages—in whose spring-time images of 'the sweet flowers' and 'gentle rivulet', with

water 'like clear air bending the soft grass', linger recollections of
the historical Rousseau's halcyon days—is broken by the arrival
of the 'Shape all light', whose enticements lead to the despairing
recognition of the universality of human delusion.

   And as the light and colour surrounding the pageant are more
vivid in Rousseau's story than in the narrator's, so the closing
part of the vision is proportionately more fearsome than anything
the narrator has to tell. Rousseau's Bosch-like vision corresponds
structurally to the sensualists' dance of death in Part II and
springs from the same emotional soil, but it carries us beyond the
impassioned statement of disturbance at a particular theme to
the still more disturbing preoccupation with *corruptio optimi est
pessima* as a universal and inescapable truth. 'Cats and monkeys,
cats, and monkeys, all human life is there', James has a character
say in one of his wry short stories. In the final part of 'The
Triumph of Life' no human quality is exempt from the excesses
which transform it into a grotesque parody of itself. Angry
disenchantment promotes Shelley's inventive variations on the
Lucretian conception of simulacra (the Loeb translation of a key
passage about them in *De Rerem Natura* runs, '. . . everything must
. . . cast off semblances . . . There are fixed outlines of shapes and
of finest texture which flit about everywhere, but singly and
separately cannot be seen').[41] Rousseau's preternatural vision
reveals the 'semblances' mocking the appearances which mask
them in life's self-seeking and opportunist headlong flurry:

              . . . some did fling
      Shadows of shadows, yet unlike themselves,
   Behind them; some like eaglets on the wing

      Were lost in the white blaze; others like elves
   Danced in a thousand unimagined shapes
      Upon the sunny streams and grassy shelves;

   And others sate chattering like restless apes
      On vulgar hands and over shoulders leaped;
   Some made a cradle of the ermined capes

      Of kingly mantles; some upon the tiar
   Of pontiffs sate like vultures; others played
      Within the crown which girt with empire

A baby's or an idiot's brow, and made
   Their nests in it; the old anatomies
Sate hatching their bare brood under the shade

     Of demons' wings, and laughed from their dead eyes
To reassume the delegated power
   Arrayed in which these worms did monarchize

Who make this earth their charnel.—Others more
   Humble, like falcons sate upon the fist
Of common men, and round their heads did soar,

     Or like small gnats and flies as thick as mist
On evening marshes thronged about the brow
   Of lawyer, statesman, priest and theorist;

And others like discoloured flakes of snow
   On fairest bosoms and the sunniest hair
Fell, and were melted by the youthful flow

     Which they extinguished; for like tears, they were
A veil to those from whose faint lids they rained
   In drops of sorrow . . . (ll.487–516)

This is a remarkable passage. It may not demonstrate the degree
of concentration and 'wisdom' which struck Eliot in the earlier
lines describing Rousseau's first appearance and remains at some
distance from the poignant vitality of the verses describing the
'Shape all light'. But it is in keeping with the new manner
signalled by the poem, where disgust and pain contend with the
writer's resolute attempt to hold the emotion under stylistic
control.

    What one senses most keenly throughout 'The Triumph of
Life' is the feeling of loss which manifests itself, at one level,
through the unprecedented tentativeness of its gesture towards
any kind of meliorism. The shift in mood in this last poem
suggests what is perhaps as yet a change of temper rather than
belief, though the change hints that hopeful idealism is beginning
to be held to with more arduousness than ardour. 'The Triumph
of Life' foreshadows that clouding over of the emotional and
intellectual climate in the years leading from the socially
committed (and by definition relatively optimistic) literature of
the late 1840s and 1850s to the more sombre speculations of

eminent mid-Victorians who held at bay with their individual brand of moral stoicism what James was later to call 'the imagination of disaster'. Shelley's 'thoughts which must remain untold', 'ills which can find no cure from thee', and the thought of which nothing will quell other than 'sweet oblivion', shows then that it is not only the still acknowledged difficulty of ameliorating the human lot but an intensifying sense of that 'something that infects' existence itself which depresses the spirit. Shelley's 'sick day' is an early symptom of 'this strange disease of modern life' from which Arnold urges his Scholar Gipsy to 'fly hence, our contact fear!'. Paradoxically, as with Coleridge's 'Ode on Dejection' (and indeed Arnold's major poetry as well), the poetry comes into being with the despondency and discovers strength and liberation in the attempt to comprehend and define it.

# NOTES

1. T. S. Eliot, *The Use of Poetry and the Use of Criticism* (1933), 90.

2. See especially G. M. Matthews, ' "The Triumph of Life": A New Text', *Studia Neophilologica*, vol. xxxii, no. 2 (1960), pp. 271–309; 'The "Triumph of Life" Apocrypha', *TLS*, 5 August 1960, 503; 'On Shelley's "The Triumph of Life" ', *Studia Neophilologica*, vol. xxxiv, no. 1 (1962), 104–34; and Donald H. Reiman, *Shelley's 'The Triumph of Life': A Critical Study*, Illinois Studies in Language and Literature 55 (1965).

3. Cp. *Adonais* (1821), ll.462–3,

> Life, like a dome of many-coloured glass,
> Stains the white radiance of Eternity . . .

and the sonnet (1824) beginning,

> Lift not the painted veil which those who live
> Call Life . . .

4. For detailed descriptions of the manuscript see Donald H. Reiman, ' "The Triumph of Life": A Variorum Edition' and 'Order and dating of materials in the Bodleian manuscript', op. cit. 136–91, 244–50.

5. *Letters of Percy Bysshe Shelley*, ed. Frederick L. Jones, vol. 11 (1964), 376.

6. The text follows Timothy Webb's reading of Shelley's holograph draft, Bodleian Library (*Shelley: Selected Poems*, ed. Timothy Webb (1977), 190). Geoffrey Matthews reads 'Seeking Life alone, *not peace*' and glosses ll.55-end, 'The fish in choosing *Life* (active enjoyment) rather than *peace* (more placid existence), are happy because the pleasure they seek blinds them to the price they will pay for it. But *Too happy* cuts both ways, meaning "fatally happy" as well as "enviably happy" ' (*Shelley: Selected Poems and Prose*, ed. Geoffrey Matthews (1964), 216).

7. *Letters* ii. 382, 406, 434.

8. Matthew Arnold's celebrated phrase first used in his essay on Byron (1881); see 'Attitudes to Shelley' p. 22 above.

9. *Letter* ii. 419, 427.

10. *Letters* ii. 436.

11. *Letters* ii. 442.

12. For example 'England in 1819' (1839), l.10, 'Golden and sanguine laws which tempt and slay . . .' and 'Lines written on Hearing the News of the Death of Napoleon' (1821), ll.34–5, 'Napoleon's fierce spirit rolled,/In terror and blood and gold . . .'.

13. *Letters* ii. 407.

14. *La Nouvelle Héloise* (1761), Première Partie, LIV—A Julie.

15. *Letters* ii. 357–8.

16. *Letters* ii. 345.

17. *Letters* ii. 434.

18. *Letters* ii. 363, 364.

19. Carlyle, *Sartor Resartus* (1838) Book II, chap. ix, 'The Everlasting Yea', Centenary edn (1896–1900), I, 152–4.

20. *Letters* ii. 374, 382, 399, 404.

21. *Letters* ii. 430. The italics are Shelley's.

22. *Letters* ii. 406.

23. *Letters* ii. 407.

24. The translation in the mid-1580s by Mary Sidney, Countess of Pembroke, 'has the distinction of being the only English version of the *Trionfi* successfully to employ and sustain the terza rima, a verse form which every other English translator of the poem from Morley to Ernest Hatch Wilkins has conceded he has not been able to render satisfactorily' D. D. Carnicelli, *Lord Morley's Tryumphes of Fraunces Petrarcke* (1971), 37.

25. *The Triumphs of Petrarch*, translated by Ernest Hatch Wilkins (1962), 6–7. Wilkins notes, 'My translation . . . retains the tercet structure of the original, but does not attempt to preserve the Italian rhyme scheme' (op. cit., vii).

26. *The Use of Poetry and the Use of Criticism* (1933), 90.

27. Preface to *What Maisie Knew* (1897).

28. Included in David Lee Clark, *Shelley's Prose, or the Trumpet of Prophecy* (1954), 298–9, with Richard Garnett's translation (used here), Appendix D, 359–61.

29. 'Lamia' l.191–2,

> *Not one hour old, yet of sciential brain*
> *To unperplex bliss from its neighbour pain,*
> *Define their pettish limits, and estrange*
> *Their points of contact and swift counterchange . . .*

30. *The Letters of John Keats*, ed. Hyder Rollins (1958) i. 280–1.

31. See above, p. 250 and n.22.

32. *La Nouvelle Hélöise*, Partie V, xiii (*Oeuvres* X 343 n).

33. See the ballad of 'Sir Patrick Spence' St. 7.

> Late, late yestreen I saw the new moone
> Wi' the auld moone in hir arme . . .

(used by Coleridge in the epigraph for his Dejection ode (1802).

34. Donald H. Reiman, op. cit. 29–30.
35. See above, p. 249 and n.19.
36. *Shelley: Selected Poems and Prose*, ed. G. M. Matthews (1964) 215.
37. G. M. Matthews, 'On Shelley's "The Triumph of Life"', loc. cit. 115.
38. F. M. Stawall, 'Shelley's "Triumph of Life"' *Essays and Studies* V (1914), 104–31.
39. G. M. Matthews, 'On Shelley's "The Triumph of Life"' loc. cit., 108–9.
40. *Oeuvres* vol. 23, 221–2.
41. Lucretius, *De Rerum Natura*, iv. 85–7.

# Select Bibliography

## Texts

The standard edition remains *Shelley: Poetical Works*, Oxford Standard Authors ed. Thomas Hutchinson (1904), revised G. M. Matthews (1970). G. M. Matthews is preparing a two-volume edition for Longmans Annotated Poets.

*Selections and texts of individual poems include:*
*Selected Poems of Percy Bysshe Shelley*, ed. with critical introduction by John Holloway (London, 1960; repr. 1964, 1965).
*Shelley: Poems and Prose*, ed. with critical introduction by G. M. Matthews (Oxford, 1964).
Shelley's *The Triumph of Life*, ed. D. H. Reiman (Urbana, Illinois, 1965).
*The Lyrics of Shelley*, ed. Judith Chernaik (Cleveland, Ohio, and London, 1972. Includes texts and critical studies.)
*Shelley's Poetry and Prose*, eds., Donald H. Reiman and Sharon B. Powers (New York, 1977).
Shelley: *Selected Poems*, ed. with critical introduction by Timothy Webb (London, 1977).

## Prose

A complete modern edition of the prose is projected by the Clarendon Press. The fullest collections so far to appear include the relevant volume in *The Complete Works of Percy Bysshe Shelley*, ed. R. Ingpen and W. E. Peck (1926–30, known as the Julian edition) and H. B. Forman's 1880 four-volume edition. The following are invaluable for ready consultation:
*Shelley's Prose, or the Trumpet of a Prophecy*, ed. David Lee Clark (Albuquerque, 1954).
*The Letters of Percy Bysshe Shelley*, ed. F. L. Jones (2 vols., Oxford, 1964).

## Biographies

Contemporary records and memoirs include *The Letters of Mary Shelley*, ed. F. L. Jones (2 vols., Norman, Oklahoma, 1944); *Mary Shelley's Journal*, ed. F. L. Jones (Norman, Oklahoma, 1947); Edward John Trelawny, *Recollections of Shelley and Byron* (1858) and *Records of Shelley, Byron and the Author* (1878), ed. David Wright (Harmondsworth, 1973); Thomas Medwin, *The Life of Percy Bysshe Shelley* (1847), revised edition H. B. Forman (1913). In preparation: *Shelley and his Circle*, (10 vols.) of which have appeared vols. 1–4 ed. K. N. Cameron, 5–6 ed. Donald H. Reiman (see also under texts of individual works). For general consultation the following are invaluable:
Richard Holmes, *Shelley: The Pursuit* (London, 1974).
Newman Ivey White, *Shelley* (2 vols., New York, 1940: the standard life).

## Critical Studies

Carlos Baker, *Shelley's Major Poetry: the Fabric of a Vision* (Princeton, 1948).

Harold Bloom, *Shelley's Mythmaking* (New Haven, Connecticut, 1959).

Peter Butter, *Shelley's Idols of the Cave* (Edinburgh, 1954).

Judith Chernaik, *The Lyrics of Shelley* (Cleveland, Ohio, 1972). See under *Texts*.

Stuart Curran, *Shelley's Annus Mirabilis* (San Marino, California, 1975).

Desmond King-Hele, *Shelley: His Thought and Work* (1962, 2nd edn., 1970).

Gerald McNiece, *Shelley and the Revolutionary Idea* (Cambridge, Massachusetts, 1969).

Glenn O'Malley, *Shelley and Synaesthesia* (Chicago, 1964).

Neville Rogers, *Shelley at Work* (1966, i. 2nd edn., 1967).

Earl Wasserman, *Shelley, a Critical Reading* (Baltimore, Maryland and London, 1971).

Timothy Webb, *A Voice Not Understood* (Manchester, 1977)

——, *The Violet in the Crucible: Shelley and Translation* (Oxford, 1976).

## Critical Anthologies

M. H. Abrams, ed., *English Romantic Poets* (New York, 1960, 2nd edn., Oxford, 1975). (Referred to below as *Abrams*.)

James E. Barcus, ed., *Shelley: The Critical Heritage* (London and Boston, 1975).

Theodore Redpath, ed., *The Young Romantics and Critical Opinion, 1807–1824* (London, 1973).

George M. Ridenour, ed., *Shelley* (Twentieth Century Views, Englewood Cliffs, New Jersey, 1965). (Referred to below as *Ridenour*).

Patrick Swinden, ed., *Shelley: Shorter Poems and Lyrics* (*Casebook*, 1976). (Referred to below as *Swinden*).

R. B. Woodings, ed., *Shelley* (*Modern Judgements*, 1968). (Referred to below as *Woodings*.)

Newman Ivey White, ed., *The Unextinguished Hearth* (Durham, North Carolina, 1938; London, 1966.

## Books containing critical references to Shelley

M. H. Abrams, *The Mirror and the Lamp* (New York, 1953).

——, *Natural Supernaturalism* (New York, 1971).

Harold Bloom, *The Ringers in the Tower: Studies in Romantic Tradition* (Chicago and London, 1971).

——, *The Visionary Company* (revised edn., Ithaca and London, 1971).

A. C. Bradley, *Oxford Lectures on Poetry* (London, 1909).

Donald Davie, *Purity of Diction in English Verse* (London, 1972).

R. A. Foakes, *The Romantic Assertion: A Study in the Language of Nineteenth-Century Poetry* (London, 1958).

R. H. Fogle, *The Imagery of Keats and Shelley: A Comparative Study* (Chapel Hill, North Carolina, 1949).

F. R. Leavis, *Revaluation* (1936).

Earl Wasserman, *The Subtler Language* (Baltimore, 1959).

W. B. Yeats, *Essays and Introductions* (London, 1961).

## Articles

Peter Butter, 'Sun and Shape in Shelley's *The Triumph of Life*', *Review of English Studies*, xiii (1962), 40–51.

Judith Chernaik, *The Lyrics of Shelley* (1972). See under *Texts*.

John Holloway, Introduction to *Selected Poems of Percy Bysshe Shelley* (1960). See under *Texts*.

I. J. Kapstein, 'The Meaning of "Mont Blanc"' *PMLA*, lxii (1947), repr. *Swinden*.

Jerome J. McGann, 'The Secrets of an Elder Day: Shelley after *Hellas*' *Keats–Shelley Journal*, xv (1966), repr. *Woodings*.

Geoffrey Matthews, 'A Volcano's Voice in Shelley' *Journal of English Literary History*, xxiv (1957), repr. *Rideour, Woodings*.

——, 'Julian and Maddalo': The Draft and the Meaning', *Studia Neophilogica*, xxx (1963), 57–84.

——, 'On Shelley's *Triumph of Life*', *Studia Neophilogica*, xxxiv (1962), 104–34.

——, 'Shelley's Lyrics' *The Morality of Art*, ed. D. W. Jefferson (1969), repr. *Swinden*.

Frederick A. Pottle, 'The Case of Shelley' (*PMLA*, lxvii, 1952), rev. 1960 and repr. *Abrams, Woodings*.

Donald H. Reiman, 'Structure, Symbol and Theatre in "Lines Written Among the Euganean Hills"', *Publications of the Modern Language Association*, lxxvii (1962), 404–13.

R. B. Woodings, '"A Devil of a Nut to Crack": Shelley's *Charles the First*', *Studia Neophilogica*, xl (1968), 216–37.

# Index of Persons

Works which are mentioned in the text without the author's name
being specified have been tacitly indexed under the appropriate author.